"*Having lived in Afghanistan myself, written my own books on Afghanistan, and read a good bit of what's out there on the subject, I'm delighted to report that this is one of the best. The depiction of life, culture, and war is accurate — without exaggeration.*"

Josette McMichael, *Images of Afghanistan: Exploring Afghan Culture through Art and Literature*

In the Warlord's Garden

Melinda J. Lewis

Dedication

To the MOLEs this book is lovingly dedicated. It is a privilege to be one of your number.

Note on names

The names of everyone in this book have been changed except for those of political leaders, our immediate family members, and those who have passed away.

Table of Contents

CHAPTER ONE

Americans in the garden

One who runs will also fall. (Afghan proverb)

Snow swirled around the Kabul airport terminal, a few flakes carried inside through the high, shattered windows. Pulling our coats close, Rich and I thrust ourselves and our children through a thicket of men, pushing beyond passport control toward the only other foreigners in the frigid building. We were relieved to see that the International Assistance Mission, the aid and development organization we joined to work in Afghanistan, had sent staff to retrieve us. Although we had not seen them for over two years, James and Greg were easy to identify. That February day in 1992, the six of us standing together in the bedraggled lobby made up a quarter of Americans then in the capital.

I threw my arms around James, relieved to see a face I recognized. "Not here," he murmured, extricating himself from my embrace. He turned and gave a bear hug to Rich – this was culturally appropriate – and led us to where office workers were rolling our barrels toward a truck. Greg towered over the Afghans, his blond hair escaping a *pakul,* one of the ubiquitous woolen caps popular in cold weather.

1

He laughed as he shook his head. "You have more stuff than I've ever seen anyone bring," he said.

It was no surprise: we had been sent pages of recommendations from IAM women – things that were unavailable (pantyhose and Tupperware), things that were available and expensive (shortwave radios and chocolate), and things that were available but of poor quality (cookware and cotton cloth). With two sons and a baby on the way, we efficiently crammed our barrels and suitcases with everything on the list.

"No one thought you'd be here in time for language school," James told us as we rumbled across the city. I gazed out the muddy windows of the van, capturing a blur of gray and barbed wire and trodden white slush. We passed Microyan, a drab Russian-built array of modern apartment buildings coveted for their central heating, then wound through the embassy district of Wazir Akbar Khan, past the Kabul zoo, and around the traffic circle at Deh Mazang. James pointed out the Russian Cultural Center, an imposing building less than a decade old, before turning into the neighborhood of Karte Seh. We pulled up near a tall, gated wall. "Your house isn't quite ready. They were going to put you in the guesthouse, but we thought it would be nicer if you stayed with us."

Our arrival *had* been abrupt: we finished raising funds for our three-year term only days before. But we thought our house in Kabul could be prepared in less time than it took a family of four to shift hemispheres. Clearly we had to a lot to learn.

James Mueller and his wife Ann (pregnant with their second child) graciously showed us to a spacious bedroom typical of homes in Karte Seh. This neighborhood, where all IAM staff settled, had once housed the hordes of Americans working for the embassy and in the various projects begun after World War II to help bring Afghanistan twentieth-century infrastructure. The American International School of Kabul, which operated from 1965 to 1979, still stood near the edge of Karte Seh, memento of a lost era. By the time we arrived, houses left by fleeing owners were easy to lease, some for as low as five dollars a month. The Muellers lived in one of these.

2

Although Russian troops had left Afghanistan in 1989, the ruling government was still under Soviet control. That meant that fuel and electricity were strictly rationed, and the Muellers (like other foreigners) kept one central room warm by the drip of a diesel stove. They tried to insulate the bedrooms by tacking up plastic and hanging heavy curtains over the windows but we arrived during a particularly harsh winter. One morning I gazed through the shrink-wrapped glass to see Ann beating ice off laundry which swayed from the clothesline like sheets of corrugated tin. We slept in our clothes, pulling the blankets around our heads for warmth.

Rich arrived in Kabul ready to work. After medical school, he had completed a family practice residency designed for doctors locating in remote areas. That meant he was experienced in doing everything from emergency room stitch-ups to delivering babies. But we knew that if we wanted to be really useful to the Afghans, we would have to hone our communication skills.

The IAM was strict about language acquisition. Before getting involved in any projects, we were required to complete a four-month course that would get us conversational in Dari, one of the major (and easier) languages spoken in Afghanistan. To our dismay, we discovered classes were beginning the day after we arrived. We knew jet lag would keep us fuzzy-headed for a week. (Kabul was twelve and a half hours ahead of Portland, Oregon, so our days and nights completely flipped). But we figured we had a jump on the other students in our course.

"We studied a year of Iranian Farsi in the States," Rich informed the Executive Director as we lunched with him our first day in Afghanistan. We knew that Dari was a dialect of Farsi – like American English is to British English. Or so we thought.

"Won't help you a bit," the ED told us. "You'll have to relearn it all."

The next morning Ann watched the children as we traipsed through the snow to begin what was known as the Long Course. Like most of the IAM buildings, our school was a converted house, each bedroom filled with desks. The bulletin board outside our classroom was plastered with articles espousing the view of the stout Finnish woman who headed the program: rote language acquisition was by far the most effective method of learning.

"You must read the book if you don't understand the grammar," she instructed us. "Do not ask the teachers to explain."

Each class we repeated a few lines of text and then made minor alterations before repeating again. My mind wandered during the early lessons. (*Say, "You." Say, "Two." You say, "Two."*) I looked around at the others in our course: an American nurse, a Dutchman, a Swedish couple, and a German mother, at twenty-three the youngest in the IAM. Her husband had finished the previous Long Course while she remained in Europe with their newborn, who had recovered from cranial surgery and lay cooperatively in his carrier while we droned on. *If only Aidan had been so docile*, I thought. As a newborn, our second son wailed through our evening Farsi class at Portland State University. After that, we left him with grandma.

Rich and I walked to language class each morning with a degree of smugness. Richard Penner, the Executive Director, was wrong. We were far ahead of our classmates and able to use fascinating nouns in the simple sentences each student constructed aloud. We joked with our teacher, an attractive woman whose dark eyes sparkled as she corrected our vocabulary: "That's an *Iranian* word," she told us. "In Afghanistan, we say. . ." And she would point out what we assumed were the few regional differences.

Not only could we speak Farsi, we could read and write a little. The other students would not learn these skills until they had mastered the spoken language, perhaps years in the future.

Language learning for us, I thought, would be a breeze.

Where my confidence came from is a mystery. I spent a summer studying Arabic in college, but made little progress. One day I stopped a Middle Eastern student in the hall after class. "Excuse me," I said, opening my textbook, "is there a difference between these two letters? They sound the same to me."

She peered at the book. "No, no," she assured me. "They are the same – like *p* and *b*."

But our professor in Portland claimed Farsi was easy – easier than Spanish. Both, like English, are Indo-European languages and we recognized some patterns in sentence construction and even a few words that were similar (for example, "no" is *"nay"* and "shoe" is *"boot"*).

My skill in Farsi languished after the second week of classes.

Richard Penner had been right after all: spoken Iranian Farsi and its Afghan sister, Dari, were substantially different. It was like beginning again as we learned the list of verbs and their conjugations. Even "thank you" was not the same. Unlike me, Rich was a natural language learner (he had become fluent in Spanish while working in Oregon after his medical residency program finished) and quickly made the shift from Iranian Farsi to Afghan Dari.

Although my classmates varied in their language-learning ability, I sensed that I was gradually dropping behind everyone else.

❖

After a week at the Muellers', we moved into our new home. The office staff tried to dissuade us. "All the pipes are frozen," they told us. "There's no running water."

"Never mind. We can make do," we said.

Our house, on a corner lot a few blocks from the Muellers, and even closer to the language school, was cavernous, its yard (like all in the neighborhood) enclosed by walls. On the front porch sat a spare toilet and one of a number of dysfunctional washing machines that Greg Oswald had collected to rehabilitate.

We walked through a hallway larger than our previous apartment to explore the downstairs. There were three rooms besides the kitchen, nook, and bathroom; upstairs were more – cold, empty, and encased in glass. We decided to ignore them until spring. The office had installed a diesel stove and beds in the room next to the nook; this would be home while we waited for the weather to warm.

A few women accompanied us on our walk-through. An American mother of three school-aged daughters who had lived in Afghanistan for more than a decade pointed cheerfully to a storage area under the staircase.

"You have a good safe place," she said encouragingly. "During fighting you'll be protected from flying glass."

She nodded toward the massive window casting dim light over the landing. I pictured our small sons huddled in the dark corner and tried to smile.

We hadn't done any shopping or cooking on our own yet; the women handed me a basket of food they had prepared as a housewarming gift. I assumed these were essentials but later discovered they had showered us with treats: English jelly, cookies, and instant coffee (the only kind available in Kabul). I pulled out a bag of peanuts and it ripped, nuts skidding across the dusty kitchen floor. As I went for a broom, the other women scrambled to scoop up the nuts, making sure each was retrieved and returned to the bag. Their frugality, I thought, would have made my mother, a Depression-era baby, proud. It would not take long before I joined their ranks, treasuring every imported delicacy.

I'm not sure what we imagined before we arrived in Afghanistan – certainly not frozen pipes, in-home bomb shelters, or the way warlords would wreak havoc on our lives. But we quickly learned the significance of all three.

The view from our house, Kabul 1992

Oregon, 1986

CHAPTER 2

Companions

Find a companion before you inquire about the road. (Afghan proverb)

Iran piqued my interest long before Afghanistan. My sophomore year in college I worked part-time at *The Oregonian* newspaper while taking classes. In the library I met Fariborz and his friends; we began talking, and they told me they were from Persia. Like most Americans, my geography skills weren't the greatest. I went home and looked up Persia in the dictionary only to discover that it was the ancient name for Iran. Only a week before, the halls of *The Oregonian* buzzed with news of the release of the hostages from the American embassy in Tehran. I understood why Iranians might want to obfuscate their background by telling me they were Persian.

As my relationship with Fariborz and his sister Jamila developed, I became more and more interested in Iran's architecture, culture, and values. I toured Jamila through one of my favorite lunchtime haunts – the Oregon Historical Society museum – and watched with amusement her alarm at being confronted by a stuffed bison. She, in turn, opened a new world to me – a world in which our perspectives on religion and politics collided and I pondered how an intelligent young woman could anticipate a conjugal match made by her father. "He picked out a good man for my sister," she explained to me, "and I'm sure he'll pick a good husband for me. We will grow to love each other."

We went to a Persian New Year's party that March. While she listened to a lecture in Farsi, I perused the political cartoons posted in the back of the auditorium. A shiver ran down my spine at the depictions of a diabolical Uncle Sam.

However, the political side of things did not quell my growing interest in Iran. I checked out books from the library and marveled over the beauties of Isfahan. A British woman who had been living in Tehran spoke at a conference I attended, sharing about the sudden death of her husband and the incredible solace and support she received from her Iranian friends. The bond of sisterhood was one of many aspects of the culture that appealed to me.

But it seemed like the door to Iran was locked and barred.

The country was engaged in a brutal war with Iraq. A student from Tehran told me with tears in his eyes that authorities warned his parents that if he did not come home, they would take his fourteen-year-old brother as a soldier. Even so, my friend refused to return. If Iranian nationals would not even go home, I could see no way that I would ever get there.

I still had the Middle East on my mind when I returned my junior year to the University of Oregon. It was such a strange preoccupation; in four years of college, I only met two others who thought about working in the Muslim world. Rich was one. He had studied with a group of pre-med students in my dorm freshman year, so I recognized him. Our class schedules threw us together for most meals our junior year; we had plenty of time to discuss our post-college goals. I resisted my increasing attraction to him; he was so *serious*.

We were both taking English classes from the same professor. While in his office I took the opportunity to ask about Rich.

"I heard you have Rich Lewis in your class," I said, toying with his paperweight as he passed me my notebook. "Is he a good writer?"

The professor looked up. "Rich Lewis? He is, but he writes about God too much. A good poet, though."

A good poet. . . this was a side of Rich I had not seen. He could not be all bad, I decided, if he wrote poetry. I skipped my political geography class a few days later to meander with him through the rhododendron-lined paths of Hendrick's Park near campus. That stroll clinched it for me. We spent much of the summer walking, talking, and boating along the Willamette River near his parents' house.

Over winter break, I received a call from a former roommate whose brother, a Navy pilot, had dropped by on home leave the previous year and taken us both to dinner. We had all spoken of our mutual interest in the Middle East; now she had an offer for me.

"Jim has invited us to come and stay with him in Bahrain!" she told me. We could get jobs and experience Arab culture up close.

The idea was irresistible. I had no idea what I was doing after graduation; I had looked at Master's degree programs but made no plans. Rich flew around interviewing at medical schools and decided he would go to the Oregon Health Sciences University, but he never proposed marriage. Why not travel? With $1800 round-the-world airline passes we could visit friends in Hawaii, Japan, the Philippines, Hong Kong, and Singapore on our way to Bahrain. My parents agreed, my brother loaned me money, and my friend and I booked flights for a week after school finished. Rich and I parted in cap and gown after the University of Oregon graduation with no commitments made.

Bahrain exceeded my expectations. I got a job at the American Mission Hospital typing transcriptions for the radiologist. (Poor man; between his accent and my ignorance of medical terminology, some of the reports were indecipherable.) A Bahraini woman worked alongside me; she did the Arabic typing while I performed office tasks in English. A Canadian nurse walked me through the wards to visit patients with her.

In the afternoon I returned to the navy base, which was another world. There were few women around – and they were almost all married. Jim's sister had taken a job as a lifeguard; I visited her at the pool, picking up my mail on the way in.

Rich and I wrote every day and mailed our letters once a week. They were tomes – pages and pages of neatly handwritten reflections and observations. Often we found we had been thinking about the same things as our ideas crossed in the mail. I could not resist smiling as I sat on the edge of the pool at the base, pouring over those letters. It must have been aggravating to the lonely sailors. (I flashed Rich's photo whenever one asked me out.) Instead of yielding to the temptation of the situation, I became more and more convinced that Rich was the man for me. After a couple of months in Bahrain, I packed my bags and headed home.

We married nine months later, after his first year of medical school. With my experience in Bahrain (including seeing a functioning hospital) we both were more animated than ever about the idea of living and working in the Middle East. So it came as a surprise when we started looking for opportunities. We chose an agency that places people in Asia and the Arab world and were told, "General physicians aren't really needed in the Middle East. What they need are specialists."

Specialists! Rich had specifically chosen a three-year family practice residency that emphasized rural medicine, learning to do it all – obstetrics, pediatrics, general surgery. We were dismayed to discover that those skills would not be useful in the Middle East.

While meeting with the leaders of our agency, we also met James and Ann. Another couple (who had taught in Afghanistan in the 1970s) showed the four of us slides of a ruggedly bewitching country. At that point, I suspect neither Rich nor I could have located Afghanistan on a map.

While we were investigating options, a telegram came to the office from Richard Penner of the IAM:

WHERE ARE THE PEOPLE WE SO DESPERATELY NEED?
URGENT
URGENT
URGENT
PLEASE SEE OUR PERSONNEL OPENINGS &
NEEDS LIST FOR SPECIFIC NEEDS. THANK YOU.

12

Afghanistan. . . we had not considered it before, thinking we would end up in one of the Gulf States. But now we were willing.

"If they want us, we'll go," we told the office staff.

We were back in Oregon when the news came from the IAM. Yes, they would love a family doctor. The IAM operated a blind school and a physical therapy school as well as an eye hospital in the capital. Rich, they wrote, could work at one of its other facilities, a mother-child health clinic. The Russian troops had left and the city was safe for families.

My mother clipped an article from the newspaper a couple of months later. "1000 dead in Kabul bombings," the headline screamed. The article painted the picture of an unstable capital plagued by rocket attacks that indiscriminately killed civilians.

Rich and I quavered a bit, but encouraged by talking to a couple who were working with the poor and raising their family in inner-city Los Angeles, we decided we would go. Surely Kabul could not be worse than L.A.

Kabul, 1992

CHAPTER THREE

Challenges

He who is wounded by a sword will recover,
but he who is wounded by a plate never will.
(Afghan proverb)

Our family philosophy toward each trip is, "It will either be fun or interesting." The first months in Afghanistan were more interesting than fun. Although we were excited to finally be there, the hardships of daily life quickly caught up with us.

The office staff had warned us the pipes were frozen in our house. So we began melting snow over our diesel heater to use as drinking water. Greg Oswald came by to check on us, and glancing into the pot on the stove, he asked, "Why don't you get water from the well?" It was the first we had heard there *was* a well. We sheepishly followed him out to one of the rooms built against the wall of our yard. There, in the middle of the floor, was the pool of water and bucket. But we still lacked hot running water and our bathroom was freezing. Too embarrassed to ask our new friends for a shower, we survived seventeen days on sponge baths. We were probably not the only ones relieved when the weather warmed and our pipes thawed. I never enjoyed a shower so much.

During the first year, we were told, we should expect to be sick a lot. My initial illness hit soon after we arrived. Four months pregnant, I vomited all night and by morning wondered if the baby had survived; I barely had. Water, we discovered, was often the culprit of our gastric complaints. To prevent the consequences of impure water, teammates drove to one of the IAM's rental properties that had a deep well. We stood in line to fill plastic jerry cans with enough clean drinking water to last the week.

When eating out, we were told to avoid raw vegetables, which were rinsed in unclean tap water or water from ditches. As part of our orientation we were given a handbook written in the 1970s by an American doctor who recommended washing tomatoes in soapy water; rinsing; soaking in more water with iodine; rinsing in drinking water; and then peeling. ("And then throw them away," Rich added, wryly reading me the instructions.) Some vegetables, the manual said, should be avoided altogether: raw lettuce and spinach, for example. Fruit should be washed before peeling – even oranges and bananas. Nuts needed to be baked before consuming. Goat cheese should be pressure cooked.

Although we tried to follow these guidelines, we still got sick.

The arid Kabul air also caused problems. At the end of a cold, I developed a dry cough which sent pain ripping through my chest wall; Rich diagnosed me with a cracked rib. Our feet also cracked with excruciating fissures nearly impossible to cure. One friend suggested filling the crevasses in our heels with superglue. I tried (like the Afghans) massaging them with Vaseline; Rich swore by malodorous udder cream.

Each morning Rich headed to the bazaar with a towel to wrap up loaves of fresh *naan,* which (after we finished the gift of English black currant jelly) we slathered with Iranian or Pakistani jam. Then we walked the children to the preschool that had been set up by the IAM. Connor, who turned four a few days after we arrived in Kabul, was fine. But Aidan wrapped his chubby arms around my legs and wailed, "Mommy, don't leave me!" I nearly picked him up but instead carefully untangled myself, promising I'd be back soon. At noon, when our language classes finished, we returned to find Aidan and the other babies and toddlers in front of the preschool, stretched out on a table in their snowsuits, sound asleep. (Although the Scandinavian mothers assured me this was good for the children, I never got used to arriving at meetings to find strollers parked in the snow with red-cheeked infants napping inside.) When he awoke, Aidan had forgotten the trauma of our parting and was happy to see us.

Often after class Rich and I went shopping. We marveled at the mountains of cauliflower (each as huge as a bridal bouquet), purple-tinged carrots, and potatoes stacked in muddy piles in front of the stores. An ignorant city girl, I wondered how they managed to get the produce so dirty.

The rows of shops in Pul-i-surkh – mostly narrow rooms filled with identical goods – were stocked with cans of powdered milk, loose tea, bags of candies and nuts, cookies, and unrefrigerated eggs and bowls of yogurt. Nearby entrepreneurs had converted shipping containers to music shops or meat markets. Most of the foreigners made trips on the weekends to the more upscale section of Kabul known as Shar-e-nao (New City) where one could find loaves of white bread and meat frozen in packets. On Sarak-e-gul-furoshi (Flower Street) we reveled in luxury items like cereal and canned processed cheese.

One of the women grew tired of paying extra for prepackaged meat, so she tore a page from her *Betty Crocker Cookbook* and showed the diagram of different cuts of beef to a butcher, who then hacked off the best pieces according to what she pointed out in the drawing. I tried this, but the group of men merely flipped the page around, studying the drawing from different angles, and shrugged.

All of our purchases were carried in bags made of old school book pages carefully glued together. Despite lagging behind in language class, at least (I comforted myself) I was able to read these snippets from Dari primers.

Even though we could find fresh fruits and vegetables, it was a struggle to shop, cook, clean, and study. Many of the IAM workers hired Afghans to help in their homes; one gave us the name of a cook seeking employment. He came mornings while we were in class, and we arrived home eager for his hot lunches. First we tried having him cook Afghan food, but when he told us he had previously worked at the Hungarian embassy, we asked for some goulash (the only Hungarian food we had ever heard of). This dish bore a striking resemblance to what he had already served us. When we finally ate authentic Afghan food, we were relieved to find it not at all like the meals our former embassy chef had prepared. (We did miss his apple strudel after he left, though.)

Since much of our house was furnished with items borrowed from the IAM, Rich began scouring the bazaar for replacements. I started sewing curtains on the American sewing machine we had brought. Unlike many of the local people, we were granted access to electricity at night. However, our office told us out of consideration to get heavy window coverings so the neighbors would not know we had energy when they didn't. Rich brought home corduroy to match the orange and purple geometric design of our family room rug. When I finished these curtains, I began work on window coverings for our upstairs rooms.

We learned after we had been in Kabul a few weeks that the Finns and Swedes had converted a storage room into a sauna. Once a week they incinerated a pile of wood to heat both the room and a tank of water. The women enjoyed it the first hour, followed by the men. The Scandinavian females pressed me to join them.

"Oh, I can't go in the sauna," I told them.

"Why not?" one woman asked.

"Well, in America the doctors say that the high heat can be harmful to pregnant women and their babies."

She laughed. "If saunas were harmful to babies," she told me, "there wouldn't be any Finns!"

I skipped the sauna but did enjoy a blazing shower in the room next door.

As the snow dissipated and the temperature rose, we decided to sleep upstairs. There were four bedrooms on the second floor; we chose the most sheltered one at the back of the house (it had only one small window) for Connor and Aidan and moved our new bed in next door. At night the barking of packs of street dogs echoed through the empty rooms. We heard stories that children caught outside their gates at night were snatched away by these wild creatures.

During language school we were so busy we did not have time to visit our neighbors. Fortunately, the man next door dropped in on us. He was a regal-looking Pushtun who relished eating my cinnamon rolls while conversing with Rich. When he and his wife invited us over for a meal, we had our first experience at dining on the floor and eating without cutlery. Afghans use a delicate procedure with rice which involves scooping up a handful (only the right hand is used for eating) and pushing the mixture with one's thumb into the mouth. We made a terrible mess. Our neighbor pointed out that one-and-a half-year-old Aidan, who shoveled the handful directly into his mouth, ate like Amanullah Khan, one of the early-twentieth century Afghan kings. We were glad that the children attracted enough attention to keep our gracious hosts from noticing how much food Rich and I were spilling.

The IAM passed around a sign-up sheet to host newcomers for meals during their first few weeks in country. Even after that period passed we continued to receive invitations from other foreigners. We loved walking home after dinner, inhaling the crisp mountain air. The stars glittered intensely; the Milky Way shined like a luminous paint swath across the black of the night. The absence of street lights had its advantages.

One night we returned late and pulled the rope outside our front gate. This was attached to a bell inside so our *chaokidar* (watchman) would know to let us in. We yanked the rope repeatedly, jangling the bell. We banged and banged on the gate, its sound reverberating through the still of the neighborhood.

"I wonder if the *chaokidar* is okay," Rich said worriedly. Our watchman, a frail, ancient-looking man, appeared to have been hired by the office as an act of charity. Rich climbed the wall and clambered down the other side. He unlatched the gate; still there was no sign of the *chaokidar,* although light from the bare bulb in his room streamed across the yard. We glanced in as we passed. A body lay on the cot, completely covered in a woolen blanket.

"I think he's dead," Rich whispered to me. "You take the children inside, and I'll check on him."

I put the boys to bed while Rich crept into the watchman's room. He appeared inside a few minutes later.

"Well?" I asked.

"I knocked on the door, and he didn't answer, so I banged on the window. Finally I went into the room and called his name, but there was still no response. So I went over and pulled the blanket off."

In a hushed voice, I asked, "What happened?"

"He sat bolt upright," Rich laughed. "I don't know who was more frightened."

The old man explained away his semblance of sleep by saying he was just trying to keep warm. Over time we learned that sound sleep was a common trait among *chaokidars.*

Our small circle of Afghan acquaintances was growing: the *chaokidar,* the cook, our next-door neighbor. One day a man stopped Rich on the street speaking English, and told him he

20

had received a copy of a religious book years before from a foreigner.

He wondered if Rich had any more like it?

Rich was recounting this story one evening for an older American couple who had dropped by for a visit. The woman suddenly put her hand up to stop him. "Is your phone unplugged?" she asked.

"No," Rich answered.

"Unplug your phone," she said. After Rich complied, she explained. "Although the Russians are gone, their secret police, the KHAD, are still here. They park outside foreigners' homes and are able to eavesdrop on conversations through the phones." She didn't want Rich to share any information that would get his new acquaintance in trouble.

At first her claim sounded ridiculous, but we began to hear evidence that foreigners were followed and watched, especially if they spent a lot of time with Afghans. We were even forbidden from wearing local dress; it made us hide too easily in a crowd. Having worked with bearded Russian immigrants in Oregon, Rich had shaved off his beard before we arrived in Afghanistan. The last thing we wanted was to be mistaken for the occupiers who had brought destruction and war to the country. But because of Rich's fair hair and clean-shaven face, the Afghans he met in the bazaar repeatedly guessed he was a Russian soldier. So he grew his beard back. We tried to fit in as best we could without looking so local that we would be arrested.

For some reason, the foreign women in Kabul in the early 1990s wore below-the-knee skirts and dresses, long-sleeved blouses, and short headscarves. In retrospect, we probably also looked more like Russians than anything else. Ann wore trousers under her dresses and was complimented on the street for her modest attire, which was similar to what the local women were wearing. After the fall of the government, we all began dressing like Ann. I was glad I hadn't invested in the ninety pair of stockings I had been advised to bring.

Walking to and from language classes, I noticed that boys were harassing me in ways the other women were not getting bothered. We were all accustomed to the cries of *"Kharijee!"* (foreigner) and *"Kachalu!"* (potato – perhaps a reference to our white skin). But when I was out alone, children pelted me with stones as soon as I passed them. Mystified, I mentioned it to our Dutch classmate, Maarten, during one of our tea breaks at the language school.

"It's the sunglasses," he said.

"The sunglasses?" I repeated.

He nodded. "The kids can't see your eyes. Plus they make you look like some kind of a movie star." Being extremely light sensitive, I could not do without my sunglasses. But I put away my Polaroid lenses and tried my less-reflective back-up pair; the rock-throwing ceased.

The English-speaking man Rich had met invited us to lunch at his house. It was the month of Ramazan (Ramadan, as it is called in Arabic-speaking countries); devout Muslims fast during the daylight hours. Our host explained that ordinarily he would not eat, but his father had told him to go ahead so that his guests would not feel uncomfortable. Awkwardly, we picked at the platters of food his sister set out before us, not wanting to flaunt our privilege (as non-Muslims) to eat. After watching us a few minutes, our host turned to me and burst out in English, "You are ashamed!" I protested at this accusation, but a week later in class learned that the Dari word for "ashamed" is also translated "embarrassed." So, in fact, he was right.

When the month of Ramazan had finished, Rich said, "We should have his family over for lunch."

I had never attempted cooking an Afghan meal by myself, but I had a cookbook; and after all, there would just be seven of us, including Connor and Aidan.

When the family arrived, I discovered my error. Our friend had brought his *entire* family, which included six adults I had not yet met. If I had realized how difficult single-handedly preparing a huge meal would be, I would have sent Rich out for kabobs right then.

I carried tea and candy to everyone and then returned to the kitchen. Someone had told me Afghans calculate one cup of dry rice for each person, so I poured ten cups of rice into our largest pot and began to boil it. Meanwhile, I set to work on the other parts of the meal. I was gone from the living room so long that our friend's sisters came looking for me.

"Let us help you," they offered.

Afghan women pride themselves on cooking rice to perfection. They soak the rice for hours to remove the starch, and then rinse it until the water runs clear. They know how to add fat and salt in such a way that the rice is blazing hot, each grain swelled but not sticky. As I scooped the rice onto platters for our guests, it plopped in gelatinous clumps. Our guests were kind and said nothing to add to my distress; a late lunch of mushy rice did that job admirably.

We have seen spreads so beautiful we could not resist taking photos: dishes with mounds of rice crowned with chunks of meat, julienned carrots, and sautéed raisins and nuts; homemade yogurt gleaming in glass bowls; fresh *naan;* salads of thinly sliced tomatoes and onions or trays arrayed with green onions and radishes; stuffed pasta with meat sauce swirled on top. Usually there would be fruit bowls piled with mandarin oranges or pomegranates or apples, and sometimes the local pudding, *firni,* a translucent pool of white sprinkled with finely chopped cardamom, pistachios, and almonds.

In light of this, the graciousness of this Afghan family in choking down the food I prepared makes me *maysharmom* (with both meanings of the word – embarrassed *and* ashamed) even now.

Mujahideen, Kabul 1992

CHAPTER FOUR

Planting season

A good year is determined by its spring. (Afghan proverb)

One can be surprisingly myopic when the world is falling apart.

As a college freshman, I was barely sentient when it came to politics. I knew about the hostages in Iran but paid scant attention to President Jimmy Carter's State of the Union address in January 1980. He announced that the US would not be sending a team to the Olympics in Moscow that summer because the Soviet Union had invaded Afghanistan at Christmas. "The implications of the Soviet invasion of Afghanistan could pose the most serious threat to the peace since the Second World War," President Carter said. That sounded ominous. But I don't remember giving the issue another thought.

Rich and I read the CIA World Factbook on Afghanistan before arriving in the country, but I was drawn more to sections on customs and practices than those covering the power brokers of the area. I knew the basics: after the USSR invaded in 1979, a number of rebel groups rose up to fight the Soviet-backed government; the Soviets withdrew in 1989. A baffling array of *mujahideen* (or "freedom fighters," as President Reagan called them) peopled the landscape, mostly united along ethnic lines. Hezb-e-Islami was a powerful faction manned by the Pushtuns (Gulbuddin Hekmatyar their spokesman); Jamiat-e-Islami by the Tajiks, with key commanders in the north (Ahmed Shah Massoud) and east (Ismail Khan) of the country. The Hazaras identified with Hezb-e-

Wahdat, the Uzbeks with Junbish-e-Mille, and (to tangle matters further) Etihad-e-Islami was a Pushtun group linking up with the Tajiks.

These forces took on personal significance in the early spring of 1992.

On March 18, Afghan President Mohammed Najibullah, acting with Soviet support since its military withdrawal in 1989, agreed to step down as soon as a transitional government was formed. This set off a chain of events: the northern military general, Dostum, defected from the government and formed a coalition that took control of Mazar-i-Sharif. The United Nations proposed to fly Afghan tribal leaders into Kabul to begin work on the transitional government. The plan was to then spirit Najibullah out of the capital. But before this could happen, Massoud's forces took control of Bagram Air Base and joined Dostum's militia north of Kabul. Hekmatyar's men were stationed to the south of the city. Najibullah was forced back from the airport while attempting to leave the country. He took refuge in the United Nations compound, where he remained until he was tortured and killed by the Taliban in 1996.

While all this was happening, life for us carried on. With the help of our *chaokidar*, we tilled and planted our vegetable garden with seeds we had brought from the US. The mountain air was crisp and clear; I smiled as I hung laundry on a line stretched over the newly plowed earth. Those myriad men poised outside Kabul were as heedless of the life in our garden and in my bulging belly as we were of their ambitions.

Spring and war seemed incongruous. I had always envisioned November as a time for death and destruction; the sky should be steel and the ground barren. But Afghan warriors waited for the snow to melt to resume fighting; winter was the time to rest and wait for dry weather. This was a pattern we would see repeated each year in Afghanistan.

Soon after Najibullah's resignation, rural teenagers appeared in the streets armed with AK-47s. One afternoon, I was walking to the Oswald's house, when one stopped me.

"Where are you going?" he demanded, fingering his rifle.

"To visit a friend," I answered. "Is that okay?"

He grunted an affirmative. I walked briskly away, a chill running through me despite the warming air. These young men, without any accountability, had been granted the power of life and death. We knew the situation was serious when our Pushtun neighbor, who had always tried to dissuade us from believing that the sounds of rockets we heard were weapons, now assured us he would guard us if there was any trouble.

The IAM called a meeting. The *mujahideen* were encircling the city, Richard Penner told us, and were ready to attack and take control of the government. Each individual and family group had to decide what to do while there was still time to flee the fighting.

We should, we were told, feel free to stay or go.

Rich and I discussed our options. He seemed confident we should remain in Kabul.

"What if we stay and the fighting gets unbearable, and we're stranded?" I asked. "What if something terrible happens and we *could have* gotten the children out of the country but *didn't?*" I did not voice my other thought: *How would we ever defend our decision to the grandparents if our children were injured or killed?* We had agreed to serve in Kabul because we had been told it was relatively safe for families.

A few weeks earlier, Ann had contacted the Red Cross hospital in Karte Seh. Would staff provide back-up support for us if we delivered our babies at home? They told her they couldn't – they were there for the war wounded. As a result, Ann and James had already left for the US. I wanted to get out of the country, too.

Rich wanted to stay. "We've only been here a few weeks," he argued. "As a doctor, I might be useful if there is fighting." Our baby was not due for at least three more months. There would be plenty of time to get out.

I talked to our classmates during the tea break the next morning; I was anxious about staying but did not want to contend with Rich. We had known when we came there were risks involved. We updated our wills before leaving the US and signed a form in Kabul stating that we knew the IAM would not pay ransoms and

27

that we agreed to be buried there if we died in country. But somehow placing our children in a preventable, dangerous position did not seem the same as making that choice for ourselves. The people I confided in were sympathetic with my concerns and urged me to leave.

That afternoon, Rich and I reached a tense agreement: the boys would fly out with me, and he would stay behind. It was the first time I felt we were truly at odds, and the stakes were high.

Despite our compromise, the decision pained both of us.

When Richard Penner got wind of our plan, he called us into his office, offering his characteristic blunt assessment.

"You're too new to be separated," he said. "And you are not useful here. You will both be evacuated."

Rich was stunned. We barely spoke as we returned home to begin packing. When it was announced the following day that *all* of us would have to leave (except for a skeleton crew to keep the projects going), I felt slightly vindicated. But the damage had already been done.

That night, peering through our small bathroom window, I could see intermittent flashes north of the city, illuminating the mountains nearby. Was it fighting or lightning? Just in case the *mujahideen* took the city overnight, I decided to enjoy our electricity and running water and take a hot shower. If I was going into captivity, I might as well be clean.

Outside raindrops began falling on our garden and the street outside our gate. The lightning – that's what I had seen through the window – passed us by. We slept soundly.

❖

Easter Sunday, the fourth day after Najibullah resigned, we met with other Christians in Kabul to celebrate the holiday. After the service, we hugged our colleagues goodbye and talked over plans. Some would return to their home countries; some would be reassigned to projects elsewhere. We had a ticket to India, but did not know what to do once we got there.

Dan Terry, whose father had been a director of the IAM years before, had an idea. He told us of a hill station in northern India (one of the cool locations the British had sought to

28

survive summers) where he had gone on vacations as a child. There was a mission hospital, and Rich would be able to work there, he suggested. Then when Kabul was stable, we could return.

With no real concept of what would happen to the capital in our absence, focused on our own plans, we finalized our preparations to fly out of Kabul the following day.

Mr. Banon's Guest House, Manali 1992

CHAPTER 5

Outside the garden walls

Patience is bitter, but it has sweet fruit. (Afghan proverb)

My first impression of India was tainted by circumstances. Our journey to Afghanistan in February had us traveling Portland to New York, New York to New Delhi, and New Delhi to Kabul. However, we were told during our layover in New York that we would not be allowed to board our plane to Delhi without Kabul tickets in hand. Although we arranged for a travel agent in Delhi to meet us at the airport with the tickets we had already purchased, there was no way to prove this to the officials in New York. So we bought a second set of tickets at JFK to demonstrate we had no intention of remaining in India.

After twenty-four hours of traveling, we spent a sleepless night huddled over our luggage in the transit lounge of the Indira Gandhi International Airport. Unable to exit without Indian visas, we eyed the dangerously tempting "drinking water" signs above the fountains and kept a close watch on our children and baggage.

Now, ten weeks after entering Afghanistan, we were back in New Delhi. (Because of tensions between Pakistan and Afghanistan in 1992, India was the easiest place to evacuate to.) This time we had tourist visas and a vague idea of what we were doing. As many people experience their first time in Delhi, our every sense was assaulted. In traffic, the bulky white Hindustan Ambassador taxis competed with open-sided auto rickshaws, private cars, bicycle rickshaws, and motorcycles (sometimes carrying entire families). Buses erupted passengers; children approached vehicles at stops to sell strips of freshly sliced coconut or to beg (sometimes feigning disabilities like blindness or missing limbs); drivers honked if the vehicle in front did not shoot forward as soon as the light changed or if they were unhappy with traffic conditions. (We had one driver who honked rhythmically to music blaring from his radio.) There were people everywhere at every time of day and night – shopping, dining, standing on street corners, sleeping on sidewalks. Men in slacks and button-up shirts and women in saris and Punjabi suits swarmed around carts displaying spicy chickpeas or advertising refrigerated drinking water, passing bakeries whose glass cases displayed unrecognizable treats formed in spheres and triangles and squares, sometimes wrapped in silver foil. The smells of Indian food, tropical flowers, and the dirt of the streets swirled together. From the safety of our taxi, we observed it all.

Not knowing where to stay in one of the largest cities in the world, we had asked teammates for advice before leaving Kabul. One couple, who frequently traveled for medical supplies and to visit their daughters in boarding school, suggested a guesthouse in Old Delhi. Our taxi pulled up at a dark, Raj-era building run by two glum old ladies and their brother. As they showed us our room, they handed us a single roll of toilet paper. "If you need more, you must buy it yourself," they said.

We crept through the dim building, hushing the boys in respect for the tomb-like atmosphere. Each day we were served the same food – dal, rice, and chapattis – for lunch and dinner. With relief, we answered the phone a few days after our arrival to find that others who had evacuated from Kabul were meeting for a trip to the zoo.

Delhi was already sweltering in April, but we exulted in reuniting with people we knew. The animals were smart enough to hide behind trees and in the shady grass of their enclosures while we dragged our sweaty children around for a couple of hours. We then bundled into auto rickshaws and headed to Connaught Place, the white-pillared circle of shops and restaurants in New Delhi

32

where foreigners and the upper classes mingled. Sitting in an air-conditioned Chinese restaurant, we discussed our immediate futures.

An older nurse named Marjorie told us she was taking a trip to central India to visit a renowned community development program. By the end of lunch Rich, who was depressed by our forced departure from Kabul, agreed to join her. Community development interested him, and there might be usable ideas for when we returned to Afghanistan after the fighting stopped.

Meanwhile, a Finnish mother and I talked about heading north together. Hilkka had been to India before and told me Connor, Aidan, and I could join her and her toddler on the thirteen-hour bus ride to Manali.

"Stay there," Rich told me, "and when we've finished looking at this program, I'll come find you." I was fine with this arrangement; he needed time to recover from our recent disagreement, and I needed to get out of the heat.

Hilkka and I boarded the relatively comfortable bus, watching out the window as we passed through the fields of the Punjab-Haryana plain and then up into the mountains. Each time we stopped for a restroom break, Hilkka grabbed the plastic potty chair she'd brought for Timo, and I accompanied Connor and Aidan to progressively primitive facilities. The first was a clean room with a toilet and sink; the next a public restroom – less pristine, but still with flush toilets. Our following break was at an outdoor row of ceramic squat toilets separated by low walls. The final stop consisted of a wall with a dirt floor and a hole in the ground.

Connor became queasy after a series of switchbacks and finally threw up on himself between stops. I exchanged his shirt for the clean one I had saved for our arrival in Manali.

While our trip had minor challenges, Rich's was worse.

Although we later anticipated Indian rail travel with pleasure – the trains were generally on time, and we rode in temperature-controlled cars in which we were sometimes served meals and tea – Rich and Marjorie ended up with seats in the third-class car. This meant that instead of relaxing with air conditioning and cushioned arm chairs, they scrunched in with others on wooden benches, hot wind rushing through the bars of the pane-less windows.

Before leaving Delhi, we had been lured into buying scoops of local ice cream at a modern-looking shop; Rich became infected with amoeba. His train grew progressively warmer as it headed south; plagued with diarrhea, Rich knew he needed to replenish his liquids. At each station, the *chai-wallahs* hawked blazing mini-cups of sweet milk tea, passing them through the open windows, but Rich wanted water. At that time bottled water was available in the major cities, but harder to find in the countryside. He became dehydrated.

The last stretch of their journey, Rich and Marjorie sat down in a local bus. "The next thing I remember," he told me later, "I woke to find I had fainted in Marjorie's lap and she was fanning my face." He chuckled. "The other passengers just stared. Who knows what they thought of the strange foreigners."

Although the journey from Delhi showed India was not all one noisy marketplace, it was Manali that really altered my initial impression of the country. The town lies in the Kullu Valley, surrounded by the pine-forested base of the Himalayas and bordering the crystalline Beas River. Trekkers, white-water rafters, and transplants from Nepal and Tibet – as well as the early summer tourists from warmer places in India – thronged the streets. The road to Leh (when snow melt allowed travel later in the summer) and strife in Kashmir led others here. Even in the main bazaar, the air was pure. From the time I stepped out of the bus, I loved Manali.

We took a taxi up the Circuit House Road to John Banon's Guest House, which Dan Terry had recommended to us. The owner was grandson of an Irish lieutenant of the Bengal Fusiliers who settled in Manali in the 1870s. He had married an Indian and planted one of the first apple orchards, along with cherries, nuts, figs, and quince. The guesthouse had been a favorite of mountaineers exploring the region; a few still made it their base.

At that time the property consisted of four buildings: the cook house, the dining room with an attached office and apartment for Mrs. Banon, and a pair of two-story lodgings for guests. Our room opened onto a large verandah facing the lawn area, which was surrounded by fruit trees. Hilkka and Timo were put in an upstairs room in the second building. Behind these other buildings was a structure housing the massive wood-fired water heater.

The suite Mr. Banon provided for the children and me was next to his own apartment; with its well-worn rugs and floral-print bedspread, I found it cozy and reasonably priced. The children had room to play in the garden and were welcomed by the Nepali staff into the cookhouse to visit while they worked. All our meals were provided in the dining hall, unless we opted to walk to the bazaar for Tibetan food. In the afternoons, staff carried tea to the verandas or to tables on the lawn where we could chat with a variety of visitors. Two were British mountaineers who served with a special services unit part of the year (one showed us bullet scars in his abdomen but wouldn't tell us where or when he received them); in the summer they led treks in the Himalayas. They were so fond of Connor and Aidan that before they returned to England they bestowed on the boys their surplus candy rations.

One week a wealthy Indian family arrived. We were appalled to find that one of the children was not theirs but a poor girl they had brought along as a servant. While they were at the guesthouse she washed their clothes and waited on them. When they went out sightseeing, they locked her out of their rooms; she sat mournfully on the steps until they returned. Our new British friends warned us not to judge too harshly. "No doubt she's better off than she would have been if that family hadn't taken her in," one said. It gave us a different perspective on child labor, but we still burned at the injustice of the girl's treatment.

Others passed through Mr. Banon's: an Indian teacher from the American Embassy School in Delhi and her husband; an English couple who puzzled at their dessert – the husband queried across the dining room, "Excuse me, but is this spaghetti in milk?" (it was); an Irish pair who told us their next stop was Kashmir and promised to send us a postcard to assure us they had survived (they did); and a German family who regularly joined us for afternoon tea and lavished affection on our boys.

We also made friends with people living in Manali, including another German family working among the Tibetans, a British nurse, and a Canadian-Indian couple who provided services to nearby tribal people.

When Rich arrived, Mr. Banon agreed the boys could eat early – at five p.m. – and then we would put them to bed before we went to dinner at seven. Between courses in the dining hall one of us would sneak back to the room to check on them; both slept well after active days outside. Rich and I enjoyed "dining out" every evening.

With a history of nourishing mountain climbers, Mr. Banon's offered an ample breakfast. First came a bowl of steaming oatmeal to pass around the table. After this were eggs cooked to order along with a frequently replenished tower of thin toasted white bread, butter, and jam made from the estate's fresh plums.

Fruit and steaming pots of tea rounded out the meal.

Hilkka and Timo met us in the dining hall each morning. Timo was the same age as Aidan, but a larger and sturdier child. (Both his parents were at least six foot tall.) He quickly adapted to the meal's routine: as soon as he was strapped into his high chair, he became agitated, a spoon waving in his chubby fist. While watching the swinging doors that led from the cook house, his voice crescendoed to a yell until the oatmeal was deposited in front of him and his mother had filled his bowl. After he downed his first serving, the scene repeated until he was given more oatmeal.

"Good morning, Tarzan," one of the mountaineers greeted Timo one morning.

"Tarzan?" Hilkka looked at us quizzically. We explained the allusion to the strapping outdoorsman and his unforgettable cry.

Morning by morning we watched as Timo was belted into his chair and began howling. And then, one day, the cook appeared, slapping a plate of toast down in front of Timo. Tarzan continued bellowing.

"Where is the porridge?" Hilkka inquired over her son's roar.

"Finished," the cook answered. "No more. All gone. None in the bazaar."

We often walked through the shops, and I distinctly remembered seeing the maroon tins of Quaker Oats on the bakery shelves. Clearly the cook had had enough of the toddler's tyranny.

We endured a noisy meal.

A few days later, Hilkka ran from her room to tell us she had received a letter from her husband.

"It's calm enough to return to Kabul," she told us. She packed her bag and disappeared with Timo the next morning.

Oatmeal mysteriously reappeared on the menu the following day.

I was six months pregnant when we arrived in Manali and as the weeks stretched on it became clear that we could not go back to Afghanistan until our third child was born. Shortly after joining us, Rich contacted the Lady Willingdon, a simple mission hospital located in the town, and was eagerly taken on as a volunteer. With the aid of a translator, he saw patients in the clinic and became friends with the Indian staff and a Scottish internist who was serving there.

While Rich worked, I watched the boys play in the garden, read books with them, and constructed castles out of discarded magazines. I was relieved that language lessons had ended and I no longer had to deal with Aidan's distress at our daily partings. Now as the children entertained themselves on the lawn, I pulled the Dari language book from my suitcase and started over, reviewing what I knew and trying to catch up on what we had covered the last few weeks of class.

Sundays we joined the Hindi-English church in town, sitting cross-legged on the floor with the congregation and singing to vibrant tunes lyrics we did not understand. We picnicked by the Beas River. Sometimes we walked down to the bazaar for momos (Tibetan dumplings) or ice cream, or up the path past ashrams and the so-called "German" bakery in Old Manali, through the mountains where strings of Buddhist prayer flags fluttered against the sky. With all the high-altitude exercise, I felt fit and strong.

As May, June, and July wore away, we became restless. The apple blossoms had been replaced with fruit; the fruit swelled to full size on the trees. Letters arrived from others who had already made their way back to Kabul. We longed to join them. We played badminton and scrambled over the mountainsides in hopes of bringing on labor.

Rich and I had come to different conclusions about my due date. But since he was a Board Certified family practitioner who had delivered hundreds of babies (and my lowest college grade was in "Personal Health"), when he suggested I had passed my delivery date and he should induce me, I agreed.

Our friend the British nurse offered to babysit Connor and Aidan. So one morning after dropping the boys at her apartment, we waded through sheets of rain across the cobbled courtyard to the Lady Willingdon Hospital.

The screenless windows were thrown open in the second floor maternity ward to allow in the moist monsoon air. A few beds covered with quilts filled the room; there were no partitions between them. New mothers rested in a room nearby. I could not help but note the differences between the other hospitals I had given birth in. Connor was born in a county hospital in Southern California where Rich had trained; Aidan was delivered in a small, private hospital in rural Oregon. Lady Willingdon lacked the starched sheets and monitoring equipment available to us for our first two deliveries.

A nurse helped Rich set up the oxytocin drip and I was soon having powerful contractions. Unfortunately, the nurse anticipated a lengthy labor and disappeared for lunch. Rich called, "Sister! Sister!" a few times frantically before resigning himself to doing the delivery single-handedly. (Of course, I helped as much as I could.)

Rich was jubilant as he announced, "It's a girl!" He cleaned and swaddled her before handing her back to me wrapped in a blanket. After making sure I was okay, he ran to bring the boys up to see their new sister.

Connor was not surprised the baby was a girl – he had told us months before that he wanted to pray for a sister. He had even picked out her name and told people, "My mom's having a baby and her name is Hannah." We wondered what would happen to his fledgling faith if another boy came along, but Connor's assurance was justified.

It had not been easy settling on a name. Rich was the fourth in a succession of Richards, and we determined to end the custom of naming our first-born after him. Having taken that step, we felt we could not choose any other family names. As the youngest of four, I marked off possibilities every time one of my nieces or nephews arrived. And having had two sons already, we had run dry on male names. The two potential girl names we had chosen as options when the boys were born subsequently became the names of Rich's mother's dogs. So we thought Hannah might be a good choice – so far no relatives or pets had been named Hannah.

One of the visitors at the guesthouse that summer was a seminary student from the US. I did not tell her the names we were considering, but one day she told me she thought all Christians should name daughters *Hannah Rose*, because it was such a biblical name ("You know – 'Hannah rose and went to the temple to pray,'" she quoted to me from the book of I Samuel). When Rich got home from work that day, I told him the story. Amused, we both agreed that if the baby were a girl, her name would indeed be Hannah Rose.

Despite the primitive facilities, this was the easiest delivery yet. We waited a few hours at the hospital and then took a taxi back to our guesthouse. The staff were thrilled with their tiny guest and gladly brought tea and meals to my room. It was a much more restful postpartum recovery than I had had in either American hospital.

We went to the post office to call our families with news of Hannah's birth. After waiting in line, Rich dialed my parents' number. "We had a girl, her name is Hannah," was about all he could blurt out before the call dropped. The prospect of standing in line again to reconnect was too intimidating. We paid and went back to our hotel.

Was it the beauty of Manali, the friendliness of people we met there, or giving birth to our daughter that endeared the place to me? Whatever it was, on every return trip to India, my feelings have been overwhelmingly positive. I'm glad I did not trust my first impression.

With Mr. Banon and the house staff, July 1992

The house across from our home in Kabul,1992

CHAPTER 6

Uprooted

"O mother, on which ledge shall I lay my egg?" (Afghan proverb)

Hannah's introduction to our family caused no ripple in our plans; she was a healthy baby and the miracle of a third thriving child was not lost on us. But Kabul's ongoing turmoil tossed us into a mini-crisis, forcing us to change our trajectory.

The guest rooms at Mr. Banon's had no television, but we found if we held our shortwave radio at just the right angle while standing near the dining hall, we had clear reception of the BBC news. From reports we knew there had been fighting all summer in Kabul, but we did not understand the details until later. A few days after we evacuated in April, various groups of *mujahideen* had entered the city; rocket attacks and street fighting began shortly thereafter. Starting at the end of May, the western part of Kabul – where our teammates were living – came under brutal attack.

I'm not sure why we thought our office in Kabul would report particulars to us in Manali. Staff probably assumed that we were aware of the living and working conditions in Karte Seh and would make decisions accordingly. For our part, we figured that no news was good news. So four days after Hannah's birth, we arranged for a driver to take us to Delhi.

A couple of days before we left, there was a rap at our door. It was the German family. Since it was early in the morning, our visitors didn't engage us in discussion. They wished us well and handed Rich an envelope. Rich closed the door and climbed back into bed. He unsealed the envelope.

"Oh, man," he said. He pulled out a note.

"What is it?"

"They've left us enough money to fly to Delhi." Enclosed was hundreds of dollars' worth of rupees. The note instructed us not to drive down to Delhi, but to fly from Bhuntar Airport, about an hour from Manali. Our acquaintances' generosity was touching, but we decided that rather than risk traveling to the airport to find the flight fog-bound (as often happened), we would stay with our original plan of going by road. While we were in Delhi, we contacted the German consul, a friend of theirs, and he returned the money to them with our thanks.

The German embassy was not the only one we visited. We had to go to the American embassy to get two important documents for Hannah. With nothing more than a ruddy-cheeked infant and a mimeographed form filled out in Hindi, we applied for a Consular Report of Birth Abroad (the equivalent of a birth certificate). Then we filled out paperwork for an American passport. Because of the strict guidelines, we were not allowed to hold Hannah for her photo. She had to be looking directly at the camera with her head filling the frame of the picture. After considering his options, the photographer laid the baby on the floor and hovered over her, adjusting his view until he was convinced Hannah's head was the right size for the passport.

As we toted our daughter around New Delhi we attracted a lot of attention. Some people counted our children aloud in wonder. One American hippie stopped me.

"I just think it's so cool you came to India to have your baby in an ashram," she oozed. I thought the real story would have sounded even odder, so decided not to go into it.

❖

Before leaving Manali, we had met a teacher from a private college who offered us accommodations in Delhi; when we arrived, we were shown to a room with rows of twin beds. It was strange having a large family in an all-male school dorm but the price was right.

We returned from a day running errands to find a message at the front desk. "A man named Richard Penner asked you to call this number," the receptionist told us.

"Congratulations on your new baby," Richard said over the phone. "I am in town with my family. Why don't you come and join us for lunch?"

We took a taxi to the Imperial Hotel. Richard seemed very relaxed and told us in his straightforward manner that we could not return to Kabul.

"We can't go back?" we repeated in shock.

"The fighting has flared up again," he said. "We're on our way out for a holiday. You should just wait awhile until things settle down."

The dormitory did not seem like a good long-term option, so we thanked our host and shifted to the cheap guesthouse that served as an office for our agency in Delhi. The building consisted of several small floors joined by a narrow marble staircase. The neighborhood around the guesthouse was far from ideal for tourists since it was a residential area without restaurants or shops. The guesthouse cook prepared food for us, but since we could speak no Hindi and he knew no English, we had to eat whatever he was offering, whether we liked it or not.

While monsoon in the mountains meant refreshing rains punctuated by clear spells when we could go out walking, in Delhi we were plagued by oppressive humidity and mosquitoes. There was no air conditioning and the electricity often went off at night; all five of us were jammed in a room so small we could barely walk around the bed. Baby Hannah cuddled on my chest. I dreaded the sound as the ceiling fan grew slower and slower during a power outage. The whine of mosquitoes engulfed us; without the breeze to scatter them they moved in, able to feast freely. We were covered with bedbug bites, Rich was ill, and I had dropped below my pre-pregnancy weight. Only Hannah seemed content. ("It's because she's an Indian," the office workers told us, smiling.)

The news from Afghanistan was bleak: non-stop overnight bombardments; continued street battles; the city water supply cut. The government estimated a thousand people were killed or wounded in one week in early August. But we held out hope of returning.

As we waited, foreigners began to pour out of Kabul. Many made a transit through the guesthouse. Some told us they were going to another country to work for a time; others were returning to their home countries. Greg Oswald and his wife Mary said goodbye on their way to Nepal. I watched sadly as they loaded into a taxi for the airport. Our Dutch friend Maarten was the only one who stayed on. Each day he headed to the airport with his bags to see if a flight would leave for Kabul. But he returned a few hours later. The answer was always the same: no flights were going that day. One day he was told not to return again; the Kabul airport had closed.

If we had stayed in the cool and calm of Manali, perhaps we could have endured the circumstances better, but now we were sick and exhausted.

"Why don't we go home for a while?" I suggested. "We can show Hannah to the grandparents, and when the Kabul airport opens, we can come back. I'm going to have a mental breakdown if we stay here."

It seemed like an admission of failure – we had spent so little time in Afghanistan, not long enough to be helpful to anyone – but Rich finally agreed. The threat of my impending insanity was enough to send us back to the US.

We were met at Portland International Airport by an entourage that included my parents and Rich's mother, who was nearly hysterical when she saw her gaunt son. We returned to my folks' house, where we had stayed several weeks before our move overseas. The boys lit up. (The cross-stitched hanging in the hall summed it up: "There's no place like home – except Grandma's.") When Aidan saw the easy chair in the living room, he turned to my mother and asked, "Rock-a-baby, Grandma?" Six months had passed, but he still remembered her singing the lullaby to him while we were taking Farsi classes at Portland State University.

As we recovered in Oregon, eating Tillamook ice cream and escorting the children to the park, our office kept us updated on what was happening in Afghanistan. We discovered that when our teammates in Kabul had fled overland to Uzbekistan (and then scattered to India and elsewhere), two families had not left the country, opting to stay in the northern city of Mazar-i-Sharif. The Muellers (with their little girl and new baby boy) and another young couple had been given permission to set up an office in Mazar. We also learned that Greg and Mary Oswald were heading to Afghanistan to join them.

When we heard this, we asked, "Can we go, too? We'd love to live in Mazar."

Foreigners had been longing for years to work outside the dingy confines of Kabul, to spread to the cities of Mazar, Herat, Jalalabad, and Kandahar. With fighting intensifying in Kabul, it seemed the dream was coming true. For the first time, security was better outside the capital than within.

The IAM office sent word back: yes, we could join the others in Mazar. After a month in America, we gladly boarded a plane to Afghanistan, ten pounds heavier than when we had arrived.

Since there were no international flights to Mazar, we flew into Kabul again. The first thing we noticed as the airport came into view was half an airplane, its guts spilling out in a pile of ash and debris. A Russian Ilyushin 76MD, it was apparently hit by a rocket before boarding Soviet evacuees. The ride through our neighborhood was shocking: Deh Mazang, where Rich's English-speaking friend had lived, now consisted of block after block of rubble. Rockets had collapsed houses or portions of houses; bombed out cars and tanks littered the roads. The walls around our yard were riddled with bullet holes. All of our possessions had been packed up and moved out by the foreigners who had remained behind during the most intense fighting. One of the women who did most of the work told me she retrieved our clothes from the yard, where they had been dumped out the windows by thieves. Everything was piled to the ceiling in a room at the guesthouse. The good news, they informed us: our garden had yielded a bumper crop from the vegetables we planted in the spring.

Before we evacuated in April, we had been urged to pack our most valuable items into barrels so that if we were unable to return, they could be shipped to us. I had dutifully put in my new sewing machine, flute, autoharp, and Rich's tools. We returned to Kabul to find that our *chaokidar,* a seemingly feeble and ineffective watchman, had apparently been an accomplice in a plan that involved stealing an office vehicle and all our best goods (which I had helpfully prepared for him).

The children and I moved temporarily into an unoccupied house with Mary and her two daughters. Maarten had returned and stayed with us as well; the kids were ecstatic and jumped all over him as soon as he awoke each morning. Rich and Greg packed up what was left of our furnishings and took a bus to Mazar to get houses ready before we came.

After our first arrival in Kabul, Connor had struggled, a sudden spate of disobedience and rebellion flaring up with the move. This time Connor adapted well; Aidan cried a lot, so I made sure I spent plenty of time holding him.

Mary, always good at making the best of a challenging situation, baked cookies in the solar oven (an all-day affair in October, since the sun was so low in the sky). We talked late after the children had gone to bed; she helped identify "incoming" as opposed to "outgoing" rockets, which alternated with the sound of machine-gun fire booming across the sky each hour. One day when automatic weapons sounded outside the gate, we ushered the children into the safe place in our house but discovered it was merely celebratory gunfire.

We were happy and relieved when word came from Rich and Greg that we should take a flight to Mazar rather than replicating their fourteen-hour bus ride. Not long after, a rocket hit the house we were staying in; many years passed before it was habitable again.

Mazar-i-sharif, October 1992

CHAPTER 7

Transplanted

Forget the past, but look out in the future. (Afghan proverb)
During the hour flight from Kabul, I marveled at the tiny
villages and lakes tucked high in the folds of the Hindu Kush
mountain range. As our plane touched down, we immediately
noted differences between Mazar and Kabul. The landing field
lacked the bombed-out fuselages littering the Kabul airport. And
the countryside was flat; mountains rimmed the plain to the south,
but otherwise shrub-covered desert stretched in all directions from
the airport.

The city was a fraction of the size of the capital, its major streets
stretching like spokes from the Raoza Hazrat Ali, the blue shrine
and mosque complex at the center of Mazar. James had traipsed
door-to-door and managed – despite the competition from wealthy
Afghans who had also evacuated Kabul – to rent three houses in
different parts of the city. The Oswalds' was nearest the airport.

"You'll be staying with us until your house is finished," Greg
told us as he showed us around their compound. The house was in
an enclosed yard hidden behind their landlady's property. She was
a spunky older woman sharing her own house with her Hazara son
and his beautiful Pushtun bride. (We came to find that such
ethnically mixed marriages were unusual, especially since the
Hazara were considered the lowest-status ethnic group and the
Pushtuns – the group from which the Taliban later came –
considered themselves the highest.)

51

Homes in Mazar tended to have two designs. With one style, the front door entered a hallway running the length of the house; doorways opened off this hallway to the individual rooms (each of which often contained a family unit). The second floor plan had rooms in a row connected without a hallway; you entered one room to proceed into the next. Guests were entertained in the front-most rooms and the family's private quarters were farther back.

The Oswalds' house was a modification of this second floor plan. On one side of the entryway were the connected rooms and on the other a bathroom and a large room which Greg had been converting to a Western-style kitchen. Since dishwashers were unavailable, he knew that they would spend a lot of time hand washing. Before we arrived in Mazar, Greg arranged carpenters to come in and build cabinets.

"I want them high enough so Mary doesn't have to lean over the sink," he told Rich. He ordered the cabinets built about four inches taller than the standard three-foot counter height. He ushered us proudly into the kitchen to show us the work he'd done. "I made the cabinets taller so it won't hurt your back," he told his wife.

Mary stepped up to the sink. Although the cabinets looked fine when Greg – who is over six feet – stood next to them, the added elevation dwarfed her. She lifted her arms. "This is too high," she said. Greg looked crestfallen. "I guess I'll have to get him to cut the bottom off the cabinets," he said.

The rest of the house looked good, though. Since Mazar has hot, dry summers and cold, wet winters, Greg had put their bedroom in the basement, which was well insulated against the outdoor temperatures. Upstairs their formal sitting room opened onto a family room and then a guest room, all furnished with *toshaks* (the long, cotton-stuffed cushions used instead of couches or beds). Encompassing the yard were rooms unconnected to the main house. The courtyard was a perfect place for the children to play without needing constant supervision.

❖

Mazar, we were told, had two seasons: the time of mud and the time of building. We arrived before the mud and were enchanted by the village feel of the place. Roads formed mazes leading to adobe-walled enclosures. Some gates opened onto compact, well-swept dirt yards; others revealed meadows, complete with cows. One house we walked past had its gates thrown wide to reveal a magnificent rose garden that forced double-takes even from us, though we had spent our youth marveling at the floats in Portland's Rose Festival parade. The dusty main arteries, laid out and named for the cities toward which they headed, were traversed by a few private cars and taxis. Our favorite mode of transportation was the *gahdee*, a horse-drawn carriage. Ann hired one to pick her up for weekly shopping trips.

The glory of Mazar was definitely the shrine to Ali, Muhammad's successor in the Shi'a line of Islam. The graceful mosque and tomb, covered in blue tiles in intricate geometric designs, drew people not only for prayer times but also for strolls in the park surrounding the buildings. It seemed so discordant with the bleak desert around it that Rich said its location lent credence to the story he had heard that Ali's camel refused to go farther with his body, so the shrine (and city) had been built there.

Because Mazar had not faced the ravages of the Russians or the *mujahideen,* the culture of hospitality seemed to have survived. Not long after we arrived, Greg and Mary's neighbors sent over bowls of thick homemade yogurt and once even a dish of colostrum from a cow that had just given birth. (Mary baked it, creating a ricotta-like ingredient which she used in lasagna.) The friendliness of the Mazaris demonstrated they had not become jaded by exposure to foreigners.

We visited our house across town. The yard was devoid of landscaping and the house just short of completion. After two weeks with the Oswalds and no visible progress on the house, we decided to move in and so put pressure on the owner to finish the work.

Unlike other houses we had seen, ours was an angular C-shaped building, set at the rear of the yard, its back incorporated into the mud wall surrounding the property. The ground floor consisted of three rooms and a bath; the rooms looked out onto a central porch, beneath which was the basement. The interior walls had all been whitewashed except in the tiny central kitchen, which still had mud exposed, and the upper half of the bathroom walls, which required enamel paint to keep the mud from splashing off during showers.

The ceilings upstairs were created by pulling blue and pink paisley taut and nailing it across the beams. (In the spring the crickets hid up there and serenaded us.) The basement ceiling – the foundation for the porch – was a tribute to Afghan ingenuity: instead of wooden beams, stolen tubes from the Soviet gas pipeline supported the roof.

Because no city-wide sewage system existed, our plumbing drained into a septic pit in our yard. When we moved in, the workers were nearly finished lining the cavernous hole with bricks. But three of the four sides collapsed, so they had to start again. Every morning they arrived early, waited for me to prepare some tea with sugar, and then got to work. Even after the septic pit was finished, I was a little nervous walking over the grass above it, fearful the top would cave in. As far as I know, it never did.

We began again the process of furnishing a house. We bought a small refrigerator (a little bigger than a college dorm fridge) and a Japanese washing machine, its undersized cylindrical tubs reminiscent of an ice cream maker. Automatic washers were not available; that meant I had to fill the washer with a hose, drain it after washing, fill it again to rinse, and then drain and put all the clothes into the spinner before hanging them outside to dry. This process was time-consuming. Sometimes I would have to return to the bathroom, where the washer was kept, when the tell-tale *thud-thud-thud* indicated the clothes in the spinner were unbalanced. But (especially with diapers) it still beat washing clothes by hand, which is what most Afghan women did. Many of the foreigners hired local women to do their washing and ironing for them, but it meant owning enough clothes to survive several days before your laundry came back.

Greg was skilled at many things; he had spent time as a contractor, so he knew about building, and he knew how to repair all kinds of appliances. (He and Mary had met on a hiking trip and she affectionately referred to him as her "Boy Scout" because of his myriad survival skills.) In the bazaar he spotted a circa 1949 Kenmore washing machine and tinkered with it until he got it fully functioning. Mary loved its massive round tub and vigorous wash cycles. It even had an old-fashioned hand-crank wringer; articles of clothing would be sucked through one side and come out nearly dry (and flatter than a pancake) on the other. The Oswalds enjoyed many months of clothes washing bliss until their house helper failed to notice that spikes had broken through the rollers; she proceeded to wring an entire twenty-five-gallon tub full of laundry. Mary forlornly held up a shirt for me to examine; it was punctured with rows of holes. "The whole load came out like this," she sighed.

Kabul's energy grid was damaged during fighting, so its people suffered with very little power; in Mazar we had electricity but it was so unreliable we put more confidence in it than we should have. At peak hours the filaments of our bare light bulbs gave a barely perceptible glow. Greg set up a voltage meter in their hallway so they could monitor the power coming in – Afghanistan was set up for machines working off 220 volts, but the needle often pointed far below that. One day I walked into her kitchen to see Mary using an American hot plate.

"I figured out that when the electricity drops enough, we can use our 110 volt appliances," she said. It worked well if she unplugged things before the power increased; they lost at least one machine to an unexpected electrical surge.

Sometimes the power went off for days, and more than once I eagerly tossed clothes in our washing machine and filled the tub with water only to have the electricity vanish again. It came an average of every third day, long enough when it did work (I wrote my parents) "to quickly do all the laundry, vacuum and take a bath while there's warm water." Fortunately our two-burner kitchen stove, not unlike an American camping stove, relied on gas. The tank connected to the stove by a rubber tube; we had to be careful to flip the gas switch closed when we weren't using it to avoid leaks. After one of our teammates lit her stove and suffered a minor explosion, we decided to bore a small hole through the wall and move the tank onto the front porch, where any escaping gas could dissipate.

As we unpacked, we discovered items missing, so we repurchased those. Some of our curtains had survived (there were a few bullet holes), but we borrowed Mary's sewing machine and I set about making more for the windows which took up far too much wall space. When Mary's machine was stolen out of a car we were using, Rich bought me a manually-run Chinese Butterfly sewing machine and we reimbursed the Oswalds for theirs.

We weren't in Mazar long before Ann, always quick to arrange things, told us we would be restarting the Long Course.

"I found someone to watch the children during classes," she said. She introduced us to Guljon, a plump middle-aged woman in a tattered *chahdri*. When we questioned her, Ann admitted that when she hired her, Guljon had been begging. Our childcare attendant spent much of her time chasing Aidan around the Oswald's yard crying, "*Beenee pawk*! (Clean nose!)" as she struggled to wipe his perpetual drip. Aidan picked up the language effortlessly and was now beyond the teary goodbyes that had made our previous lessons so miserable.

While the boys played outside, Rich and I (with baby Hannah on my lap) sat in one of the compound's rooms across from our new teacher, Daoud. In his early twenties, Daoud was a gracious and bright young man who had befriended some of our American colleagues in Kabul before the fighting. Gifted with languages, Daoud could not only speak Dari and English, but also Uzbeki, Pushtu, and later, Russian. He had fled ahead of his family and was relieved to run into James Mueller as he stepped off the bus in Mazar. Half Uzbek and half Tajik, Daoud had learned from his father (formerly a member of parliament) the art of dealing suavely and diplomatically with people. As eager a student as he was a teacher, he quizzed us on American idioms he had heard or read.

Daoud was not only our language teacher, but also an interpreter for Rich, who began work immediately. Before our language classes Daoud and Rich would make the rounds of the forty-five local schools housing about five thousand Kabuli refugees. In the classrooms, families clustered in little groups with whatever possessions they had been able to haul out of the capital. No doubt some of their medical complaints were stress- and loss-related. Rich examined patients and handed out medicine provided by the UN.

Due to hygiene, many people in Afghanistan suffer from intestinal worms. One day a woman told Rich she had worms and then asked the question patients always posed: "Is there any special diet, anything I shouldn't eat?"

With a twinkle in his eye, Rich responded, "Well, you shouldn't eat any worms." The family (and the crowd which gathered when a patient was being seen) roared with laughter.

Feeling pretty pleased with himself, Rich left the classroom.

Daoud, who had joined in the hilarity, turned to him in the hall.

"That was very rude," he said. "You should not have suggested she would eat worms."

Rich was mortified and a little confused at why Daoud had been laughing if his comments were inappropriate. But we discovered that humor is very culture-specific; sometimes *we* were angered at Afghan laughter over dropped goods or injured children. Needless to say, Rich never made any worm jokes again.

Mazar-i-sharif, 1992

CHAPTER 8

Bouquets

One day you meet — you are friends;
another day you meet — you are brothers.
(Afghan proverb)

When people ask, "Do you miss Afghanistan?" I am not sure
how to answer. It is not the most beautiful place we have been;
trees are scarce and where there is no water, the land barren. Some
of the best aspects of the culture have dissolved in many places
because of years of conflict. Keeping body and soul together took
an inordinate amount of time. But Afghans drew us into their
family circles and treated us as kin. We made connections which
are difficult to maintain despite technology; emails from the few
we knew with access to Internet cafes are infrequent and the
English so garbled it is hard to know what they are really trying to
communicate. So when asked, I usually respond, "I miss the
people."

In Mazar we finally had time and opportunity to develop
friendships. Our yard bordered a wide unpaved street, but the
front gate actually opened onto an alley. At the end of this alley
lived a man with his two wives and their children, including a
grown son and his wife and a widowed daughter-in-law — eighteen
people in all. They came by frequently to check on us because they
knew we were far from family and they didn't want us to be sad
and lonely. They became a prominent feature in our new life and
we referred to them as our "near neighbors."

Each person won a special place in our hearts.

One day I sat with the young widow as she carefully pressed the pleats in her powder-blue *chahdri*. She arranged the fabric in minute folds, flattening them with something like a yardstick and then running a charcoal-filled iron over the pleats.

"My husband died in Kabul," she told me. "He was crossing the park in Shar-e-Nao when a rocket hit. He was killed instantly." She leaned over awkwardly, maneuvering around her pregnant belly. "I won't be here very long," she told me with a sad smile. "As soon as my baby is weaned, I will leave him here and return to my family."

"Leave your baby here?" I echoed, afraid I'd misunderstood.

She nodded. "It is the Afghan custom," she explained. "Children belong to the husband's family." While I heard many stories of suffering due to years of conflict in Afghanistan, for me this woman became the face of those in pain. Sent back alone to her parents, she was unlikely ever to remarry, doubly bereft of husband and child.

We spent a lot of time with the teenage sons and daughters of our near neighbors. They did not seem as conscious of their family situation as we were; we puzzled over relationships. Which were whole and which half siblings? They discussed this among themselves at length before answering. Each wife had separate living quarters, so the primary way the youth untangled their own relationships was by considering which mother each lived with.

One of the sons had a mental disability; his father brought him by after the boy grabbed his string during kite fighting. While this might have resulted in a minor rope burn in the US, in Afghanistan the kite string is impregnated with glass. As his kite slipped away, the string sliced like a knife through his thumb. Rich stitched up the wound in our kitchen.

We had tacked a world map in the entryway of our new house. One day another son saw it and asked Rich what it was a map of. After explaining, Rich asked the sixteen-year-old, "Can you find Afghanistan?" He shook his head.

His older sister gazed at it thoughtfully. Each country was colored differently; Afghanistan was green. After a moment, she pointed confidently.

Rich leaned over. "Close," he said. "That's Nepal. This one is Afghanistan."

"Oh," she said, only slightly taken aback. "On our map at school, Afghanistan is the purple one."

Another day one of her brothers announced to Rich he wanted to move to America. "Everything is better in America," he said.

"Well, there's no *pilau* there," Rich told him. Most Afghans eat rice on a daily basis.

Shocked, our neighbor recanted. "Well, if there's no *pilau*, I don't want to go," he said.

This young man took everything we said seriously. One day he and Rich were sitting out on our porch chatting. I joined their conversation. Teasing is a sign of affection in our family. At one point, responding to something Rich had said, I tried to poke fun at him with my limited vocabulary. In Dari, I told the teen, "His head is empty."

The boy glanced in horror at Rich. He looked at me, and back at Rich, clearly waiting for something to happen. Finally, he asked, "Aren't you going to beat her?" I left it to Rich to explain my strange sense of humor and mentally filed this incident away in my lessons on Afghan culture. Apparently any show of disrespect toward my husband (even in jest) was off limits.

Despite our relational clumsiness, we were showered with kindness by our neighbors. This often appeared in the form of food. Sometimes a son or daughter would be sent with a plate of warm pinto beans and yogurt; sometimes, fresh *naan* baked in their home tandoor; at holidays, pudding made from wheat sprouts. We had discovered Afghans loved American pancakes. After cooking a batch, we carried over a large platter with a cup of syrup I'd made with maple flavoring from the US. However, as one of the girls gently informed me later, I had mistakenly replaced *pohder-e-cake* (baking powder) with *soda pohli* (baking soda), rendering the pancakes bitter and inedible. It seemed like we were always receiving more than we could give.

Visiting this cheerful group was a pleasure, despite my primitive language skills. I could understand conversation – and realized with delight one day that I was no longer translating word for-word but following whole phrases. Once I sighed inwardly as the eldest son's wife turned to the others and declared about me, "She doesn't understand anything." Afghans seemed mystified at why we found Dari challenging, and assured us that our mother tongue was easy. But usually the only English we heard came from the elementary school primer. Children chanted to us on the street, "What is this? This is a pen." Sometimes I felt like their linguistic equal.

Fortunately, like their father, Connor and Aidan quickly acquired the language. They were rewarded for their efforts with gifts of money, candy, and fruit by local people smitten with their blond hair and pale skin. And although Hannah was still an infant and merely babbled, the girls in the family created dresses and hats for her and happily bounced her blonde curls. Whenever I showed up without her, they complained; when I brought her, they took turns passing her around.

Along with our near neighbors, we were spending a lot of time with Daoud. One afternoon he and Rich were out together. Daylight faded with no sign of them and I began worrying. Hearing banging at the gate, I looked out. When the *chaokidar* unbolted the gate and a vehicle pulled into the yard, I realized it was not the Land Cruiser Rich had left home in.

"I was getting concerned," I said, kissing him in greeting. "I was just praying for you."

"You should have prayed sooner," he said grimly. "Daoud wanted to get some practice driving on Silo Road." (The Soviet bakery still produced tough loaves of bread that gave the street its name.) Although Rich warned Daoud repeatedly to slow down when they spotted an elderly man leading his donkey across the road, Daoud ignored him. As they hurtled toward the man and animal, Rich yelled for Daoud to pull off the road. The Land Cruiser slammed into the donkey, sending its load of hay through the air. To their surprise, the donkey staggered to its feet and headed on its way.

"What about the old man?" I asked.

"He got up," Rich said. "And then Daoud started berating him and telling him he should have gotten off the road. I finally got

62

Daoud to leave. The Land Cruiser had a lot of damage, so I took it back to the office and switched vehicles."

Although Rich was reluctant to let Daoud behind the wheel again, their friendship remained unimpaired. Daoud ate frequently with us and despite the excellent cooking he had grown up with, he was always complimentary about what I served. Once when I was out of the room he leaned across the table to ask Connor, "What is this food called?"

Four-year-old Connor hated fried rice and told Daoud, "It's called 'garbage.'"

When I returned, Daoud piped up enthusiastically, "This garbage is very delicious! We should have it every day!"

His diplomacy extended to the street beyond our gate. I told him that local boys had been verbally pestering me and throwing rocks. When we were leaving one day, he told me to point out the ringleader. I indicated the worst troublemaker.

Daoud squatted down beside him and said, "You seem like a clever boy. You see this woman here? I want you to make sure that whenever she's out on the street, no one bothers her. Can you do that?" The boy nodded vigorously, and remembered his promise – for a couple of days.

Besides his skills with language and diplomacy, Daoud was also a gifted artist. At one point he showed us his portrayal of the ideal woman. She was beautiful, a scarf delicately draping her head and neck. What stood out to us was her Frida Kahlo-esque unibrow.

Not long after this, Daoud announced that he had hired a woman to join him in teaching Dari. In walked a teenager looking suspiciously like the beautiful drawing. She was gorgeous, but appeared painfully shy and soft-spoken. She lasted one lesson.

Daoud later had a crush on one of the new IAM workers, a woman with black, curly hair and a pearly smile. She was staying with the Oswalds. Every day as she entered the yard, Daoud stopped lessons to watch, awed by her beauty.

Then one day she opened her mouth. "Koobasty?" she asked, her own version of the greeting, *khub astee?,* discordant but recognizable. Daoud cringed and sighed. Any potential romance ended there. Death by pronunciation.

Daoud announced that one of his friends was getting married and he invited Mary, Ann and me to the celebration as his "family". It was my first wedding in Afghanistan, and I had no idea what to expect. Daoud showed up the morning of the women's party in a smart new suit and seemed particularly charming. He picked up Hannah, who immediately spat up on his blazer. This ruffled him a bit, but after we cleaned him off he regained his suavity and led us into a home where the bride and her family were sharing the wedding dinner.

"You can eat here," he told us. We sat on the floor with the women of the family, honored by the privilege of joining this group even though we had never met. The bride was a stunning sixteen-year-old. Both families were fairly well off, and the bride unusually happy. (Women are supposed to demonstrate grief at leaving their parents' home to live with their husband's family; wedding photos tend to be devoid of smiling newlyweds.) She greeted us graciously and asked questions as the women arranged the skirts and veil of her traditional white gown.

After eating we said goodbye and were escorted to a gymnasium-sized room where the other guests were waiting. There were over a hundred women of all ages in an amazing array of fashions. I had been expecting the same modest clothing we saw on the streets – unlike in Kabul at that time, many women were completely veiled in *chahdri* outside their homes. The dimly lit hall dazzled with glittering, shimmering dresses of rainbow hues; among the guests I was even startled to see a six-foot tall woman in a sleeveless gold lame' pantsuit. Not only were the women flamboyantly attired, they also wore elaborate makeup and many had hair tumbling down their shoulders, something a discreet female would not do on the streets of Afghanistan.

A live band sat toward the rear of the room and women took turns dancing for a few minutes before sitting down and giving others a chance. Several men – all members of the family – took videos and photos. Other than that, no men were allowed; they had a separate party. Daoud clearly enjoyed roaming through the crowds of beautiful women.

"Would you dance?" he asked each of us in turn. Ann, who always leaned toward the most conservative behavior, declined; Mary danced for a few minutes. I love to dance, so I gladly passed Hannah off to Mary and headed to the center of the room with Daoud.

I was astonished as the floor cleared when Daoud and I began to dance. Daoud was a good dancer, and every move I made, he mirrored. I was enjoying the actual dancing, but every time I looked around I could see rows of women somberly watching us. Was it the novelty of a man and woman dancing together? Was it the oddity of how I danced – emphasizing footwork rather than the curving of wrists overhead, as an Afghan woman would? Or was it the fact that the band seemed to be playing the longest song in Afghan history? It reminded me of one of those awkward junior high school moments. When the dance finally ended, I gladly took baby Hannah and melted back into the crowd.

Later, Daoud informed me that many of the girls wanted to learn to dance like me and wondered: Was I doing the Lambada? (The Lambada was a sexy dance craze of the late 1980s; considering we did not even touch during the song, I am not sure any of them had actually seen it.) I wanted to put the episode out of my mind, but weeks afterward when a woman waited to be examined by Rich, she told me she had seen me dancing in a video. "Was that the Lambada?" she asked. I feared pirated copies of "Daoud and Melinda do the Lambada" were being marketed in the bazaar. I vowed that I would never dance at another wedding in Afghanistan.

Our near neighbors invited us to our second wedding a few months later, this time in a village close to Mazar. Rich had bought fabric for me at Christmas to make a dress for fancy occasions. The outfit the tailor created I called my "Liberace dress" because of its red velveteen swirled with black and gold. Before we left for the party, our friends expressed disappointment at my understated cosmetics. They insisted on performing a make-over on me, thickly covering my lids with gray eye shadow and my lips with purple lipstick and black lip liner. They tried to persuade me I was gorgeous; as I told Rich later, I felt like the biblical Whore of Babylon.

Rich had also dressed for the occasion, in his fancy embroidered *payron* (shirt) and *tumbon* (trousers) and a tweed jacket for warmth. The neighbors piled into the vehicle, and then Rich discovered that he was not actually invited to the wedding – he was only there to transport us. Although dismayed, he did haul us out to the village and dropped the ladies off.

This time the wedding was even more crowded than the previous one. Every room of the house was jammed with women on *toshaks* lining the walls, shoulder to shoulder, for the meal. Outside there was some dancing, but in keeping with my pledge, I refrained from joining in. Hannah was hungry and fussy, and my long-sleeved, tight-fitting dress with a zipper up the back was not very accommodating to the discreet form of breast-feeding Americans do. The Afghan women cheerfully urged me to pull off my dress to nurse; I did my best without exposing myself to hundreds of women, and waited miserably for Rich to pick us up.

We later re-hashed the event. We suspected my invitation had been a ploy to get Rich to drive rather than a real desire to include us. For some reason this wedding served as an eye-opener. We longed to fit in, to be accepted as though we, too, were Afghans. Suddenly we knew the painful truth: no matter how hard we tried – how well we spoke Dari, or dressed and moved like locals – we would always be *kharijee,* foreigners. After that, a day never passed when this idea was not part of my consciousness.

And yet I miss the people. My friends.

Naan-baai, Mazar 1993

CHAPTER 9

Food, fainting, and family

Some people ask: What shall we eat?
Others ask: What shall we eat with?
(Afghan proverb)

One of the challenges of leaving our home culture was figuring out what and how to nourish our family. Should we try to stick as closely as possible to our normal diet? As Oregonians, that meant fresh, low-fat, low-salt foods. Or should we "go native" and live on palm kernel oil-drenched rice topped with chunks of beef or lamb? We attempted a modified version of both menus.

Addiction to *naan* came effortlessly, especially in Mazar. The Kabuli *naan* was stretched thin by bakers pulling their fingers across the dough, leaving long impressions. Nearly white and cracker-like in places, *naan* in the capital came from Pakistani wheat. The bread in Mazar was far tastier, the local whole wheat flour flavorful and the loaves thick and bagel-like. We took turns going to the *naan baai* around the block to buy the cheap loaves warm. While in Kabul the tandoor was in the floor – bakers swaddled their faces and arms to prevent burns – in Mazar ovens were built into the wall so we could see the glowing embers and watch the men slap the disks of dough onto the side walls, splash the tops of the loaves with water to give them a glossy coating, and then pull them off with long forks. The bakers were friendly; one even dubbed Connor with an Afghan name, "Nahdir," which stuck.

We had to relax our standards on food quality and hygiene; bakeries with dirt floors and walls could not be expected to live up to the requirements of a shiny American restaurant. It became a breakfast pastime to look for any surprises baked into our *naan* – chunks of charcoal, mud, strings, or pieces of cloth. We figured the high heat of the tandoor killed the germs.

From the Afghans, we learned how to choose the best long grain rice and what to do in early spring when fruit was scarce. (The pale green football on the fruit cart, they informed us, was in fact a melon skin with dried strips of its flesh stitched inside.) We were told we could eat watermelon seeds, apricot pits, dried mulberries, balls of desiccated yogurt, and raw rhubarb sprinkled with salt. We discovered the secret to delicious Afghan French fries: ground grape seed sprinkled on top.

I missed black beans but cooked pintos; we tried slow-cooking beef only to discover that it was still too tough to swallow.

(One of the boys chewed for several minutes before finally asking, "May I spit it out now?") We added more salt to our food to counter the dizziness of summer dehydration, and I became adept at rolling out flour tortillas. The bazaar lacked broccoli, our favorite vegetable, but there was an abundance of others; we probably ate more produce there than we did in the US. Although apples disappointed, we enjoyed a few of the hundred variety of grapes in Afghanistan; sweet and sour cherries; different types of melons; plums, peaches, and apricots; and wonderful Mandarin oranges (more like Clementines than the canned Mandarins my aunt had popped into marshmallow salads).

In terms of convenience foods, there were noodles of various shapes, all made from soft wheat that produced mushy pasta; tomato paste; and dry milk powder. Other than that, everything was either fresh or non-existent. We were eating about five pounds of rice each week with beans and chickpeas; we splurged occasionally on a cut of veal at a dollar per pound. *I have not figured out*, I wrote home, *how to get the butcher to stop smashing the bones with his ax.*

Including our family, our first Thanksgiving included twenty people – the Oswalds, the Muellers, and guests from the UN (none of whom were American). A photo of the meal would not help in identifying it; nothing was quite right. Ann stewed the turkey because she had no oven at that point; Mary made yeast rolls but found too late that the yeast was dead, so they were flat and dense. The mashed potatoes we brought were okay but the pumpkin pies had taken two days to bake in our solar oven so we weren't sure if they were safe to consume. There were no cranberries. Mary, who once told me to always prepare dessert first ("If the food doesn't turn out well, at least everyone leaves happy") baked a pineapple upside-down cake. Not a traditional Thanksgiving dessert, but like the rest of the food, it was happily devoured by our European friends, who seemed mystified when we laughed about the menu.

By Christmas, we had it all figured out. Most modern cookbooks do not take into account the challenges of cooking without a butter-infused bird and a pop-up timer. But we poured over *The Joy of Cooking* (the only cookbook I had seen with recipes for porcupine, beaver, and bear) and after Rich and James killed and plucked the turkey, we trussed and basted it through an oil-saturated tea towel. The Oswalds and Muellers and some Afghan friends joined us for the meal. Our children seemed content that morning with a few gifts and some candy; Christmas in Afghanistan helped free us of materialistic customs and set us on a course of experimenting to make it a *holy day* and not just a *holiday*.

❖

While we adapted to the locally-available food, we did miss chocolate. In Kabul it was available in Shar-e-Nao on Flower Street, but Mazar was a different story. Apart from Russians, the city had not seen foreign traffic like the capital and so had not developed the extensive trade in international foods. We were longing for anything cocoa-flavored. One day James called us on the radio and said he had found an eight-year-old case of Iranian chocolate (known as "Tak Taks" and looking suspiciously like "Kit Kats"). Catching a *gahdee,* we hurried to the shop and bought a box ourselves. The bars were stale and the chocolate white from melting and re-hardening, but we didn't care. A custom developed for visitors from Kabul to bring chocolate and an expectation that those who went abroad from Mazar would bring both chocolate and cheese back, since cheese was not available, either.

One shopkeeper had escaped Kabul with his imported foods. He set up business in the bazaar, and I went to examine the delicacies which could be found nowhere else. To my shock, he was asking eight dollars for a bag of yeast (I later discovered the inexpensive Iranian equivalent for about a dollar) and even more for a bottle of Tang drink mix. We referred to him as "The Extortionist" between ourselves, and boycotted his shop.

Rich and I had been encouraged as newlyweds to take regular date nights. But by this point we had seven children between our families, and no babysitters. So we began taking turns watching the kids so each couple could go out to lunch at the UN guesthouse, where for $2.50 we enjoyed a meal of meat, rice, and cooked vegetables. Sometimes we took along the children after our weekly worship services. Since the other non-governmental organizations (NGOs) banned staff from bringing children into the country, ours were the only expatriate minors around, and we heard many expressions of envy by fathers from around the world who missed their own kids. One day while eating lunch at the guesthouse, Connor wandered the dining room. He soon ran back to our table, excited.

"Dad," he said, "there's a man over there from the country that tried to kill Samson!" We turned and with one glance were able to correct him.

"He's from the *Philippines*," Rich told Connor, "not the *Philistines*." When we met a UN worker from Ghana named Hazel, Connor again misheard, looking around and asking earnestly,

"Where's Weasle?" We were glad our children could grow up in the diverse community of aid workers from Asia, Africa, and Europe.

We were spending more time in Afghan homes, too. Daoud took us to see a family whose mother had been one of Rich's patients. After a few minutes in the formal parlor, we were separated: I ended up in the women's quarters, where an Australian soap opera (dubbed into Russian) blared on the television; the men dined while watching Bollywood films and recent videos by Michael Jackson and Madonna. Although we preferred visits without mandatory television viewing, it seemed to be an important element in the upper class's show of hospitality. We appreciated Daoud's help in acquainting us with the culture.

Despite the end of the mobile medical clinics, Rich kept busy. He was often pressed by Daoud into treating his friends, many of whom had moved from Kabul. Rich also provided medical advice to our teammates.

At the beginning of January 1993, Ann called us on the radio. "Could we come over and talk to you?" she asked. She sounded agitated.

"Sure," we said.

Both James and Ann seemed somber as they sat down.

"James has been having fainting spells," Ann told us. He couldn't connect them to anything and they happened without warning.

"This morning, he was in the bazaar buying *naan*," Ann said, "when he collapsed. He woke to find a man in a turban leaning over him with a large knife." We looked at James, shocked. "The man gently scraped the mud off James' face with the knife before helping him up."

"Well, that was nice of him," we agreed.

"But clearly, you need to get worked up by a doctor," Rich said. "If you were in America, a cardiologist would run tests on you. I'm afraid you'll need to leave the country to get help."

James scheduled a trip to Uzbekistan but the problem was not properly diagnosed; he continued blacking out. Finally he and Ann planned a vacation to Islamabad in Pakistan, where James could be examined at Shifa International Hospital.

73

While James and Ann were out of the country, we spent our spare time trying to maintain our hastily constructed house. Rich climbed on the roof to shovel away inches of snow with a cookie sheet – the flat roof design would not allow the melt-off to go anywhere but inside, and it was already leaking. The increased humidity caused doors to swell, preventing them from closing, and the main water line to our house froze and burst. (We had to draw water from our seventy-five-foot deep well until things thawed.) The sidewalk from our gate to the porch buckled and sections of the driveway collapsed. We had not had time to paint our poor-quality concrete floors before moving in, and whenever I swept, about half a cup of sand would come up with the dirt. There was plenty of mud in Mazar, as we had been forewarned, and it was a challenge to keep at least *some* of it outside.

We also decided it was time to try to contact our families.

From the time we left the US in October 1992 until the first of January 1993, we had received only two letters from the States. In Kabul, we had had a phone, although we never used it; in Mazar, a phone in the home was not an option. James and Ann kept the office radio set at their house, and attempted twice-weekly calls to our headquarters in Kabul. (If the fighting was bad, no one would answer at the other end.)

With the advent of the Internet and mobile phones, it is almost unimaginable to consider that twenty years ago we would hear about major life events long after they occurred. My uncle and grandfather both died and my brother married while we were virtually inaccessible.

We wrote letters each week to chronicle what was going on. We were advised to post and receive mail through Delhi; letters were carried there from Kabul. When someone left Mazar for the capital or headed north through Uzbekistan, we would quickly finish the correspondence we were working on and deliver it to the traveler to send. We always hoped visitors might bring mail, too. Sometimes family members heard through the grapevine someone was coming to Afghanistan, and they would send plastic bags thoughtfully packed with Legos, chocolate chips, and clippings from *The Oregonian* newspaper. Oddly, I found I could tolerate absences from family until their letters came. Then I spent a day feeling homesick.

When I became pregnant with our fourth child we wanted to call home, so we decided to drive across the northern border of Afghanistan to the city of Termez in Uzbekistan. This would also allow us to stock up on whatever goodies were available. Termez still glowed with the aura of the former Soviet Union; when we stopped a traffic cop to ask for directions to the United Nations office, he demanded we show our ID. The shops were empty except for one or two products stacked in a pyramid inside. But on the street we were thrilled to find men guarding boxes of Snicker bars. We stopped the car and bargained with the vendors – we did not want to buy one or two bars, we informed them, but their entire stock.

Considering the scarcity of chocolate in northern Afghanistan, finding Snickers in Termez was like striking gold. One of the girls whose family had newly arrived in Mazar even wrote a poem suggesting parents would sneak out and enjoy candy bars after their children were asleep. ("It isn't just my father/it's the other fathers, too/They say, "Tonight let's get together/for a father Snickeroo.") It's amazing how delicious anything from the US started to taste.

Kabul, 1993

CHAPTER TEN

Edges of the garden

What difference does it make if there is a door or a mountain between us?
(Afghan proverb)

It is easy to misjudge distances and the degree to which events in one location affect those elsewhere. For example, the distance between Mazar and Kabul by road is only a little greater than the distance between Phoenix and Las Vegas, or Chicago and Dayton, or New York and Washington. If Chicago dissolved into a state of anarchy, would it have any effect on Dayton? To those abroad reading the news, the conflict might seem to swallow up the entire North American continent. But to those on the ground, life in Dayton would probably appear relatively normal.

In the same way, our day-to-day lives were generally unaffected by Kabul's turmoil, although we did have contact with the skeleton team left in the capital. We were financially dependent on our Kabul office: since there was no international bank open in Afghanistan, we wrote blank checks which were transported to the capital and either deposited in our IAM account to pay for expenses like rent, or sent back transformed to currency. It was a risky business; at one point, the police returned a thousand dollar check to us that had been stolen in route. On another occasion, the money changer who was carrying our checks out of the country was murdered.

Many of the Afghan and foreign workers in the capital were friends and we followed their descent into hell by listening to the BBC and gleaning what we could from the intermittent radio calls between the Mazar and Kabul offices. The city had fallen into such disarray that our colleagues could barely work. The head of the IAM Board of Directors sent a bleak report out in February 1993:

> As I write this we are almost deafened by a large volley of very loud explosions. There have been direct or very close hits on every residence [of IAM workers] (except one) . . . . For our projects CWH is closed as is NOOR, PSK [the physiotherapy school]. Blind School and Motor Vehicle Workshop are burnt out. MCH [the Mother-Child Health] Clinic struck by missiles and coming and going is dangerous for workers. . . . Office is operating but not very encouraging. Not much work but heavy expenses.

The blind school and NOOR – the eye hospital – were the initial projects of the IAM when it began in 1966, so it was particularly disheartening when they closed. The rocket that hit a container next to the motor vehicle workshop (we had our own group of mechanics) burned down that building as well as the blind school and the optical shop, where eyeglasses were made. Afghan employees lost family members as fighting continued; three relatives of a *chaokidar* died, and a carpenter had five children killed. Greg and Mary's former house helper and friend was hanging clothes outside when a rocket hit her house, killing her seven-year-old daughter and blowing off her husband's legs.

We heard that at one point during heavy fighting, teammates in Kabul took refuge together in a basement. Periodically someone would announce which homes and buildings had been hit by shelling. There were collective groans as each report came in. As of February 4, the office reported to us, the sauna had suffered some damage, losing windows and the front door, but still stood. Not long after, it was destroyed; a roar of misery went up that was almost audible in Mazar. Of course we all recognized this loss was nothing compared to the human casualties.

Northern Afghanistan was like a different country – in fact, we heard rumors at times that its leaders sought to break away from the central government and form a new land. The Uzbek warlord Abdul Rashid Dostum controlled several provinces, including Balkh, in which Mazar lay. Although at the time we were unaware of the atrocities Dostum would later be accused of, while living in Mazar we appreciated the stability of the area under his oversight. His Junbesh soldiers could be seen around town in their distinctive blue-and-green plaid turbans and *payron* hitched up so high their lower legs were exposed. But trade in the food bazaars, the carpet and tin markets and other enterprises around town seemed lively, and transportation flowed smoothly. Herds of camels watered toward the edge of town. On the corner near our house, a man tossed stacks of wheat, sending clouds of chaff into the air. We frequently heard celebratory gunfire from weddings – or when the electricity came back on after an absence of several days – but other than that, Mazar was fairly peaceful.

But at the beginning of February 1993 we started hearing a different kind of gunfire outside the city. Checkpoints were erected; we lived between two and had to be in our yard by ten p.m. Rich's spoken Dari was so good that he made friends with all the soldiers, and they waved as we passed by. Only once was a warning shot fired – when Rich unwittingly drove into an area where Dostum himself was traveling.

Increasingly frustrated with medicine ("They can't differentiate between the severity of a sniffle and a gunshot wound"), Rich anticipated a new job in the IAM. Working in development – an idea fostered by his trip to central India during our evacuation in 1992 – was now on the table as a viable option. Rich, Greg, and a dentist who had joined us in Mazar drafted a proposal for an official Community Development Program that involved using the city as a base and doing the actual projects in surrounding villages. Greg was interested in dry sanitation; he assured us that odorless pit toilets were a possibility. (This stretched our credulity; we had camped in places in the US where we had been obliged to take a gulp of fresh air before dashing into outhouses.) Rich wasn't sure what he would be doing in the CDP but was open to trying something new.

❖

In early March Daoud appeared at our door, cheerfully informing us that his family had arrived from Kabul by bus. For an Afghan, the worst fate possible was being alone; Daoud had missed his family so much, he slept over at our house about once a week. Although he was not the oldest son – his brother had been sent to Russia under the Soviets to be educated, as was their practice, and never resettled in Afghanistan – Daoud took on the role of eldest, finding housing for his family. With the burgeoning population, rentals were neither plentiful nor cheap.

Daoud's sweet mother and younger sister, his older sister and her husband, two younger brothers, and his father – a man whose presence must have once filled the parliament building – finally settled in a few rooms with the items they had been able to stow on top of the bus along with the possessions of others fleeing the capital. We marveled at their dignity and hospitality, especially considering that they had left behind one of Karte Char's mansions to move into these cramped, dusty rooms in Mazar.

Despite the stability of Mazar and good news – like the arrival of Daoud's family – there were things to discourage us. Workers with other aid groups in the area left after three UN workers were killed in Jalalabad, a city east of Kabul. The UN diminished from sixty to nine; Oxfam completely pulled out. Besides our small team, only about four people with Medicin Sans Frontieres (Doctors Without Borders) remained.

Sometimes we also had pangs of culture shock as we were repeatedly reminded we would never be Afghans and never fully understand them, or be understood by them. Trust, a foundational requisite of Western friendships, was not part of our relationships with Afghans; mutual indebtedness was the core ingredient. Neighbors would grace us with a platter of steaming *aushak* dumplings one day; the next they would expect a ride or money or an appointment with the doctor *saeb*. We also discovered people would lie about all kinds of things, important as well as insignificant. Our straight-forward declarations ("I was too busy to come") began to sound like blatant untruths even to us; we fumbled to sweeten our responses but often failed.

The attitude that *The foreigner can afford to pay, so why not charge more?* drove us crazy. When we first moved to Mazar, Daoud went carpet shopping with Rich. After selecting some rugs he liked, Rich left the shop and discussed them with Daoud, who returned to bargain. The shopkeeper berated him for helping foreigners instead of his own people. Another day following a language lesson, I almost relished using a new verb – "to cheat" – on a butcher who tossed a rock onto the scale to bring my meat up to the half kilo I had ordered.

We never went anywhere without being noticed. About eighty percent of the women in Mazar wore the full *chahdari*. Respecting the conservative culture of the city, we had chosen to dress like the local women, but opted to forego the *chahdari* in favor of the large scarves the older women usually wore. These kept our faces visible, draping over our heads and upper bodies. Apparently our fair skin was alluring, and men could not resist staring. Once while riding in the back of a horse-drawn carriage, I watched as a young man bicycled close behind and gazed at me admiringly.

"How white you are!" he exclaimed in Dari.

Considering none of us were stunning by American standards, the response we got from men in Afghanistan was surprising. We decided we should apply for visas to Uzbekistan, in case an emergency required evacuation. All of us dutifully went to a local photographer. We were led into a room with an old glass-plate camera; we covered our heads and tried *not* to smile for the pictures. When James went to pick up the photos, he discovered that there was one less photo of me than of other people.

"What happened to the fourth picture?" he asked the photographer.

"Fourth picture?" the man echoed, feigning ignorance. "Yes, there should be four pictures of each person," James pointed out. "This one only has three."

James persisted with the young man, who finally relented. He pulled back the blotter covering his desk. Beneath, James saw stacks of photos – all portraits of young women that the photographer had kept. He sheepishly returned mine to James.

Our physical appearance in itself was not an automatic giveaway that we were foreigners; there were a few blond Afghan men and more than once people ran after us to "return" children they thought we had left behind – brown-eyed, fair-haired children like our own. Rich's spoken Dari was so good, an Afghan once told me, that "if your back was turned and you heard him speak, you'd think he *was* an Afghan."

But people realized quickly that we were not natives. Afghan women actually hold their bodies differently as they move (one of the physical therapists explained it to me – something about shifting their weight back over their pelvis) and American women tend to walk briskly. Not only could local women recognize us from a distance, but they astonished me by identifying other veiled women on the street. They would walk through clusters of women clad in blue *chahdari* and suddenly stop for conversations.

"How did you know who they were?" I asked once after observing this.

"By their shoes," they answered. I wondered if I could even identify my immediate family members by what they had on their feet. This acute power of observation was yet another reminder of the distance between us and the people among whom we lived.

Mazar, 1993

Pirate birthday party, 1993

CHAPTER ELEVEN

Weeds

Look after your property,
and you won't accuse your neighbor of being a thief.
(Afghan proverb)

We were privileged to have a number of retirees serve in Afghanistan. One was an ophthalmologist who had helped start the NOOR Eye Hospital in the 1970s; he made repeated trips to train local physicians. During one of his last visits, he stood up at a meeting and announced he had SARS.

At that time, SARS – a potentially deadly respiratory disease – was spreading across the globe. So Dr. Friesen had our attention when he spoke. "I have SARS," he said. "Severe Afghanistan Return Syndrome."

We instantly understood: there is something addictive about Afghanistan. Life is raw and real; hardly a day passes without leaving behind a story. Life in the US seems prosaic by contrast. Dr. Friesen couldn't resist coming back again and again.

Our friend James seemed to have more than his share of stories. He and Ann had spent six weeks in Pakistan both for a break and to see if they could get a clear diagnosis on James's fainting spells. When the doctors found nothing obvious, the family decided to return to Mazar. Ann and the children flew in, but James stopped in Kabul to do some work in our main office before rejoining them.

After several days without communicating, James stumbled into the Muellers' yard late one day, exhausted and without luggage.

He had left Kabul by bus. Heavy snow caused an avalanche, covering the Salang Pass, which wound through the mountains along the major road between Kabul and Mazar. Several busses and cars were trapped in the nearly two-mile long tunnel built by the Soviets. After four days on the bus, James decided to walk out.

On the bus was a woman with a baby and a small child, and James was afraid they would freeze to death, as others had already done. So James took the children, and they tried to make their way down the highway. But the mother, clad in high heels, kept falling. Blizzard conditions had set in again, and James told the mother, "If I wait for you, the children will die." So he took both children and trudged five hours through the snowstorm until he reached a place where he could wait for the mother. Not only did the baby cry the whole way, but James also had to put up with trekking in his sport jacket and dress shoes – not exactly perfect cold-weather attire. Fortunately, he did not get frostbitten or have a blackout – especially significant since he had ridden part of the way holding onto the back of a truck.

After hearing James's harrowing story, we were all so relieved at his safe return it took us until the next morning to wonder if anyone had initiated a full-scale rescue operation. We discovered that the Oswald's landlady was on one of the trapped busses; her son wanted to look for her. Greg, James, and Rich contacted Medecins Sans Frontieres and arranged to head back to the Salang Pass to see what they could do. By that time food was being brought in to people, and a number of passengers had walked out. Greg and Mary's landlady said she wanted to stay with her bus to console other women who had been stranded. The crisis was nearly over when James and the others arrived. But it was reminder again of the hardships Afghans faced in everyday life.

❖

We missed the transition between winter and spring. Overnight blossoms appeared on the cherry and apple trees Rich had planted in our yard and the beautiful purple jacaranda trees around the central shrine. Undesirables began to appear inside, too: in one week we found a locust, a scorpion (which Rich annihilated with a hammer, splattering its guts everywhere), and a snake (which the neighbor children assured us was "very dangerous").

Celebration ushered in spring in Afghanistan. According to the Persian calendar, New Year's Day is not January 1, but March 21, the date of the spring equinox. While living in Kabul we had attempted creating the traditional *Nao Roz* dish of *aft maywa* – a mixture of seven dried fruits and nuts. Unfortunately it fermented, so we could not share it with our Muslim neighbors. This time there was no *aft maywa,* but our near neighbors brought bowls of *halwa*, a surprisingly delicious pudding made of sprouted wheat germ. We did not anticipate the noisy revelries that night: gunfire, artillery, and rocket explosions filled the evening air, and tracer bullets and flares lit up the sky. We were relieved when our *chaokidar* assured us the war in Kabul had not shifted north.

Our formal language classes ended in April, a year later than they should have. Ann hired refugee musicians to perform for our graduation party and we dined on *pilau* and kabobs. The last few chapters of our textbook were a blur (there are still a few verb tenses that perplex me) but we were done with the Long Course and could get on with life.

For me, that primarily meant taking care of the family. We had hired a middle-aged woman, Bibijon, to help with the cleaning but I continued to do all the cooking from scratch. I also decided to start kindergarten with Connor, who had celebrated his fifth birthday with a pirate-themed party in February. Using the publicschool kindergarten curriculum I brought from the US, we sometimes had to improvise. "We did 'The farmer in the dell' the other day," I wrote my parents, "and let [baby] Hannah be the cheese. Of course, we had to change the words: 'The cheese *sits* alone.'"

I had never felt completely comfortable with Bibijon; it seemed un-American to have a "servant" and the wages were pitifully low by US standards. Plus I always felt in the way when she was cleaning. One day I was in my bedroom and heard what sounded like water gushing from the taps in the bathroom. I tried to push the door open to urge our house helper not to be wasteful. We had to pump water with electricity to the roof, where we stored it in barrels, and the electricity was not reliable. Bibijon pushed equally hard from the other side of the door, preventing me from entering the room. "I'm cleaning," was all she said.

I had resolved before she arrived that morning that this was the day I would let her go. At the end of the morning, I explained that now that I was finished with language lessons, I could do the work myself. She was very unhappy when I informed her of my decision, but accepted her final salary, which I had previously laid aside for her. The children and I waved goodbye as she walked through the front door, down our cracked sidewalk, and out the gate.

A few days later Rich went to get some money, and started searching our room. He could not find it in the cupboard where we usually stored it. He went through everything, including our passport pouch, and then discovered all our cash (including our Indian rupees) was gone. The total came to about a thousand dollars, enough for us to live several months in Mazar. We were heartbroken, and chided ourselves for ignoring admonitions from other foreigners to lock up our valuables. Adding what had been stolen in Kabul to this, Rich told me, "We've lost more money than we've spent here." Word spread through the community that we had been robbed. The only people who had been in our house with any opportunity to steal were one of the teen sons of our near neighbors (who would no doubt have been discovered by his family if he'd shown up with large sums of money) and Bibijon.

Bibijon returned a few days later in tears, hearing rumors that we might send someone to arrest her, and she swore that she would never steal from us. We knew that regardless of who took it, that money was gone for good. I suspect that on the very morning I fired her, while running water as a cover she had actually been stuffing cash into her bloomers.

Another theft soon occurred on a much larger scale. One Friday we all went to the UN guesthouse for lunch. When James and Ann returned home, they discovered that the office money, which they managed – ten thousand dollars – had been stolen. They called a friend at the UN, and he urged them to notify the police. The loss of the money almost seemed minor compared with what followed.

The police rounded up everyone on their street for questioning, and then went after the Muellers' employees. Ann's cleaning woman came to her in tears, begging her, "Do not let the police take me away." She had heard enough stories of what happened to women in jail, and of course she was not really a suspect. James spent hours at the jail getting friends and neighbors released. To add to their other troubles, the Muellers noticed that the police had apparently stolen their hand-held radio during the investigation.

"I think the landlord must have taken the money," James told us. "He doesn't live very far from us, and he knows when we're going to be gone." But like our cash, the office money was never recovered.

When their lease came up for renewal, the Muellers' landlord refused to rent to them. As James and Ann prepared to move out, they began exchanging the expensive German faucets they had installed in the bathroom for the original, cheaper taps. But the landlord stopped them; he would not permit them to take the parts they had paid for.

We heard later that a rocket hit the property. I confess feeling justice had been served when discovering only one room had been destroyed: the bathroom.

Rich began spending time with two brothers, Faizullah and Rahimullah. Faizullah was small, with a thick black beard and turban. He rarely smiled and, unlike most of Rich's friends, made me feel like women were meant neither to be seen *nor* heard. I gladly steered clear of him, hiding beneath a scarf when he was near. Early on he warned Daoud about spending time with Rich, since we are Christians, and Faizullah's own devotion to Islam was evident. During one visit, the call to prayer sounded from a nearby mosque, as it did five times each day. Faizullah made a show of going onto our front porch to perform *namaaz*, the ritual prayer, kneeling toward Mecca. I was puzzled why he would come for a visit so close to prayer time; someone later explained Faizullah believed he would get extra spiritual merit for praying in front of infidels.

Faizullah shared a number of legends with Rich that hinted at his worldview. Rich recorded them in a journal he was keeping:

> The turtle was once a man who did not honestly weigh out the goods he was selling, and was thus cursed by God to wear stone on his back. The baboon was a man who cleansed his son's bottom with a chapatti, and was cursed to forever sport a red rump! The lizard was a man who urinated on Adam from a tree; the porcupine a needle seller who sold her goods too expensively.

> The moon was originally a woman, the sun a man. But the woman was afraid of the night and asked the man if she could take his place in the day. And we know that the sun is now a woman, because you can't look at her!

Rich noted after these stories that "F. & R. actually believe these things."

After a few months, Faizullah astonished us by inviting us to his house; apparently I had passed inspection and was deemed modest enough to be introduced to his younger sister. The family lived at the end of one of Mazar's maze-like alleyways; Faizullah warned us they kept a wolf on the roof in lieu of a watchdog, so we scanned the edges of the building as we entered the courtyard. Faizullah ushered me into the ladies' quarter where I met his sister.

It was no surprise that Faizullah kept her cloistered. She was very beautiful by any standard, with fair skin and tawny brown hair.

She greeted me and then asked, "Do you know where I can buy whitening cream to bleach my skin?"

"Your skin is beautiful," I told her.

"Well, I have these freckles," she complained. I wondered how she had acquired those; considering her brother's protective attitude, I guessed she received little sun exposure.

When other guests appeared in the courtyard, she motioned me away from the window and pulled the curtain, afraid we would be seen. We talked for a while and the room filled with women from the extended family.

After the men had finished lunch, the women served me. They watched attentively as I ate. It was awkward, eating while they observed. Trying to enjoy the meal like an American, I asked the women questions and conversed. But suddenly I realized what was going on. Quickly finishing – and eating less than I normally would – I thanked them for the meal. As soon as it was clear I was finished, the women dived into what was left of the rice and meat. There was no talk now; they all concentrated on the food. It rankled me; not only had they been forced to wait for the men, but had to eat *my* leftovers as well.

Faizullah took us to the home of his cousins, and it was one of my most unpleasant visits. Again I was sent alone to a room full of women. They immediately began questioning me about my body. What color was I "down there"? (They demonstrated what they meant, in case I misunderstood.) They made suggestive movements and laughed. Considering the outward modesty of Afghan society, I had not expected this. I tried to change the course of the conversation and was relieved when Faizullah and Rich called me out of the room to walk with them in the family garden.

In retrospect, I suppose these women had been deprived of opportunities to meet others dissimilar to themselves. When we looked at Afghans, we saw differences in color and facial structure between people, but they seemed far less noticeable than the variety we saw in the US. But Afghans were attuned to the characteristics that separated them from others. I knew racism was a problem in my home country, but did not realize until then it was an issue in Afghanistan, too.

While Faizullah was visiting one day, an Uzbek friend showed up. Faizullah leaned close to Rich as the guest crossed the yard. "Be careful," he said. "Uzbeks cannot be trusted."

Rich went and greeted his friend, who – seeing Faizullah -- whispered, "Watch out for Tajiks. You cannot trust them." Despite this blatant show of racism, and the violence of one ethnic group against another occurring in Kabul at that time, we later heard – and witnessed – people from different communities protecting each other, especially from the Taliban. But like in our own country, racism is a weed not easily uprooted.

The shrine by night, Mazar 1993

The street outside our gate, Mazar 1993

CHAPTER TWELVE

The mud and the Eids

If you can kill a man with sugar, why use poison? (Afghan proverb)

Even though we came from Oregon – a state known for its unremitting rain – we had never experienced anything like the "season of mud" we'd been warned about in Mazar. Nearly all the streets became goopy sinkholes in the winter and spring. When we were out visiting, we picked our way along the edges of the yards, clinging to the walls as we sought solid toe-holds. Most of the women wore silky white trousers under their dresses; we adopted this style, too. But mine seldom survived an outing; the mud clung like tar and did not seem to wash out. I marveled at men in their plain white or pale gray outfits and the women in their shiny black stiletto-heeled shoes walking around town. They never seemed covered with mud as we were.

On one of his trips to the bazaar, Rich took the boys. Aidan, at two-and-a-half, lost his footing and fell face-first in a chocolaty puddle. Immediately a passerby pulled him up, unwound his own turban, and carefully wiped the mud from Aidan's face. I marveled, when hearing such stories of people's graciousness, that the Afghans were at war with each other.

Not only was it a challenge to keep to one's feet; even in vehicles, the mud made roads almost nontraversable. The Land Cruiser Rich was using had four-wheel drive, but that didn't prevent it from getting stuck in the alley outside our gate.

95

Our yard was certainly a mud pit, but Rich planted beans, corn, and watermelon, and bought fruit trees to line our walkway. We hoped that by summer we would have enough greenery to keep the topsoil from blowing away in a cloud of dust.

One evening after we put the children to bed, a downpour started, an almost monsoon-like rain. When we went to check on the boys, we saw something we had never seen before: sheets of liquid mud streaming between the juncture of the wall and floor of their basement bedroom. We rushed across the rising water and plucked them and their covers from their beds, envisioning furniture floating upstairs on a brown river. It took two weeks to dry everything out.

In 1993, Ramazan, the month of fasting, began during that muddy late February. Since the Muslim calendar is based on the cycles of the moon, Ramazan falls at varying times each year. Occurring during February was an advantage: it was not yet hot, and observant Muslims do not drink (or eat) during the daylight hours. We were frequently asked in the bazaar, "Are you keeping the fast?"

Rich often did skip meals during the day, not for religious reasons but because he was working around others who were fasting. But since I was home, I made lunch for myself and the children. As Ramazan wore on, a pattern emerged: friends dropped by at noon and then mentioned that they were sick and not fasting that day. If this was meant as a hint, I tried to ignore it – I did not want to be known as the infidel chef. After a while, I realized it was inappropriate for men to be coming by when Rich wasn't home, anyway, so I asked the *chaokidar* to turn them back at the gate.

Two *Eids* were observed after the month of fasting. The first, *Eid-al Fitr,* came immediately after Ramazan. "Little *Eid,*" as Afghans sometimes called it, consisted of three days of celebration. The first day was reserved for the immediate family; the second and third days were dedicated to visiting other relatives and friends in socially concentric circles, from most to least intimate connections.

Our first *Eid* we tried to participate as the people around us did, buying kilos of bakery cookies and candy and nuts. I spent the day rushing tea from our little kitchen to the variety of guests who were being greeted in our living room (on one side of the kitchen) and our bedroom (on the other). We had to take into account that women should be separated from men, and some men – particularly those from hostile ethnic groups – separated from each other.

After two days of this, we were exhausted, and stopped answering our gate when someone pulled the bell rope.

We noticed that Afghans had an elaborate system for dealing with these holidays. Men and women took turns hosting and being hosted; the house was never left empty, and a hot thermos of tea stood ready for any visitors who might arrive. At the very least, sweets were arranged in little bowls – *nuqul*, candy-coated almonds or apricot pits; a few pieces of hard candy; and some toffee. If a family could afford it, there were elegant trays of arranged cookies (sugar cookies that all tasted the same but were formed in a variety of shapes), cakes, and nuts. The hosts even served half-glasses of tea for our children in clear mugs, pouring the tea from cup to cup until it was cool enough for Connor and Aidan to drink. Since we were missing out on Halloween trick-or-treating, we figured the kids could go ahead and enjoy the candy that was urged on them at each house we visited. It would have been hopeless to restrain them, anyway: Afghan hospitality meant that our wishes would be overridden and the children indulged. More than once I had to fetch a piece of candy out of Hannah's baby grasp and explain the danger of choking.

The first *Eid* was festive, and women sewed new dresses for the occasion. Everywhere in Afghanistan sparkly, shiny clothes were the fashion for these holidays (although the more "hip" younger women preferred to wear *cow buoy*, as they called denim). Children were beautifully attired and anticipated that guests would give them a little cash to celebrate. If they had female relatives adept at the incredibly regular and intricate local handiwork, the men wore special embroidered *payron*.

Eid-e-Qorban was different from the first *Eid*. This occurred forty days after the end of the fast, and was a more somber occasion. There was still tea and treats; but this *Eid* recalled the story of the patriarch Abraham's sacrifice. We knew the biblical account of how Abraham had taken his wife Sarah's son Isaac to the mountain and been stopped by an angel while in the act of sacrificing him to God. Instead, the Lord provided a ram to take his place. The Muslims had a different version of this story. It was not *Isaac,* they said, who had nearly been killed, but his half-brother *Ishmael.* (According to the Bible, Ishmael, Abraham's son by his wife's maid, became the father of the Arabs, which made the Islamic variation on the tale interesting.) At any rate, *Eid-e-Qorban* was a time to remember this sacrifice. Any family who could afford to slaughtered a sheep or a goat. They often sent a portion of the meat to the poor.

Our old neighbors (formerly our "near neighbors") had built a house at the northern edge of town. We were saddened by their move; we had enjoyed the daily visits both directions. Since they had no car, we borrowed an office vehicle or took a *gahdee* or taxi to see them. It was an hour's walk each way for them to drop in on us, but they did so many times. One of the teens was sent to invite us to celebrate *Eid-e-Qorban* with them.

They had a sheep ready when we arrived – not ready to eat, but ready to kill. Rich and Connor wanted to watch; I thought it would be better for the younger children not to see it. Rich told me they fed the animal sugar and petted it before taking its life. We sat in the basement, our neighbors' new sitting room, and heard the pathetic cry as the lamb's throat was cut and the blood drained out. The creature had seemed so passive up to the final assault that I could not help but think of the expression "as a lamb to the slaughter…"

They flayed the sheep by blowing air between the flesh and the skin to separate them and then our host came down to ask us what cut of meat we wanted to eat. In an attempt at being accommodating, we said, "Anything but liver." He looked crestfallen – apparently that was what he intended on serving us – and made kabobs for us instead. After that day I could never think in the same way about the personified sheep in children's books or cartoons.

As they explained the significance of the celebration, we knew our Muslim friends secretly hoped we would see the light and join them in their faith; for our part, we explained that we viewed Jesus as our *qorban*, or sacrifice.

As the weather continued to heat up, we learned ways to live without air conditioning. Rich rigged up burlap shades to cover our windows and had a metal frame built over our porch; we tied on this one of the ubiquitous blue UN plastic tarps (designed for refugees, but somehow finding their way into the bazaar for private sale). We began freezing small cartons of mango juice, which we cut in two and ate like sherbet. Daoud's mother showed me how to take sour cherries and repeatedly boil them in fresh water until they were leached of flavor and turned white; strained, chilled, and sweetened, this juice made a refreshing drink.

When we went visiting, sometimes rather than tea we were offered locally bottled Mirinda (an orange soda) or Coca-Cola. We had doubts about the purity of the products; we weren't sure how much company oversight the plant had. (Usually people stood outside shops drinking the soda before returning the scuffed bottles to shopkeepers. Sometimes the liquid inside did not even match the brand on the bottle.) It was hard to resist on especially hot days when a host set a bottle of soda in front of us, chunks of ice floating in the top. I stayed away from it; I began carrying bottles of water, telling people the children needed boiled water to drink because we were "weak foreigners." But Rich imbibed almost everything.

Although I was trying to run errands and visit friends in the afternoons, the local Jamiat-e-Islami commander (from the group led by Ahmad Shah Masood) told Rich I should "not go everywhere." Someone suggested I take a child with me when I went out, so Connor became my "bodyguard."

Rich was busy with James, finding housing for new members joining our team. We were glad to have single people and new families (which added eleven new playmates for the children) from Canada, New Zealand, the UK and the US. Our group meetings became a high point of the week; we hired a former IAM chef to cook a vat of *qabili pilau* for us, and we ate and talked while the children ran and played in the yard. A veterinarian from Australia stayed in our house a week until Faizullah, who was obviously smitten with her, scared her away.

Rich was also seeing three or four patients a day out of our home as his reputation spread around town. A neighbor we didn't know came to tell Rich his infant was sick; Rich followed him home to find the tiny (Rich guessed a little over three-pound) baby with a low heart beat and respiration rate. He tried CPR to increase his heart rate without effect. The parents realized their preemie would die; Rich said they were shaken but confident that it was the will of God. Mazar hospitals didn't have sophisticated enough equipment to deal with this kind of problem.

Since the local doctors owned the pharmacies, there was an incentive to overprescribe, and usually patients left the drug stores loaded down not only with antibiotics, but needless vitamins and other drugs as well. A foreigner claimed he overheard the following conversation in a pharmacy one day:

First man: "Dr. Lewis only prescribed one or two medications. What kind of doctor is that?"

Second man: "Yes, he doesn't give a lot of prescriptions. But if Dr. Lewis says you need it, you *need* it."

That summer rumors spread that cucumbers were being injected by Pakistanis with poison and that people had already died in Herat and Kabul. (It sounded like a time-intensive plot, I thought.) Supposedly four hundred people died in the city of Pul-i-khumri from these tainted vegetables. One shopkeeper even warned me not to buy the beloved mango juice packs; some of those were suspect as well. We were mystified about the story, but everyone knew it, and the price of cucumbers dropped so low the shopkeepers were practically giving them away.

One day Rich was walking home when two women ran screaming past him into an open gate. After a moment, another woman appeared and cried, "There's the doctor, bring him in!"

He hurried in and found what he later described as total mayhem. Four women were hysterical; one was stuffing strained yogurt into the mouth of a man lying unconscious on the cushions. His nostrils flared, indicating he was having trouble breathing, and his body was rigid. "What happened?" Rich asked.

"He ate a cucumber!" they reported. Rich tried everything to rouse the man – including giving him a painful sternum rub – but without success. "Let me get a car," Rich said. "We'll take him to the hospital."

The patient was completely limp as Rich and two of the men of the family carried him to the car and then into the hospital.

"Quick!" Rich said to two young men in lab coats. "This man ate a cucumber."

One of the doctors turned nonchalantly to the other. "Bring an ampule of sterile water," he instructed him.

Horrified, Rich stopped the doctor. "You can't just inject him with sterile water," he insisted. "This man needs real medical help."

The young doctor motioned for Rich to be calm. He carefully injected the patient with water. Rich watched with concern. After a few minutes, the nearly-dead man sat bolt upright.

Within an hour he was ready to go home.

Stunned, Rich asked the doctors, "How did you know?"

"We have seen several cases over the past few days," they said. "People hear that the cucumbers are poisoned, they get dehydrated and eat a cucumber for liquid, and then they faint. The families all assume they've been poisoned."

Later we heard that the BBC investigated the alleged Pakistani plot and could confirm no cases of death – or illness – from cucumbers that summer. And our family was able to enjoy an abundance of cheap, nontoxic produce.

Typical Mazar street, 1993

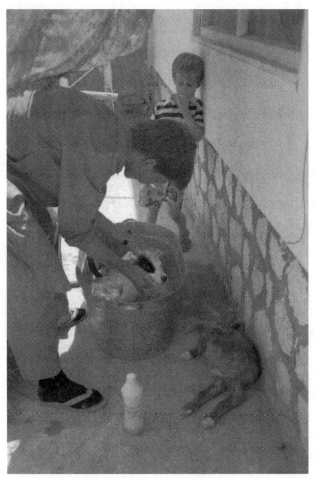

Rich and Connor with Patch and Cocoa, 1993

CHAPTER THIRTEEN

In sickness and in health

What God decides will happen, but tie the knee of your camel anyhow.
(Afghan proverb)

Like all conscientious parents, we wanted the best for our children. In the United States, we knew that meant attending a good school, playing a sport from an early age, learning a musical instrument, and having at least one family pet to care for. But we did everything wrong by American standards. Because of the nature of our nomadic lifestyle (and lack of options early on), our children were homeschooled, they had no access to team sports, and we did not possess the only instrument I was any good at. However, during our time in Afghanistan, we did claim six dogs as pets.

A UN worker brought us our first two puppies from the same litter. The female, Patch, was white with brown spots; the solid brown male we named Cocoa.

About ten days after we received the dogs, Patch became listless. In deference to our neighbors, who viewed dogs as spiritually unclean, we kept our animals outside the house. All day Patch lay on the porch, refusing food and water. Elisabeth, the Australian veterinarian, came by and examined her. "If she doesn't drink, she's going to die," Elisabeth warned me. We tried that day to nurse the puppy back to health with oral rehydration solution.

The next morning, as we were lying in bed, Rich moaned, "I don't feel well."

"Would you like me to bring you something to drink?" I asked.

"No," he said. "I'm not thirsty."

The children were still asleep in the basement. I went out onto the front porch. There in the yard lay Patch. As I approached her, the truth sank in: she wasn't napping – she was dead. I went back to tell Rich; he could not get out of bed.

I have always had a worst-case-scenario mentality. Patch had been languid; Patch wouldn't drink; Patch was dead. Rich, who braved illnesses that kept others home from work, was reclining lethargically in bed and would not drink. Might it be, I worried, that Rich had contracted whatever killed our dog?

The summer sun had baked our muddy yard to concrete. There was no way I could dig a hole to bury the dog, plus I had to take care of Rich and the children. I dragged Patch's little corpse into the unused outhouse in the corner of the yard until someone could deal with her. The next day, a German friend came by and retrieved her body (bloated by the heat) and dug a grave.

Rich was vomiting about every forty-five minutes and got weaker and weaker. "I need an IV," he told me, trying to insert the tube himself. After his three failed attempts, I called Mary on the radio.

"Could you come over and put an IV in for Rich?" I asked. "He's really dehydrated."

Over the next few days she and Ann took turns buying and changing the IV fluid. I marveled at Rich's lucidity, even in his impaired state, as he dictated to Ann what percent saline solution she should get him. The only nourishing item Rich could hold down was milk; his weight dropped dramatically (and he had little to spare before his illness) and he could barely get out of bed. I knew there was no better care available in Mazar than Rich was getting in our home. At one point the Medicin Sans Frontieres doctors, who could overhear our radio conversations, suggested we have him airlifted out of the country.

Visions of widowhood swam in my head. I was so distracted, caring for him and dealing with the children, that I expressed surprise one morning when Mary showed up to change his IV bag and set a chocolate cake on the kitchen table. "What's this for?" I asked.

Mary had her two daughters with her. "I thought we might want to have a little party to celebrate Hannah's first birthday," she said. In my anxiety, I had completely forgotten. While Mary took care of Rich, we held a mini-party. I wondered if Rich would be around to celebrate our daughter's second birthday.

We soon realized he had hepatitis A. Our office had advised us before leaving the US to get gamma globulin shots every six months while in Afghanistan, the suggested protocol before the vaccine became available a few years later. We were lax in getting the gamma globulin shots but ate out often; our neighbors were eager to show hospitality to the foreigners in their midst. I shunned the bottled pop and fresh salads, but Rich dug in to everything with gusto, and now he was suffering for it.

As word spread that the doctor *saeb* was sick with *zardi* (named after the color yellow, because of what hepatitis does to one's eyes), friends and acquaintances began showing up with advice and gifts. Certain foods are thought to help hepatitis; one is watermelon, which happened to be in season. A small mountain amassed on the kitchen floor. Faizullah and our landlord both offered to bring in a *zardibur*, a man who would suck the jaundice out with an onion. This proposition I politely declined.

Although Rich was weak and nauseated, he became delirious about food. This disturbed me more than his other symptoms, because he had always been indifferent about what he ate. Suddenly, lying in our darkened bedroom, he started fantasizing.

"Melinda," he began, "remember that great beef stroganoff that Sandy used to make, the kind with real sour cream, and huge mushrooms, and tender beef?"

"Yes," I answered slowly.

"I would love to have some of that! Or Chicken Kiev," he went on, smacking his lips at the memory of a childhood favorite, "or some Chinook salmon barbecued with lemon. . . some Tillamook cheese. . . or a hamburger at Hudson's Grill. . ."

I tried not to tremble. *He must be dying*, I thought.

But he wasn't. Day by day he grew stronger and was able to sit out in the living room for short visits with his friends. Once he was walking around we decided that we should take a break somewhere he could get his strength and weight back. Before the hepatitis he had been thin, but now he looked skeletal. His then-stylish glasses frames – with big ovals over each eye – did not help. They only shrunk his gaunt face further.

We bought tickets on a bus bound for Kabul. Most of the other passengers had celebrated a wedding in Mazar and apparently contracted food poisoning. Much of the eight-hour ride was spent with vomit sloshing up and down the aisle of the bus. We tried to keep a positive attitude without losing our own lunches.

Kabul was a quiet mess. We spent a night at the guesthouse and realized with shock that even though Mazar was a much smaller, less-developed city, it actually boasted more amenities than the capital. Candlelight illuminated the elegant marble bathroom where we scooped water out of barrels to flush the toilets.

The next day we traveled by van to Peshawar in Pakistan. The road consisted of the most terrifying one hundred and eighty-nine miles of highway travel I had ever experienced. Between Kabul and Jalalabad we wound along what had once been paved but now consisted primarily of potholes. The road was narrow, and van and taxi drivers insisted on veering toward the two-thousand- foot cliff above the Kabul Gorge in an attempt to avoid areas of missing concrete. Near here in January 1842 nearly seventeen thousand British had been massacred while withdrawing from Kabul toward the end of the First Anglo-Afghan War. It was easy to imagine sharpshooters picking them off a path clinging to the sides of these craggy mountains.

The IAM ran a guesthouse in Peshawar for those in transit, and I was always horrified to step through the front door and confront my own face in the full-length mirror. Usually we were covered with dust and sweat – none of the vehicles traversing the road had air conditioning, so we drove with the windows down. The first task on checking into our room was to wash our stiff, dirty hair.

The next day we made it to our vacation destination: Murree, a beautiful hill station north of Islamabad. There was an English-medium boarding school there and we enjoyed interacting with other foreigners and their children. The shops and restaurants thronged with Pakistani honeymooners, some of whom begged for photos with our families. We rented a pony and gave rides to the children outside the Raj-era cottages we leased. A month eating and walking helped restore Rich to health.

While in Murree, we met a family who was living in the Sindh province in southern Pakistan. This was an area dominated by Hindus (unlike most of Pakistan, which is Muslim with a Christian minority), and the Canadian doctor and his wife who lived and worked among them extolled the virtues of village life. By the end of our time, Rich was persuaded that we, too, should move to a village.

I had a little trepidation about this. In terms of lifestyle, it seemed the direction we continually headed: from a spacious mansion in Kabul to a compact house in Mazar; from cosmopolitan to semi-rural. Maybe village life was the natural next step. It would be hard to leave our friends, both foreign and local. But we had a few months to discuss and prepare for such a move.

Returning to Mazar, we found that the German friend who buried Patch and took care of Cocoa in our absence had a request. His children, he explained, had grown attached to the puppy. Could they keep him? Considering all he had done for us and the little time we had spent with the dog, we agreed.

Now that Rich was better, he could inspect the changes I had made while he was bedridden. The design – where guests had to walk through the tiny kitchen to get to the living room – annoyed me. With his fatigued consent, I switched the living room and bedroom, turning our kitchen into a sitting room. The office workers moved the kitchen cabinet into our former bedroom.

There was no plumbing, so I put a barrel with a spigot over the sink and drained the water into a bucket. Not an upgrade, exactly, but I was happy to have a bigger, more private kitchen.

There hadn't been time to finish the painting before we left for Murree, so we hired the brother of our devout friend Faizullah, Rahimullah, to do this when we returned.

Before he arrived to work, I pondered the dried bread we had left during our absence. We had appalled our neighbors a few months before by throwing half-eaten rice and bread on a rubbish heap in the street. (Mazar did not have trash collectors, so this was the normal procedure for waste.) Food is considered holy in Afghanistan, especially bread, so instead of throwing it away, people try to keep it for cows or other animals. To allow bread to touch the ground was unthinkable to them; they picked up an inadvertently dropped piece, kissed it, and touched it to their foreheads. In an effort not to violate this cultural norm again, we faithfully kept our old bread until we could carry it over to a neighbor who owned a cow. But we had forgotten to do this before leaving on our trip, and our *chaokidar* had not taken care of it, either.

Now the ancient *naan* was rock-hard and covered in dust. We could not throw it out on the street and it was inedible; no cow would want it. I suddenly thought, *Why not burn it?* I threw a piece of paper in the bucket and lit it; the bread smoldered like wet wood but would not catch fire. I stirred it unsuccessfully. The bucket was still smoking when our painter arrived. Realizing the delicacy of the situation, I looked up nervously as he walked through the gate.

To my chagrin, Rahimullah immediately crossed the yard and peered into the bucket. "You're burning *bread?*" he asked in horror. "That's a sin."

Stammering a response, I escaped to the house as quickly as possible. From there I chided myself for my lack of cultural understanding. Then I looked outside and saw something bewildering.

Since we now had an office vehicle to use, we kept a barrel of gasoline near the driveway. Rahimullah, with one eye on the house, was pumping fuel from the barrel directly into his motorcycle! I suppose from his perspective, what I considered wrong – stealing – was only a cultural norm: if it was accessible, it was meant to be taken. After letting the painter know we considered *theft* wrong, I terminated his contract and painted the room myself. But for a long time afterwards, I marveled at our differing ideas of what constituted a sin.

The neighbor's house after fighting, 1994. Our gate is visible to the right.

CHAPTER FOURTEEN

Trouble in the garden

He who has the power to fight doesn't negotiate. (Afghan proverb)

Home security in Mazar-i-Sharif did not involve installing cameras or putting sophisticated locks on our gates or homes. In fact, we discovered there were only a few patterns of keys sold in the bazaar, so any confidence in our padlocks and door keys was ill-placed. Someone told us that most Afghan families kept a sword to defend their house (our landlord was happy to reclaim one hidden in a cupboard) and homes were never left empty because of the risk of theft.

For this reason, the office insisted we hire a *chaokidar,* even though our previous experience made us wary. They sent us a wavy-haired young man barely out of his teens. He spent most of the time in his room listening to music on his shortwave radio and sketching pictures of girls. Others in the IAM had watchmen buy bread and groceries or even wash their dinner dishes, but we were content just having ours answer the gate.

We had already discovered another theft, items perhaps nabbed while we passed through customs on our return from Pakistan. We might not have noticed this loss until our next trip abroad. But Rich received a message that he was wanted at the World Food Program office. Mystified, he drove to the building, where he was shown into a private room.

The Afghan behind the desk, whom Rich recognized, greeted him.

"Hello," Rich said. "How can I help you?"

The man reached into a drawer and pulled out a stack of papers. "Could you sign these, please?" he asked, pushing them across the desk.

Rich glanced at the papers. They were hundreds of dollars' worth of traveler's checks – ours – already signed at the top by Rich and waiting the second signature, which was done at the time they were cashed.

"Where did you get these?" Rich asked, shocked to find himself in this surreal situation.

"I bought them in the bazaar," the man said, handing Rich a pen. "Could you sign them?"

"No, I'm not going to sign them," Rich answered. "These belong to me."

The man became agitated. "But I bought them. I paid a lot of money for them."

Rich shrugged. "Well, you made a mistake. Look," he went on, "they're worthless unless I sign them, and I'm not going to sign them. I'll give you twenty dollars for them right now."

Upset and unwilling to give up any hope of recouping his costs, the man refused. Rich left.

Right before leaving the US, we had seen ads showing an all-terrain vehicle traversing rocky outcroppings and jungles to replace lost or stolen traveler's checks. So we were a little disappointed: when contacted, the American Express office informed us we would have to pick up replacement checks the next time we were in Pakistan's capital city. I guess Afghanistan was a little farther than those American Express vehicles were willing to go.

Our relocation from Kabul was to get us – and other IAM families – away from active fighting. Although Mazar's airport had been used by the Soviets in the 1980s to launch attacks on other parts of the country, the city had remained a peaceful and stable place, even after Dostum and his fighters took control when the

Soviets left in 1989. At the beginning of 1994, however, intense fighting broke out between General Dostum's Junbesh and Massoud's Jamiat-i-Islami militias. We ushered the family into the boys' bedroom in the basement, the safest room in the house, and taped X's across the small windows facing our yard to protect us from shattering glass.

Someone had told us that children watch their parents and react to their responses, so we determined to stay as calm as possible. We used the time to play and read stories with them while above and nearby gunfire, rocket propelled grenades, and other artillery echoed through the streets. The children showed no signs of trauma, merely interest in what was going on. They were probably happy to have undivided attention from Rich and me.

The first day of fighting our *chaokidar* did not show up for work. The second morning, we ran out to answer pounding at our gate. He stood in the alleyway, glancing nervously around. We opened the door a crack to let him in.

"Why are you here?" we asked.

"My father sent me to make sure you were okay," he said.

We didn't want to dispatch him into the fray again, so we led him to the house. For the rest of the day he did nothing (apart from looking at children's books) and by late afternoon I resented having another mouth to feed. We urged him to go home when the fighting eased, and he was glad to comply.

Because we had nothing like convenience foods, feeding the five of us (six, when the *chaokidar* was there) meant that Rich and I had to leave the safety of the basement to go upstairs to scrounge up something to eat. The sound of bullets whizzing past the windows was unnerving – we later discovered five bullet holes in our roof-top water barrel, and more in the metal frame Rich had constructed over the porch.

At one particularly noisy time, Rich went upstairs to get some drinking water. A couple of minutes later, a boom rocked the house. Rich hurried down and told us something had hit the building. After the fighting we went out to see that a mortar-fired shell filled with shot had hit our roof, cracking it right at the corner above where Rich had been standing. If it had landed slightly above or below that point, my fears of widowhood would have been realized.

Since this was our first experience of fighting, we didn't know what to expect. We were surprised when – about noon the next day – we heard more banging at our gate. Rich ventured out. A neighbor had come by to tell us there was a one-hour ceasefire so we could all go shopping. Rich ran out, bought what he could grab from the shops nearby, and returned to the basement.

As evening fell, a sniper hid in our alleyway, right in front of our door, and again the fighting seemed too close for comfort. But by the next morning all the sounds of war stopped. We ventured out to see the results of four days of battle. The neighbors across the alley had just completed an upstairs addition before the fighting; a rocket blasted through the opposite end, leaving a gaping hole and effectively destroying the room but sparing our yard from an explosion.

Militia controlled the main roads and Daoud, wanting to check on us, risked crossing town to see how we were. Soldiers stole his watch while he was in transit, he told us with a smile, but otherwise they had not harassed him. His mother and brothers were okay but anxious because Daoud's father departed for Kabul days before and had not returned. I offered to go back and stay with her, and Rich agreed this was a good idea. He offered to keep the boys so I could go.

Daoud, baby Hannah, and I rolled across town in a *gahdee* and noted soberly how Mazar had changed overnight to a warzone. It was not as devastated as our neighborhood in Kabul, but there were armed men at every intersection.

Our family never saw active fighting in Mazar again, but the city did: in 1997 the Taliban wreaked vengeance after the citizens destroyed invading fighters.

Daoud's mother seemed sincerely glad to see me. I told her I thought she might be lonely and she appreciated my understanding. (I congratulated myself that at least I had figured *something* out about the culture – a small victory after the bread-burning incident.)

"*Mahdar-jon*, teach Melinda some cooking," Daoud suggested. A gracious woman who had adapted her environment as best she could, Daoud's mother invited me into the bathroom (now a kitchen). Together we prepared *shola,* made from short-grain rice and considered one of the less glamorous Afghan foods, and so rarely served to foreign guests.

Daoud expressed his displeasure with his mother when he saw what we had made, but I was happy to be considered part of the household. Another family – Afghan friends of Daoud's parents, newly displaced from Kabul – arrived that afternoon as well, and it was a wonderful evening enjoying their company and the extra language practice. Hannah and I were given our own room to sleep in with *toshaks* on the floor. The other families separated into the two larger rooms. Before we said goodnight, I watched Daoud's mother at her prayers, her lips silently but urgently entreating for the safe return of her husband. A few weeks later, he rejoined his wife in Mazar.

When we had returned from Pakistan, Rich told the CDP team that our family was interested in moving to a village. Elisabeth, the veterinarian, indicated her desire to work there, too. At the end of December, Rich, Kevin, and a Finnish dentist headed to Baghlan province for several days to find a suitable location for the initiation of our resident-CDP project. They were hosted by the son of Saeed Mansoor, the religious leader and feudal landlord of the Kayan Valley and districts surrounding it. This looked like a promising connection since Saeed Mansoor's control meant the area was peaceful, plus he was open to accepting outside help.

While Rich was gone, one of the teenage sons of our old neighbors walked every day to check on me – an hour each direction. I have never forgotten that act of kindness.

A month later, Rich headed out again to look at potential villages. This time two Afghans joined the group. None of the vehicles for sale in Afghanistan came with seatbelts, and the weather was miserable. At one point the car hit a patch of black ice, fishtailed, and rolled off the road, doing a complete flip before landing upright. Other than one woman who had slight abrasions to her scalp, no one was injured. But the group was shaken, and they returned to Mazar to repeat the trip another day.

I was surprised to see Rich at the door but thankful that he had made it back intact. Only an hour after he returned, another drama began to play out.

A thirteen-year-old neighbor had been warming himself near a hay-fire when his long shirt or *payron,* on which he had earlier spilled some diesel, caught fire. Before the flames were extinguished, the boy was severely burned from ankles to waist. Rich visited the hospital and after seeing how the youth was being treated, begged hospital staff for proper care. But they merely bandaged the boy and kept him two more days in the hospital with little treatment. His family brought him home, and Rich and Mary (an experienced pediatric emergency room nurse) tried treating him there. Mary, who was usually very tough, could barely speak when describing his injuries to me. She told me she had never seen such a terrible burn on a child.

For three weeks, Rich went to the boy's house to change his dressing, administering the anesthesia ketamine to reduce the excruciating pain caused by the bandage changes. Our friend Frank negotiated with the Red Cross to fly the boy to Peshawar where he could get skin grafts, which would be impossible in Afghanistan. We were filled with hope but found out there was a downside to this plan.

"The Red Cross will not allow the parents to go," Frank told us. "They do not fly Afghan passengers, only patients."

"We can't send him on his own," Rich said.

Frank volunteered. "I'll go and stay with him," he said. "I'll make sure he gets the food and care he needs." As an American, Frank would be allowed on the flight.

The parents were frightened to send their son abroad with a stranger, but we all assured them this was the best chance for the boy's recovery.

Frank did as he said, spending his days by the side of the burn patient. But a month later he sent us word: despite the best care available in Peshawar, the youth had died.

Died! Rich himself had spent over one hundred hours doing painful dressing changes on his wounds and had grown to love the boy; his family had become our friends. We wept at the tragedy, and wondered how we could ever tell the parents. Rich summoned his courage and went to their house. In his journal, he wrote:

> Now I've been through a second cry with the family. Their grief was horrible. Some people can watch the grief of others coolly, objectively, detached. I can do it sometimes. I could not do it with them. For 1 ½ hours the mother and girls went through waves of wailing, the father sobbing for some time. The noise in time attracted a few neighbors, one of whom told the grieving woman not to cry and preached at her about how this was A's fate, even saying "it was written on his forehead." Strange how these "answer people" are found universally, and how hollow their comfort sounds in every culture.

Despite their doubts and agony, they did not resent us; they knew we had been motivated by compassion to send their son to Pakistan. Perhaps one of the most painful aspects for them was that the Red Cross would not return his body for burial, so they never got to say a proper goodbye.

❖

Not long after this Rich was confronted with another concerning medical case involving a village near Mazar where a rabid dog had bitten eight people. (The owner refused to put the dog down). One, a young girl, was brought to our house, her cheek covered with a cloth so soaked with blood I thought it was the chewed up remains of her face. Our colleagues made two trips to Termez in Uzbekistan to get enough vaccine to treat the victims, and Rich and others went to the village to urge the owner to destroy the rabid animal.

While in the village, Rich was also able to help a mother (who, he noted, had been pregnant seventeen times) with a retained placenta. The family couldn't afford to reimburse the team for the medicines Rich used to help the woman, so they offered a chicken. He became the center of a minor dispute the next morning when locals tried tricking each other so that they could have the honor of hosting him for breakfast.

Two women from the same family as the mother sought Rich's advice for their fertility struggles. From their conversation, he surmised they were not ovulating and prescribed them Clomid. We never heard if they had babies, but we were glad at least that some options were available to them.

Those early months of 1994 were full of death and life.

Soldiers on the streets of Mazar, 1993

The road to Qarya Beykh, 1994

CHAPTER FIFTEEN

The Village at the Foot

He ran out from under the leaking roof and sat in the rain.
(Afghan proverb)

There is a difference between being a risk-taker and being restless. I am not by nature a risk-taker. But I am restless. When I hit the three-month point in my first job – the time at which college quarters would end – I was shocked to find I would have to keep working in the same position. And I loved to move; in nine years of marriage Rich and I had already lived in three cities in the US and two in Afghanistan (not to mention several months spent in Manali, India). I actually relished the challenge of packing household items efficiently. Moving, I thought cheerfully, was an opportunity to throw things away.

With every move, however, there was loss. Leaving Mazar was no different. The bouncing of the *gahdee* as it rolled to market, the soft, hot *naan,* the way the sun's glow reddened as it descended in the dust hanging along the streets like a Los Angeles sunset, the exquisite taste of fresh kabobs and French fries wrapped in newspaper and luscious pomegranates spilling out garnet packets of juice – we would miss these things.

Most of all we would miss people. The Oswalds and Muellers had been acquaintances even before we arrived in Afghanistan; this would be the first time we would live far from them. Other expatriates had settled in Mazar, too, including some families (both larger and smaller than ours) and teachers of the new school opened for children of foreigners working in the city.

Among the Afghans, Daoud was our closest friend and like a younger brother to both Rich and me. Sometimes he and his new sidekick, a Kurdish refugee, would come for dinner and stay the night. During the cold months, we let them sleep in our tiny central room, where we had put a *sandali*. This consisted of a low, square table over which was stretched a huge quilt; underneath was a tiny charcoal heater. Afghans huddled around their *sandali* during the day, drawing the thick quilt over the front of their bodies while they talked. At night, they would lie on *toshaks* around the *sandali*, using the quilt and the heat beneath it to warm them as they slept.

One morning, Daoud and his friend stumbled out of the room and told us they had been having the strangest dreams. Daoud pulled out the charcoal burner and set it on our porch. "I think we were getting carbon monoxide poisoning," he told us. We felt terrible and purchased an electric heater for their next visit.

We still met with Daoud for Dari lessons. One afternoon, on my way into the language school, I heard whimpering from under a truck parked nearby. Crouching down, I saw a puppy apparently abandoned by its mother. Extricating the tiny dog, I wrapped him in a plastic bag to keep the mud off me and carried him to my lesson. No doubt Daoud was surprised – I think our love for dogs always mystified Afghans – and I thought it best to conceal the puppy from the taxi driver on my ride home. Our kids were thrilled when I showed up with a new pet. We dubbed him Oliver, in honor of the orphan from Charles Dickens' famous story. Oliver would accompany us when we moved to the village.

We would also be bringing our fourth child in utero. This baby was not due until August; I don't remember discussing whether it was a good idea or not to move before it was born. We knew we would have to leave Afghanistan for the birth, so we probably figured we should get settled before that happened.

Rich wanted me to join the exploratory journey to the final two villages under consideration for our resident community development project. We left the boys with Greg and Mary and accompanied a local military commander from the city of Pul-i-khumri (about three hours south of Mazar) to the first village. The walled compounds testified this was a conservative Pushtun community. The commander showed us a newly mudded house we could live in if we chose to move here. It was light and airy, the interior walls smooth adobe.

We then drove to the second community. There were ruins and a canal to pass, then we drove over a long open stretch before arriving at the dried tangle of muddy tire tracks heaving itself between the recognizable road and the village. We followed the single road which quickly passed between the scattered houses.

The commander stopped at a two-story mud building at the farthest end of Qarya Beykh. "This is a fort right now," he told us, "but if you decide to move here, we'll fix it up for you."

The window panes were dirty, so we pressed our faces against them to peer inside. One room was stacked with mortar shells. Several more were piled against the outside of the house. It would take a bit of work to get the building habitable.

Qarya Beykh itself was attractive. Unlike in much of Afghanistan, the properties here were not enclosed. There were a few walls, but mostly the village was open, dotted with trees. Grassy hills rose up behind the houses; in the other directions fields stretched across the flood plain toward the mountains beyond. Women garbed in bright blue, green, and pink clothing and long scarves that left their faces exposed shared the paths with men. The social freedom was very appealing and we decided this looked like a better choice for the program than the village we had visited earlier. We insisted all the rockets be moved from in and around the fort, and arranged to have the walls and floors re-mudded and smoothed in our house as well as the building next to it (which would be Elisabeth's) and the house across the yard, which would have an office upstairs and a home for our Afghan co-workers below.

After the bumpy drive and the setting sun in my eyes, my head throbbed; I was nauseated by the time we arrived back at the commander's house, where we had been invited to spend the night. His daughters showed us into their sitting room. It was tastefully decorated, red *toshak* cushions on the floor with white pillows all around to lean against. I looked at the pillows – they were elaborately embroidered with florescent flowers, in the local pattern. I complimented our hostesses, then relaxed, waiting for the food to come and my headache to ease.

As the family chatted with us, I noticed something strange. The teenage daughter who did most of the talking had an extra finger on each hand, an additional "pinky" coming off the side. I blinked hard, thinking my migraine had affected my vision as well. The girl seated herself cross-legged on the floor and I looked at her bare feet. . . six toes on each. I leaned over to Elisabeth.

"Elisabeth," I whispered, "Is it my imagination, or does that girl have twelve fingers and toes?"

Elisabeth looked closely and whispered back, "Yes, she does." We giggled quietly. *Like a spider spinning a web,* I thought to myself, deliriously considering the needlework on the pillows the multi-digited girl had produced. No doubt my pain made connections where there were none.

After dinner, Rich and I were shown to our room. Clearly the women of the household had fun picking out our bedding – satiny sheets embroidered with hearts and flowers. The honeymoon suite, I guess. I was so weary I don't think I fully appreciated the romance of the surroundings.

Once we had determined our destination, we began in earnest to pack and prepare for the move. Elisabeth and Rich interviewed Ibrahim and Nooria, Kabulis who had fled the fighting, to work as equal partners in the project. An intelligent, articulate couple with one small daughter (who became Hannah's playmate), Ibrahim and Nooria agreed to relocate with us.

We had to leave most of our furniture in Mazar; as I suspected, our housing situation was a move downward in both size and comfort. The main part of our house was a room that would serve as a combination living/dining room; for this we had two *toshaks* and our table and chairs. We brought along a couple of planks which Rich hung as bookshelves.

This main room was reached through what had once been merely an entryway but now became our kitchen. Carpenters from our office in Mazar built a counter with open shelves below (we hung a curtain over them to keep the dust out, but that did not deter rats from chomping through our Tupperware). They also hung shelves on the wall above the counter. We set our two-burner stove on one end of the counter. With a strip of linoleum partially covering the bare mud floor, the room was complete. There was no sink.

The side of the kitchen opposite our living room opened into the storeroom. If there had been another door out of the storeroom, it would have led into the children's bedroom. But there was no other door. So in order to get to the children's room, we had to go outside. Their room, like our main room, was entered through a square entryway; this became our bedroom. We had a bunk bed bolted to the wall for the boys (in case of earthquakes) and put Hannah in a travel crib.

There was little space for our mattress on the entryway floor; besides, we discovered one night that we were sharing our bed with a frog. So we had a platform built for the mattress, and stored our clothes underneath, freeing floor space so we could completely open our door. We had to climb to get in bed, and were careful never to sit completely upright while there – if we bumped the ceiling, fine dirt would sift down through the cloth hung to hide the bare beams and mud.

A steep outdoor mud staircase (without railings) led to an upstairs room which served as the sitting room for company. This room we shared with Elisabeth. I made bright blue curtains for the two windows and we put our best woven rugs on the floor, as well as our maroon corduroy *toshaks* (considered the finest kind). The room had an excellent view of the village as well as the road which wound behind our house and out into the countryside beyond. We could also enjoy the single red poppy blooming from Elisabeth's roof next door.

Elisabeth's house consisted of one room with another entryway kitchen. She had ambitiously decided to "live like the natives." We had all noticed that most Afghans with money would invest not in furniture, but carpets. So Elisabeth thought she would try to get by with nothing but rugs and *toshaks*. Within an hour of moving in, she complained she missed having a table; she soon bemoaned her lack of chairs. Some things are just hard for Westerners to give up.

We did have a "shower" which we also shared with Elisabeth; this was a four-foot-by-four-foot room with concrete walls and floor and a drain that emptied the water outside. (This pooled up near our bedroom, attracting swarms of frogs, like the one that had ended up in bed with us.) We took our own bucket of warm water in and poured pitchers over our heads. This method of bathing worked fine in hot weather. But when it was cold we had to put a kerosene heater inside to heat the room and the water at the same time.

One of the first things we discovered about Qarya Beykh ("The Village at the Foot" of the mountains) was that there was not a single outhouse in the entire village. Unfortunately, our home was at the extreme end, so the area behind our house served as the public latrine. We were adaptable to a point, but that was too much. We hired someone to dig a pit toilet before we moved into the compound.

Our outhouse was located at the end of the yard between our house and Ibrahim and Nooria's, near where Elisabeth lived. All eight of us shared the one facility, which sometimes caused problems. We appreciated the view from the outhouse – the doorless room looked south over wheat fields to the mountains beyond. But the concept of a completely open bathroom was unappealing, despite the scenery, so we hung an old curtain for a door. That solved the first problem. The second – how to "knock"? There seemed something too personal about talking to someone squatting inside. We didn't know what to do until we noticed that whenever Ibrahim or Nooria heard someone approach, they emitted a forced cough. That was our warning; we would come back a few minutes later. We all adopted this technique.

The pit had been dug three meters (nearly ten feet) deep, and we followed Greg Oswald's plans to avoid foul odors by installing a pipe to draw the smells out. We also periodically scattered ashes in the pit to help with the composting. A few rolls of toilet paper were lost down the hole by accident; once one of the children dropped the roll and came tearing across the yard wailing, the free end of the toilet paper clutched in his fist, the rest flying behind him like a kite. Another time one of the boys had a terrible case of diarrhea and did not quite make it in time – so he cleaned himself up and "accidentally" dropped his clothes down the hole.

I found another good use for that toilet. Connor had a habit of collecting bullets – an easy hobby, as there were plenty lying around from the war with the Russians. After Ibrahim showed Connor how to pry them open and extricate the gunpowder, I was worried he might get hurt. So I spirited his supply away and emptied them into the pit. If an archaeologist ever excavates that particular site, he or she is going to have an interesting time piecing together the customs of our little civilization . . .

❖

When we moved to the village, we brought a Land Cruiser. There was not much travel planned; Rich, Ibrahim and Elisabeth would make weekly trips to Pul-i-khumri for perishables and other supplies, and we would all go up to Mazar occasionally for a getaway. I was happy to minimize time in a vehicle, considering the state of the road and my ever-expanding belly.

The actual move occurred in late May 1994. The drive, usually a four-hour trip, took eight hours. We were stopped several times with requests for rides and once to loan a tire to a jeep that had blown one. The drivers promised they would find us and return our spare. (To our amazement, they did). We found out later they had been carting a body to town for a funeral.

When we finally arrived in the village, Frank, who had come to help us move, informed me we should provide dinner for everyone – thirteen adults (including employees from Mazar) and five children. I was mortified. There were no stores nearby (and of course, no restaurants) and our cookware was not even unpacked. I was incredibly relieved when the Afghan drivers decided to head back to the nearest city, and Nooria said she would cook for her own family.

Our first disappointment was the state of the house. Although Rich had hired someone to improve it, the mud on the walls was so crudely plastered that dirt flaked off whenever we touched them.

(In the spring, the hay mixed with mud actually sprouted.) The floor had apparently not been repaired at all; cow tracks were clearly visible. We tossed a carpet over it. As the months went by, we watched dust work its way up through the rug.

There were three small windows in our main room – one faced the yard, one Ibrahim and Nooria's house, and one the village. This window had a view of the *aoz*, a mud-walled reservoir where villagers would water their animals. Sometimes we heard the low thud of cattle trooping past our house on the way to drink.

None of the windows had screens or curtains, and curious children peered in to figure out what we were doing. I hung some lace – it discouraged the children a little, but they still tried their best to see in.

They were afraid of our dog, Oliver, and I had to stop one girl from beating him when he barked at her. He had already had a rocky start to village life, first being bitten by a large dog that then proceeded to steal his food, and then getting stung by something (perhaps a scorpion) that caused his little muzzle to swell up. Elisabeth performed one of her first procedures in the village by giving him a shot of dexamethasone, a steroid that reduced the swelling. We had already had one dog die and were not ready to lose another. Later Ibrahim carried Oliver into the yard after he had gotten in a fight with a huge dog, his hind leg dislocated. Elisabeth again came to our rescue, resetting his limb so that Oliver could get out and resume picking fights with the neighbors.

Despite his hardships, Oliver did manage to indulge himself occasionally when a flock of chickens or turkeys paraded through our yard. More than once we plucked a fluttering chick from his mouth, but usually he was too quick for us.

Seeing fowl wander across the property gave us an idea: raising our own chickens. Although the villagers were willing to sell us eggs, it was impossible to come up with enough at one time to cook for the entire family. Rich and Ibrahim brought back hens and roosters from town on one of their weekly shopping trips. To our dismay, within a few days the chicken began coughing.

We didn't know much about animals, but even so it was pretty obvious that our birds were growing sicker by the day. Elisabeth had no cure, and told us we should put them out of their misery.

Not wanting to eat the meat ourselves, but not wanting to waste it either, I decided to cook it for Oliver. I popped an entire dead bird into our pressure cooker. Soon the jiggler on top bobbed back and forth, emitting steam.

Farzia, Ibrahim and Nooria's daughter, wandered over. *"Khala* (aunt), what are you cooking?"

"Chicken," I told her. Her brown eyes flashed with delight. We weren't getting much meat in our diets.

"For who?" she asked hopefully.

"For Oliver," I answered. I watched her face sink in disappointment, then told her about the sick chicken. She nodded and toddled off.

Oliver hovered nearby, licking his chops at the smell emanating from the cooker. I couldn't explain the situation to him; I finished cooking the meat and dumped both chicken and broth into his food bowl. He was in agony. The meat was too hot to eat, but based on previous experience Oliver knew that if he didn't get it quickly, some *larger* dog would. He circled the dish, testing it every few minutes and whimpering longingly. When it finally cooled down enough, he devoured the entire chicken.

Rich built Oliver a little mud house of his own in the corner near the stairway. From here the dog could watch both our house and Elisabeth's. Everyone in the village had a dog for this purpose; we found their dogs trained to attack trespassers. Whenever we entered a yard, we would yell to whoever was around to call off their dog. Once I watched in amazement as a girl of about six or seven came over and spoke to the dog, which lay down. The girl proceeded to place her foot on the animal's neck to show that she was the mistress. The dog allowed us to pass into the house without even a growl.

Although Oliver proved he wasn't the best watchdog, the children could see that he was the most fun dog around. We treated him like a pet and a friend, and after watching us play with him, the Afghan children asked, "Can you get us a dog like him?"

"What do you mean?" we asked.

"A friendly dog, that likes to play," they said. We told them all dogs were friendly if they were treated kindly. This was clearly a new idea.

Having come from a country where dogs were pampered and included as a part of the family (even in Christmas photos sent by friends), it took us some time to figure out why Afghans viewed dogs as unclean. We understood better after Ibrahim trekked with us across the wheat fields to see a donkey that had been killed by wolves. A pack of dogs was ripping flesh off the carcass – intriguing on a National Geographic special, but chilling in real life. Oliver himself dragged a donkey leg home, squirreling it away in his house, and despite our attempts to get it out, he wouldn't give it up.

After that we were reluctant to let him lick us.

Since Oliver was feisty and always up for a fight, we were prepared for the worst. One night, after washing the dishes, I went to hurl the dishwater out the kitchen door. (This solved the problem of no indoor plumbing and helped keep the dust down outside.) When I pulled the door open, I saw a white bundle lying in the doorway. I set the dishpan down.

"Rich!" I called. "Come here."

In the dim lantern light cast from the house, he gazed out.

"It's finally happened," Rich said quietly. "Oliver's gotten into a fight and dragged himself home to die."

We went outside and were assaulted by a foul smell that told the real story. Oliver had found a dead chicken and dragged its rotting corpse to us as a token of affection. Our beloved dog stood beyond, wagging his tail. We were relieved and made quick work of disposing of the nasty bird.

Dust was a bigger challenge to deal with than dead animals. It came off the walls and floors, and it entered through the windows and doors – even when they were closed. None of the windows sealed properly. And Afghanistan is known for its amazing *khahkbods* – storms that rise up suddenly, swirling dust everywhere. Once after cleaning I watched in horror as a cloud moved toward our house and visibly seeped under the windows, coating everything brown. And when the children played inside, running in circles, I watched another *khahkbod* rise from the very house itself. Sometimes we would drag the heavy rugs to the yard and snap them back and forth to return the dirt to the outdoors. But it was a pretty hopeless endeavor.

Another challenge was water. The CDP team had originally written in its philosophy statement that, "Afghanistan must get away from this absolute dependence on foreign assistance." After seeing how the people of Qarya Beykh were living, the team realized the arrogance of this: the Afghans *were* surviving, although sometimes under incredible hardship. The CDP goal was to assist local people in solving problems they self-identified, and acquisition of water was one of the first mentioned. For some reason (unknown to us) the people who had founded the village chose to build on the edge of a floodplain, near mountains but far from a water source. Of course there was no plumbing here, nor were there wells. Boys in the village spent hours each day walking with their donkeys to the canals we had passed when arriving; there they would fill water containers and walk home. With so much time spent collecting water, there was little time for school. We hired a teenager to bring us eighty liters (around twenty gallons) each day to fill the large *aodon*, or water barrel, outside our front door. We got more than we bargained for – dirty water teeming with plant matter and even the occasional fish. We let it sit undisturbed for several hours before skimming off water to boil for drinking. This, too, was a daunting task. With five people and the summer heat – well over one hundred degrees Fahrenheit every day – we drank more water than we could boil and cool in a day. We even tried the villagers' trick – half-burying a pot in the ground and trying to chill the water by using the cooler ground temperature.

Rich's father and stepmother had been planning to visit us, a scheme complicated by the rigid rules of the Uzbek government. They were required to book a stay at an expensive government-run hotel in Tashkent and needed a special visa to travel from the capital down to the northern border of Afghanistan. We still had

133

not heard if they would be able to come, but Rich wrote and asked if they did, would they buy a water filter so we could eliminate the boiling? I looked forward to the possibility of not lighting the sooty single-burner kerosene stove outside each morning to get something clean to drink the *following* day.

Sometimes the murky water seemed to defeat our purpose in using it. Once, while giving the boys a bath in a little tub we had brought, I poured a cup over Aidan. I looked again – river plants dangled from his forehead. *What a waste of time,* I thought.

After hearing the challenges villagers had in getting water and their unsuccessful attempts at digging wells, Rich and the others began to survey and hired men to dig a deep well that could be attached to a pump. The hole went down and down; after seventy meters (two hundred and thirty feet), the diggers quit. There was no groundwater near enough the surface to use. A geologist visited Qarya Beykh a few years later and determined the water table was about one hundred meters – three hundred twenty-eight feet – below ground. It was no wonder hand-digging could not reach it.

Like the Afghans, we needed bread each day. We brought a burlap sack of whole-wheat flour and hired a woman to bake a few loaves for us each morning when she made bread for her family. It was wonderful to have the hot, thick slabs brought to our door for breakfast. But one day our baker informed us the flour was gone. We discovered she had been using it to prepare bread for her own family as well as ours. She quit before we could fire her. Now I added baking bread to my list of daily tasks.

That list was already long. The lack of basic amenities, the unprocessed state of the food (I could not figure out how Afghan women cleaned rice by pouring it on a pan and shaking it gently up and down to separate the rice from the rocks and dirt), and the reality of three small children in an unfenced yard were keeping me busy. I wrote my parents that we were up at 5:30 a.m. and I did not sit down until 3:00 p.m. except to give Connor his lessons. Then at 5:00 I had to cook dinner; put the kids to bed at 7:00; and wash dishes by hand before falling (or climbing) into bed at 9:00 p.m. It rankled me when Elisabeth suggested that I didn't really *want* to go visiting the village women with her. I was just trying to keep body and soul together.

The low point came when I told Rich he had been crazy to bring a six-months-pregnant woman to such a place. My restlessness had been overcome by exhaustion.

The Lewis home, 1994

CHAPTER SIXTEEN

Language and loss

Debt is the scissors of love. (Afghan proverb)

Americans are notorious for being terrible at languages other than English. (The British might say we fall short there, too.) Although I attempted to learn French in college, the only phrase I really mastered was *Je ne sais pas* – I don't know. My professor had great fun with this one day by asking me a number of questions, all of which provided me with an opportunity to use my single statement. He ended with the question, *Qui est ton pere?* knowing that I would provide my answer, "I don't know." The entire class burst into laughter; a classmate leaned over to inform me, "He just asked who your father is."

I had been getting a grasp on Dari while we lived in Mazar. It was slightly different than the dialect spoken in Kabul, but I could communicate and comprehend most of what was being said. The dialect in the village was so different, however, it was known as *Hazaragi* after the ethnic Hazara who spoke it. Although the men articulated a clear city Dari, the women were difficult for me to understand.

One of our first days in Qarya Beykh, while Rich, Elisabeth, Ibrahim and Nooria were having a staff meeting in the office above Ibrahim and Nooria's apartment, a group of women came by our house. I was not as careful in noting the subtleties of sound as I should have been. I realize in retrospect that this

137

conversation must have seemed ridiculous from the local women's viewpoint, as I confused the word *duktar* (doctor), which they were using, with the word *dukhtar* (daughter, or unmarried woman). The fact that in Dari there is one word for "he," "she," and "it" further complicated this dialogue:

"Is the *duktar* here?" one of the women asked (with Rich in mind).

"No, she's not," I answered (with Elisabeth in mind).

"Well, when will he be back?" she asked.

"I don't know," I answered. "She comes and goes as she pleases."

"Well," the woman continued, "doesn't he eat here?"

"Sometimes," I said, "if I invite her."

The women exchanged incredulous glances. "But doesn't he *live* here?" she queried.

"No, no," I corrected her. "She has her own house. If I want her to come here, I invite her."

More astonished looks. "Well, where is he now?"

"She's in a meeting across the yard," I told them. "You can find her there."

No doubt my mistake generated some interesting speculation among the villagers about the kind of married relationship Rich and I had.

We still had our hand-held radio to communicate with staff in Mazar, and they relayed the news that attempts by Rich's parents to get visas from the capital of Uzbekistan (Tashkent) to the Afghan border had failed. So we decided we'd leave earlier than planned for our delivery and travel to them. The Uzbek border crossing was about a one-and-a-half hour drive north of Mazar, so we had a long trip ahead of us.

When we first arrived in the village the local commander, Khan Ali, asked if he could borrow money from us. We quickly discovered a new philosophy of lending: if you don't request something back, it is not returned. Before we left for Uzbekistan, Rich began asking around for Khan Ali. He had suddenly (and suspiciously, we thought) disappeared. Since Rich's efforts to get the money back failed, I decided to try.

As we drove through the village on our way to Tashkent, I asked Rich to stop outside the compound of houses belonging to Khan Ali's family. "Wait here," I urged him and the children. I entered the yard, and asked if I could see Khan Ali.

"He's gone," the women told me. As I stood there, more women amassed.

"Gone?" I repeated, putting on my most pathetic air. I rubbed my huge belly. "But he owes us money, and we need it."

"He left this morning," one of the women said. "He'll be back tomorrow."

"Tomorrow is too late," I told them. "We have to leave the country now to have our baby, and we need the money." I moaned and rubbed my belly. "Oh, *baychara,*" I murmured softly, rocking back and forth.

Baychara is a Dari word which literally means "without option." It is used as both an explanation and a complaint – a hand-wringing outburst: "What shall I do? I am *baychara.*" We had heard it used by those who suffered any variety of misfortunes. I dredged up what was left of my adolescent acting aspirations, trying to look sufficiently miserable.

The crowd surrounded me, the women clucking sympathetically. "She's having a baby," they repeated to each other. "She needs the money."

Some of them disappeared and returned with a couple of male relatives. I retold my story, and they conferred together. "We'll give you the money," the men said. "Khan Ali can pay us when he gets back."

I was surprised at my success and took the money gratefully. Hopefully they were equally fortunate in getting their money repaid by Khan Ali.

From Mazar, we planned to ride to Termez, the nearest city inside Uzbekistan, with our friend Frank. He had a pickup truck and years of experience living in Asia. Frank said he would drop us off at the train station in Termez so we could travel overnight to Tashkent.

We got the usual security check on the Afghan side – for me a thorough frisking by a woman who seemed to take more pleasure in her job than appropriate – and crossed the Amu Darya River on the narrow bridge built by the Soviets in 1985, the only border crossing between Afghanistan and Uzbekistan.

As we traversed the bridge, Frank informed us that he had cash left over from a previous trip to Termez. It was illegal to transport *sum* across the border, but he only had a little and decided to hang onto it.

"I'll just stash it under the rug by the front seat," he told us. That sounded as obvious as putting a house key under a door mat, but there was no time to argue.

The Uzbeki side of the bridge was a different world. Men in white lab coats approached and directed Frank to park his car over a hole in the ground where they could descend and check under the vehicle (for explosives or contraband? I don't know). We all got out and went inside the customs building to deal with the officials.

The office reminded us of a Cold War era film. Spartan, gray, and unwelcoming, the building and its staff discouraged banter even though the workers spoke some English. We thought our visit would be brief, but suddenly one of the men returned from checking the vehicle, and motioned for Frank to follow him. Minutes passed. We finally wandered around the building and found the room where Frank was being questioned.

If we had not been in a hurry, the situation would have been humorous: Frank sat under a bare light bulb in the darkened room while two men interrogated him about the *sum* he had hidden in the car. (As I recall, it was worth about $14.) This questioning went on for hours.

At last he was released and we drove to Termez.

"I'm sorry about the lost time," he apologized. "I'll take you right to the train station."

We had missed the train. We drove to the bus station. The bus pulled away as we arrived.

A row of taxis was parked at the bus station, and Rich hopped out of Frank's truck and approached one of the drivers.

"Where do you want to go?" the man asked in English.

"Tashkent," Rich told him.

"I will take you there," the taxi driver offered.

"Tonight?" Rich asked. "How much?"

"One *lakh sum,*" he answered. Rich did the calculations in his head. We had spent enough time in Pakistan and India to know that one *lakh* is equal to one hundred thousand. The ride would cost $160. This was even better than the train price.

"Great," Rich said.

"But first," the driver told us, "you must come to my house and we will have something to eat."

That sounded good to us. We followed the taxi to a nearby neighborhood and entered the courtyard of the driver's house. Outside under the trees was a wooden platform; our host's family brought cushions for us, and we sat with them on the dais and ate grapes and fresh *naan.*

"So," the driver said, apparently computing in his head, "that will come to $1600."

"$1600!" Rich gasped. "No, you said one lakh *sum* – that would be $160."

The taxi driver grinned. "Let's see – a *lakh* is one million…"

Rich interrupted. "No, a *lakh* is one hundred thousand."

The taxi driver shook his head. "No, it is one million."

"I have traveled all over Asia," Rich said, "and a *lakh* is always a hundred thousand."

The driver shrugged. Rich turned to us and said softly, "I think he's realizing it's not the great deal he thought it was, so he's trying to twist the price. Well, never mind. It would be cheaper to fly." We thanked our hosts for the snack, and set out again, this time for the airport.

It was twilight now; the airport was deserted except for one man talking on a pay phone in the lobby.

After he hung up, he walked toward us. Frank began a conversation and we were all glad to find the man understood English.

"When is the next flight to Tashkent?" Frank asked.

"There are no more flights today," the man said. "You will have to come back in the morning."

We were crestfallen. Termez was a bleak, Soviet-style city, and we had no idea where to go for the night.

"Do *you* have a place we could stay tonight?" Frank asked the man.

"Frank!" we exploded together. He motioned for us to be calm.

"Don't worry," he said quietly, "they do this all the time here."

The man surveyed us thoughtfully. "Yes, you can stay with me," he said. He accompanied us to the truck and, squeezing in next to Frank, directed us to his house.

Rich and I kept our reservations to ourselves; Frank seemed confident that this was a reasonable plan. He wove through Termez, turning into a large yard. We pulled up to a house and parked. It was dark now, but we saw two women and a few men emerge. Our host explained to them in Uzbeki who we were and that we were staying. They brought cushions to the dais under a tree and offered to prepare food for us.

I was too exhausted to eat. I lay down on a cushion and listened to the conversation. The men asked Rich and Frank a lot of questions; at one point I felt uncomfortable as they began asking questions about me. *Where were we from? Where were my clothes from – were they American?* It seemed odd, after living in Afghanistan, to have men talking about me to my husband; that would not happen among strangers. (In fact, even Rich's colleagues would not discuss their wives' pregnancies until *after* a child had been born – and then would only mention it if they had been blessed with a son.)

At last we were ready to retire. We would sleep outside under the stars, which suited us well. Our hosts brought blankets. Before turning in, Rich took our computer out of the back of the truck and put it inside the cab, locking the doors. Our suitcases remained in the bed of the truck.

"You don't need to lock up," our new friend told us. "It is just us here."

"No problem," Rich said with a smile. "It is our custom."

The "our custom" line answered every awkward query in Afghanistan, and it seemed to work here, too. We all said goodnight and curled up under the blankets.

After waking early we prepared to head to the airport. We thanked the family and gave them a bag of sugar we had brought to bestow as a gift on someone. (Sugar was a scarce commodity in Uzbekistan). They thanked us.

I opened one of the suitcases and began looking for a bag of raisins to give the children to munch on the way to the airport. Despite riffling through the bag, I could not find them, so I zipped up the suitcase and we all hopped in the truck. We waved heartily as we drove away, thankful for a sound night's sleep.

We arrived at the airport and Rich went to buy tickets. We were the first passengers there.

Again, as Rich, Frank and our host were at the counter, I began looking through the suitcase for the raisins. They were not to be found. I now noticed that our clothes seemed strewn around the suitcase. Checking thoroughly, I discovered many items were missing – a dress I had sewn for Hannah; my swimsuit; our newest clothes; my wedding band. My fingers had swollen so much with heat and pregnancy that I had put my ring in a toiletry bag, and now it was gone.

As soon as Rich returned with the tickets I pulled him aside. "There are things missing from our bags," I told him quickly. "Things have been stolen." I gave him the rundown on what I knew was missing.

Our host looked shocked.

"My family would never steal from you," he assured us.

"What other explanation can there be?" we asked. "Our suitcases have not been left alone except during the night."

He seemed sincerely disturbed. "Come back to my house and look," he told us.

Frank told us to wait at the airport. "I'll go look," he said. They drove away.

Others came and bought tickets. Our flight was announced. As passengers went to board, Rich exchanged our tickets for the following Tashkent flight. Even though we had been the first at the airport, we would not be able to leave until we recovered our property.

Frank returned, alone. "Well, the whole family denied taking your things," he said. "I didn't see what more I could do, unless you want to go back to their house and talk to them."

Our host had stayed behind with his family. "I don't think I could find the house again," Rich said. Sadly, we decided to head on to Tashkent. My wedding band – engraved with the second half of a Bible verse engraved in Rich's – was never seen again.

Frank left and we got in line. There were a series of checkpoints to board the plane, and at each checkpoint, we had to get our tickets stamped. Without luggage carts, we were also required to drag our bags (and children) to the plane, so it was a challenging endeavor.

When we arrived at the last checkpoint and were ready to head out onto the tarmac, the airport worker glanced at our tickets.

"You missed one stamp," he told us. "You must go back."

Having spent most of the day at the airport and dealt with problems from the time we'd crossed the border into Uzbekistan, Rich was completely out of patience now. "No," he told the official, "We *won't* go back." He showed the man the row of stamps, indicated our large and growing family, and made it clear he'd had enough. The airport worker relented, stamped our tickets and ushered us out.

The flight had no assigned seating so we all pushed our way on board after depositing our bags near the cargo hold. Fortunately, it was a short flight and the only one we ever had to take on an old Aeroflot plane. (The airline had a reputation for being poorly managed; our friend and former IAM Executive Director Richard

Penner died when the same Termez to Tashkent flight crashed in bad weather a few years later.)

Tashkent was just what we needed. It felt like a European city, with spacious parks, elegant subway stations, and restaurants. After demolishing bowls of ice cream in an open café, Rich shocked the children by offering them seconds. (They all said "Yes!") We were informed we were required to stay in a government hotel; we showed up, checked in, and then went to a private guesthouse run by Americans nearby, "forgetting" to return to our hotel.

The guesthouse felt luxurious after even a few weeks in Qarya Beykh. There was a porch swing for nearly-four-year-old Aidan, a shady outdoor platform where toddler Hannah could nap, and a video collection for Connor, our six-year-old. We tried unsuccessfully to watch a movie but the machine didn't seem to work, so we called the woman who ran the place to our room.

She took a quick look at the TV and video player. "You have to plug it in," she said with a smile. It was so long since we had access to electricity, we had forgotten to check.

Daoud had moved to Tashkent to study Russian and work after we relocated to the village. When he found out we were in town, he took us sightseeing while trying to help us locate Rich's parents. After unsuccessfully attempting to get a visa from Tashkent to Termez so that they could cross the border into Afghanistan, and hearing nothing from us, the Lewises decided our rendezvous was not going to happen. To make the best of a disappointing situation they, too, spent their days sightseeing with a guide. At last we got word of which government-run hotel they were at; they had been compelled to book their room while in the US at a price ten times what we were paying.

Rich and the boys knocked on their hotel room door, delighting everyone. They joined Hannah and me in a park nearby, the beginning of a few happy days together before they returned to the States and we headed to India.

Our daily water supply, 1993

Manali, India, 1994

CHAPTER SEVENTEEN

Arrivals and departures

Unless God does it, what can the doctor do? (Afghan proverb)

My philosophy of children is this: one child requires constant attention; two children are manageable (each parent can keep an eye on one of them); after three the adults are outnumbered, so chaos ensues and it doesn't matter how many more you have. At least if we stopped at four, Rich and I figured, we would have enough hands between us to hold onto all of them.

Even though we had a hand to spare at this point, we appreciated that the other passengers on our flight from Tashkent to Delhi took one look at us and cleared a path so we could board the plane without pushing.

India was now familiar; we rented a taxi, arriving in Manali after dark. We were discreetly heading to our room in Mr. Banon's Hotel when a voice called out from one of the verandas. "Richard? Melinda? Is that you?"

While I was glad to see the British mountaineers we had met two years before, I was a little embarrassed. I looked the same as the last time I'd been there – massively pregnant. Educated Indians have been thoroughly instilled with the idea that families should be limited to two children, so we were already a parade when we walked down the street. People occasionally stopped, pointed to us one by one, and expressed amazement in a variety of Indian languages over our total number.

We revisited friends and I was invited to the burgeoning Nepali church to talk about the situation in Afghanistan. Rich did not work this time: we planned to stay only long enough for the baby to be born. A British couple volunteering at the hospital brought their children to play with ours. We hiked and waited.

The nurse we knew had moved to another country, so we weren't sure what to do with our other three children when I went into labor. While chatting with guests, we met a young Canadian couple staying at the hotel. We asked them if they would watch the children when it was time for us to go to the hospital. They agreed.

On the first day of August, Rich was ill. We had been bringing food back from the bazaar to eat each evening rather than joining the other guests in the dining hall. Too weak to make the trip down to fetch dinner, Rich asked if I would do it. I did – walking a mile down and then back up the steep hill. That was enough to start contractions, and at about eight p.m. full-on labor started. We informed the Canadians we were going to the hospital. They brought their blankets down to our room, offering to sleep in our suite with the kids.

With each succeeding pregnancy, our babies had gotten smaller. Connor was nearly nine pounds; our last child, a mere seven pounds five ounces. Despite feeling unwell, Rich again acted as attending physician at the delivery. The labor went so fast that when, exhausted, I moaned, "I can't do it!" Rich responded, "Too late."

Returning to the guesthouse at ten p.m., we knocked on our bedroom door. It opened a crack, and the young Canadian woman peered out.

"We're back," we announced.

"Where's the baby?" she whispered.

"Here," we said, holding out the bundle. "It's a boy."

"Wow," she said, "I didn't know it took such a short time."

"It does with your fourth," I answered. We thanked the couple, and everyone went back to their own beds. Only Aidan woke

when we came in; he sneaked out of the back room to peer at his
new little brother.

We knew the ropes by now: rest a few days, then return to
Delhi. We needed to go to the American embassy to get a
consular report of birth and then get a passport photo with Owen
looking straight at the camera, his head regulation size. This time
we stayed at an inexpensive hotel with air conditioning; unlike our
last trip, we left Delhi with a new child but without an emotional
meltdown.

We retraced our steps to Qarya Beykh. When we showed up at
the guesthouse in Tashkent to retrieve all that Rich's parents had
brought for us, we discovered our bags had been opened in our
absence. Another family working in Afghanistan had stayed at the
guesthouse after we left.

"A friend of yours thought maybe your folks brought some
medicine for him from the States," the woman in charge told us,
"so he looked through your bags."

We realized to our disappointment that a vacuum-packed
salmon sent to us was missing; apparently our friend had forgotten
to replace it after going through our luggage. When we had seen
this delicacy from Oregon, we imagined relishing it back in the
village. We mentioned to the woman running the guesthouse that
we couldn't find the salmon. She admitted she had eaten it but
shrugged the loss off unapologetically. "Oh, I thought it was
mine," she said. "I'm on a diet where I eat a lot of fish." We were
a little heartbroken. At least we still had the red and white
peppermints and maple syrup extract Rich's parents had brought
us.

We hired a car to drive us to Termez. It was easier to leave
than it had been to arrive, although something electronic buried in
the depths of our bag looked suspicious on the x-ray machine, so
we had to unload everything to prove it was nothing harmful. The
guard checking our things shuddered when we offered some sugar
as a parting gift, thinking it was a bribe.

Afghan women spend forty days indoors after the birth of a child, resting and chatting with friends. Usually family members provide the requisite tea and treats to these guests, but I returned to the village with baby Owen and no mother or sister to act as hostess for the women who dropped by to see our newborn. They seemed shocked at not being fed, but went ahead and showered Owen with *af* notes (the Afghan currency). I appreciated this show of affection.

They had all asked me before we left whether we wanted a boy or a girl. Since we had two boys already, we told them we wanted a girl. (Of course it didn't really matter to us, but we looked for opportunities to communicate that girls were precious.) When the women visited and asked which it was, I told them the baby was a boy.

"*Dest-e-khudah,*" they responded cheerfully. "It's in the hands of God." It was evident they viewed the gift of another son as an indication of divine favor.

One of the surprises for us living in a village like Qarya Beykh was the structure of the local economy. As Americans, we figured that people would be happy to work for money. We were wrong. Our experience with the *naan* baker was the first eyeopener. Then we hired a woman to wash our clothes, but she refused to do diapers and in the end I had to do all the laundry myself. We had no washing machine; women came by and watched me hand-scrub clothes, insisting that my technique needed improvement. One friend saw a photo of our laundry line, strung end-to-end with cotton diapers that were less than white, and said, "There's a story right there." With two children in diapers, I did my best.

People travelled through our village on their way from the mountains to the city of Pul-i-khumri. Sometimes they came for medical care; Rich tried to set up afternoon office hours once news spread that he was a doctor. (He had been trying to keep it a secret so that he could get work done in a broader community development context.) But it was impossible to hold the patients to the hours he had established. No matter how far they had come, they always told him plaintively that "*Az dur ahmadaym,*" – that is, "We have come far." They stretched out the word for far – *duuuur* – to indicate the length of the distance they had travelled (or wanted him to *think* they had travelled). These interruptions frustrated Rich as he tried to get other work accomplished.

We had a different sense of time than the villagers. We relied on clocks and watches; they lived by the sun. As the days and nights got hotter, Rich and I decided to move our mattress outside to sleep. (The children seemed content inside our mud house.) One morning we woke at about four-thirty to find an old man leaning over us saying, "*Duktar Saeb, Duktar Saeb*, I am sick." Somehow he seemed baffled by the doctor's response to this wakeup call.

While seated on a wicker mat in front of our house eating breakfast, we were interrupted one day when a man rode up on a horse.

"One of the young men has been found face-down in a *joiee*," he told Rich. "Please come."

Rich mounted the horse and rode off with the villager returning hours later, distressed, to tell me what had happened.

As they headed through the village, a procession met them. The young man, stretched on a cot, was being carried our direction. Suddenly a group of men dragged a calf into the path and slaughtered it right there as a sacrifice to beseech God's mercy. The calf's heart was torn out and placed on the man's chest.

Rich dismounted and thoroughly examined the young man as the crowd continued to increase. He looked up and spoke to a few men.

"I'm so sorry," he began, "but I'm afraid he's passed away."

Everyone stared blankly. Women started making comments. "He's still warm," they said. "You can feel his pulse."

Rich obligingly performed a second examination.

"I'm sorry," he said again. "He's dead."

At this point the group said, "Get your car." We were the only ones in the village with a vehicle.

"What for?" Rich asked.

"We'll drive him into town to see a doctor," they told him.

No doubt a little pride mingled with his compassion.

"What am I?" he asked.

They tried another approach. "Maybe," someone suggested, "the drive will shake him up and get him breathing again."

Rich softened. "Look," he said, "If God wants to bring him back to life, He can do it here as well as in Pul-i-khumri."

But they were unconvinced. And Rich would not yield. Since the road to town went through the village, they waited until a truck came and persuaded the driver to carry them and the young man's body to the city.

Of course, the doctor in Pul-i-khumri was even less pleased than Rich with the situation. The day was hot and several hours had passed since his death before the patient made it in for the second consultation. The Afghan doctor glanced at him and said, "Why are you bringing me a corpse?"

They were sent back, chastened, and hastily arranged a funeral and burial.

Elisabeth, Nooria and I went to visit the widow, a teenage girl. I had never seen the kind of grieving that occurs in a community like that – the waves of keening, the continual feasting. (Like with the birth of babies, at funerals Afghans are obligated to feed any guests who come.) The young man's death was both tragic and costly.

In the end, Rich determined that an epileptic seizure caused the young man to collapse into the ditch face down. The sad irony was that in a village desperate for water he drowned in a few inches of it. Not long after the funeral, Rich treated the young wife for self-inflicted poisoning.

The doctor did what he could.

Aidan with a friend, 1994

CHAPTER EIGHTEEN

Village life

If you sit with us, you'll become like us;
if you sit with the pot, you'll become
black.
(Afghan proverb)

Camping was the best preparation for life in an Afghan village. Hauling water from the nearest spigot, using outhouses, quickly dismantling our tent in the dark during rainstorms, cooking on a camp stove and washing dishes in a basin, jerry-rigging laundry lines and surviving without refrigeration: all the challenges honed our problem-solving skills in primitive environments.

Camping in Oregon, however, I developed a narrow view of natural beauty: it usually involved lush greenery. Moving to Afghanistan taught me that every place has something beautiful, even when it might initially appear bleak. One of our teammates shared that she never realized before living in Afghanistan how many varieties of *brown* there were.

Qarya Beykh captivated me despite its dearth of trees. The village was surrounded by fields – watermelon crops grew part of the year, wheat the rest. The children discovered a threshing floor lhidden away in the middle of the golden stalks, and named it "Flower Island" because purple, red, and yellow wildflowers sprung up there after the rains. We walked along the dirt road early in the morning watching the iridescent blue-green Indian rollers in flight, relishing the peacefulness of life far from traffic. On Friday afternoons – Fridays are the Sundays of the Muslim world – we often hiked in the surrounding hills. This was a treat that most foreign workers did not get to enjoy, because much of rural Afghanistan still had landmines dating from the Soviet era. But since the mines around our village had been cleared, we indulged ourselves in weekly jaunts. Once Elisabeth even suggested – when she and I were alone and out of view of the village – that we run. We threw back our head coverings, and plunged forward along the road winding between the grassy mounds, exhilarated, liberated.

One Friday we walked to the ruins of a village which had been destroyed during the war. We pondered why it had not been rebuilt; it lay in an ideal spot along the banks of a river flowing through the floodplain. We picnicked on the grass, then guided the short donkeys we rented back to our village. The children only tumbled off a few times, evoking laughter rather than tears.

The stars in Kabul were brilliant, but in Qarya Beykh they were beyond belief – so vibrant, it was a challenge to pick out the few constellations we recognized. During full moon, one could almost read without a lamp. (I tried.) One chilly night in the autumn, I crawled into a mummy bag and lay outside after the others had gone to sleep, not wanting to close my eyes and miss the spectacular meteor shower overhead.

In the spring and summer, morning arrived like a slap, the sunlight searing a path across the terrain. We lived outdoors in the cooler hours, and debated the best way to keep the indoor temperature down during the day. The mud walls insulated more effectively than the concrete of city houses. My approach was to leave everything tightly shut during the heat. But when the local women came to visit they complained that there was no breeze, and insisted I open the windows. The villagers had built wicker huts to rest in on summer days; this permitted air movement. Torn between my neighbors' advice and my own intuition, I finally asked Elisabeth, who was out visiting most of the day, if it was true that our house was worse than the local homes. "You have the coolest house in the entire village," she said. But we still would have appreciated electric fans.

In the middle of the day during the summer we were compelled to take a siesta; it was impossible to work. Of course, lying on our *toshaks* in the heat being tormented by sandflies – nearly invisible insects with bites that pricked like needles and transmitted the disease leishmaniasis, which had pockmarked the faces of many Afghans – well, there was little rest to be had. Dust storms provided some relief, as they briefly blocked the sun. When the sun sank behind the mountains each evening, we luxuriated in the dropping air temperature. We ate a late dinner outside before going to bed.

Fear of djinn kept most the villagers from leaving their homes at night, we heard, but during the day we had plenty of visitors. The village girls, who spent most of their time lugging around younger brothers and sisters, often turned up in our house. They entered without knocking (like their mothers) and settled themselves on the *toshaks* in our family room. No doubt the difficulty in getting water kept them from bathing often. One night I dreamed God told me to give them all combs to disentangle their grimy, chopped hair.

Actually it was not too hard to overlook their dirt – our children were little better. Aidan, whose nose ran continuously for the first six years of life, had a persistent black mud mustache that one of our American friends told me enviously he wished he could replicate. All three children shuffled around in little plastic slippers or sandals, and although they became proficient at squatting on their haunches so that their backsides did not touch the ground, they were constantly dirty.

But unlike our kids, the Afghan girls did two things I could not bear. One was spitting on the floor. If it had been washable, perhaps I could have overlooked this transgression, but the thought of saliva embedding itself in our rug was too much. The other practice which I wouldn't tolerate was allowing their infant brothers and sisters to urinate freely in the house. They seemed surprised that I cared, but I insisted they wrap something around the bare-bottomed babies if they were going to bring them inside.

Of course, from the Afghans' perspective no doubt *we* were unclean. Handkerchiefs and Kleenex must have seemed particularly vile: a local person would merely go outside, lean over, pinch his or her nose, and blow mucus out on the ground. We were also careless about our feet; Afghans are conscientious about keeping them clean, especially since they take off shoes indoors. In the city, we saw boys in the bazaar lugging cardboard boxes lined with plastic and filled to the brim with Vaseline for sale – the perfect remedy for the cracking that occurred because of the dry, dusty environment. It took us awhile to appreciate the value of washed and well-lubricated feet.

After my initial appraisal of the girls – who all had the same short, bluntly cut black hair and colorful badly-fitting dresses – I began to appreciate their individuality. My favorite was Sozan, the same girl who had beaten our dog Oliver. She was about twelve, curious and intelligent. When Elisabeth and Nooria started the girl's school, she was in the first class. She helped teach the next new class; when she grew up (we were happy to learn) she herself married a teacher.

Another girl, who always showed up with a baby in tow, arrived one morning asking for medicine. Her little sister had a cold. Rich told her that the baby would get better in a few days. Her mother didn't like this answer; she carried her child to town and came back with the usual bundle of medicines, including injections. Day by day we watched as the baby grew weaker. Finally, Rich told the girl, "If you keep giving her those medicines, she is going to die." She did. Elisabeth and I went to the funeral, but I had a hard time comforting the mother. I knew she was trying to do what was best for her child, but in her ignorance she had, in fact, killed her.

Due to the hygiene and lack of clean water, children sickened often in the summer, and we saw about one child a week die from diarrhea-related dehydration. Rich and Elisabeth urged people to give their children a simple treatment – oral rehydration solution (ORS), a mixture of boiled water, salt, and sugar. Most people were sure that we had a magical medicine we were giving our own children to make them so robust, and were equally persuaded that we were unwilling to share it with them. We told them repeatedly that we did not have any special drug. But they didn't believe us, and children continued dying.

One morning Hannah woke up, languid and without an appetite. Refusing to eat or drink, she got weaker and weaker as the day wore on. The next morning Rich took one look at her, and said, "I'm staying home today." He mixed up a batch of ORS, sat Hannah on his lap and began reading her children's stories, every few minutes ladling a spoonful of ORS into her mouth.

People came by, searching for the *duktar saeb*. They were astonished to see him caring for his own child this way. "What are you doing?" they asked.

"I'm giving her ORS," he said.

"Why don't you give her some medicine?" they asked.

"She doesn't need medicine," Rich told them. "She just needs ORS."

The next day found Hannah outside, toddling around. She was a living demonstration of the effectiveness of the treatment the villagers had been resisting. Her apparently miraculous recovery signaled a turning point in the people's attitude toward ORS. After that we heard that other families in the village began using it to treat their own children.

Of course, they still seemed bewildered as to why we would get sick when we had a doctor in the family. After Rich had been asked this question a number of times, he developed two questions in response: "Does a mechanic's tire ever get punctured? Do you know any two-hundred-year old doctors?" He would then explain that like them, we all got sick and would eventually die. This apparently was an idea they had not considered.

The village women were not afraid to ask other health-related questions. They wanted to know if having a husband who had undergone a vasectomy meant sex was impossible. Rich walked in on this conversation and indicated with a smile that it was no problem.

One middle-aged lady brought her pregnant daughter-in-law to see Rich. They had with them a number of medications for the mother-to-be. The older woman listened thoughtfully as Rich explained that the daughter-in-law should not take the medications during pregnancy. After a pause, the older woman looked up at him and asked, "Well should *I* take them, then?" In her mind it seemed a waste to throw away drugs that might be beneficial, even if they didn't relate to any condition she had.

They also had questions about our children. Our boys were pale, but Aidan was a brunet and Connor's hair was dark blond. Hannah's hair, when it finally came, grew out into tight golden curls. One day a villager asked me, "What did you do to her hair?"

"Her hair?" I echoed.

"Yes, what did you do to get it that color?"

I laughed. "Nothing. That's the way she was born."

The woman sniffed. "Well, I like *your* hair better," she said, nodding at my dark brown braid. "Your hair is like *our* hair."

Rather than feeling offended, I was glad that the women liked their own kind of beauty best. Unlike Faizullah's sister, they weren't buying bleaching creams to whiten their skin; they seemed content with the way they were. As Hannah's hair grew in dense and wavy, I was also glad we had ignored both our old neighbors' advice to sacrifice a chicken and Ibrahim's advice to shave her head as an infant in hopes that her hair would come in thicker.

The children loved catching animals. They found a hedgehog, but it was dead (or playing dead, we were never quite sure which). They also found a tortoise that had been crushed by a passing vehicle. Rich spent an hour cleaning the wound and pulling off maggots, but the poor thing died and Aidan buried it in a shoebox.

The easiest to catch were the frogs. They hovered outside our shower and near the reservoir. The kids caught them and put them in a crater a rocket had blasted in our yard, and then carved little tunnels for them to hide in. The story began to circulate that the foreigners ate frogs. One day, Hannah marched into the house, beaming and holding up the edges of her dress. It was filled to the brim with frogs. The village children had given them to her, she told me. We hurriedly explained to everyone we could that we just liked to *look* at the frogs, not eat them.

162

We did eat something strange, but it was not our idea – it was Ibrahim's. While serving in the army, he had learned to make snares to catch sparrows. He hung the small, wire loops from the eaves of the porch; when the birds flew near, they were captured as the loops tightened around them. We were dubious about this enterprise, but Ibrahim marched over eagerly one day with a plate of cooked sparrow. Unfortunately, there was more bone than meat. Even less tasty than the stewed sparrow were the sparrow meatballs he brought another day – the ground bones reminded me of pebbles. After that, we all gave up on the prospect of sparrow as a protein source.

There *was* meat available in the village; occasionally word would spread that a goat was going to be butchered, and everyone would hurry to buy a piece. And flocks of turkeys paraded frequently through our open yard; the boys learned that they could inspire a chorus of gobbles by slamming the front door.

Knowing we could buy a turkey, we decided we'd give an American Thanksgiving a try with Elisabeth and our Afghan coworkers. Gracious as ever, the Afghans feigned enthusiasm about the unfamiliar foods we served. Ibrahim took a bite of pumpkin pie and said, "It is very *qowi,*" a word that literally means "strong or powerful." We knew this was really his way of saying the flavor was too robust for his palate.

I would never have predicted that pumpkin pie would be harder to swallow than sparrow meatballs.

Cooking outside with my homemade oven, 1994

CHAPTER NINETEEN

Women and beasts in the garden

In this world it's either religion or women. (Afghan proverb)

American culture changes so quickly that each time we reentered the US we had to acquire new skills, lingo, and styles. When we married in 1984, the wedding norm for our circle of friends was a simple ceremony followed by coffee and cake in the church basement. Rich volunteered for a drug study to purchase my wedding ring and rent his groomsmen's tuxedos; the most expensive part of the celebration was our cake.

That changed while we were abroad, so I'm afraid I misrepresented the cost of an American wedding to Afghans. I empathized with the men, who often had to wait until they were well into their thirties to marry because they could not afford the dowry demanded. When taxi drivers suggested coming to America to find a wife, I told them, "In America, getting married is cheap.

It's *after* you're married that a wife's expensive."

Although Islam allows a man to have up to four wives at a time, very few Afghans could afford this. In one of the more bizarre cases in the village, Rich and Ibrahim met a family with an even more pragmatic decision to make: if there was only *one* wife, whose would she be? A widower had a twelve-year-old son; he realized that he could either afford the dowry to marry again, or get a wife for the boy. He needed a woman around the house to do the work, so he decided he would go ahead and marry his son off.

Rich said it was odd seeing this pre-teen visiting with his guests, mimicking the demeanor of a grown man while his seventeen-year-old bride served tea and cookies. We all agreed it was better not to think about the logistics of their intimate relationship.

Usually marriages in Afghanistan were arranged with near relatives, and we saw some bittersweet results of this. It had the advantage that one could make sure the family was a good one; but there were risks. One graceful young mother brought her toddler and infant to be examined by Rich. The older son was clearly deaf. As Rich checked the baby, snapping his fingers outside the child's field of vision, he saw that this boy could not hear, either. He leaned back.

"What's your relationship to your husband?" (This is a common question in Afghanistan.)

"He is my first cousin," she answered. (This is a common answer.)

"I'm afraid," Rich told her gently, "that all your children may end up with this problem." He explained that the condition was genetic. I watched sadly as she led her family away, knowing this woman would have a houseful of deaf children to care for.

Although we had attended a wedding in Mazar, we didn't realize the difficulties of hosting the same event in a village. Because the family was obligated to provide food for all the guests, celebrations in their small, mud houses involved staggering the arrival of those they had invited. Not aware of this, we were surprised when a child appeared at our door at eight in the morning.

"Come to the wedding," she said.

"We'll come," we said. "But it's too early."

"You need to come *now*," she pressed us.

"No," we said, "we'll come later."

We wandered over at eleven o'clock to find the feast was finished. The hosts scraped together what were clearly leftovers from the meals of others and served them to us heaped on platters.

I decided in the future I would take our assigned time more seriously.

Elisabeth, Nooria, and I went to the ladies' party. All the women were crammed into an upstairs room; there was barely space to step over guests sitting on the floor as we found places to squish in beside them. Individual women took turns dancing in the tiny open circle in the center of the room. The bride, dressed in sparkling clothes and painted like a porcelain doll for the occasion, sat stiffly on the side, crying. This was one element of weddings we could never get used to: the more the brides expressed anguish at leaving their parents, the more they appeared to love their family.

Sometimes this grief took an extreme form. Once when Rich and Ibrahim were headed into town to shop, they were asked if they could transport a bride-to-be and her parents to her wedding in Pul-i-khumri. They agreed, but grew concerned as the girl (who was covered in a *chahdri,* so they couldn't see her face) not only cried, but sobbed and moaned the whole trip. The family assured Rich that the girl was fine, but it was hard to believe she was secretly looking forward to her upcoming union.

We met a few females who told us they did not want to get married. It was a risky choice, but I could understand, having seen how unhappy many women were. (Sitting around complaining seemed a common pastime at women's get-togethers, so their misery may have been exaggerated.)

In the region surrounding our village marriage was not only a matter of family concern. The area was under the political and religious control of an Ismaili leader by the name of Saeed Mansoor. The system reminded us of feudalism: Saeed Mansoor provided the villagers with sheep; they raised the sheep, sheared the sheep, and spun wool. Then the women wove two rugs: one they kept; the other was returned to Saeed Mansoor. The people seemed happy with this arrangement. If peaceful existence was the goal, this was the best system we saw functioning in Afghanistan.

Occasionally Saeed Mansoor made an appearance to bless and name children and solve disputes. One of the most interesting that occurred during our time there involved a marital conflict.

167

The husband had gone to the city for a time and when he came back he announced that he wanted his wife to move out. She returned to her father, but was not allowed to take the children. This was heartbreaking to everyone, and when Saeed Mansoor visited Qarya Beykh, the wife complained.

He took her side. He told the man that not only did he have to take his wife back, but he also had to pay compensation to her father. She had done a lot of work while at her father's house, Saeed Mansoor pointed out, and that would be missed when she returned to her husband. The man listened to Saeed Mansoor and did as he was told. We rejoiced to see the woman and her children reunited.

Villagers explained the devastation the war with the Soviet Union brought to Qarya Beykh. One older man — white-bearded but robust — told us he had lost his wife and five children when a grenade was thrown into his house. He managed to raise money to marry again; this time he chose a beautiful teenager. Despite their age difference, he seemed to treat her kindly and she appeared content. Another widower claimed that when his wife was killed, he breastfed his infant. Afghans never ceased amazing us with their adaptability to changing circumstances.

One elderly couple Rich met was childless. Curious, Rich asked the man why he had never taken a second wife. "I felt like God wanted me to just have the one wife," the man told him. Rich noted that they were a particularly tender couple but marveled at the economic consequences of their decision. Sons are the Social Security system in Afghanistan.

Because infertility was particularly heartbreaking in a culture where aged parents are financially dependent on their children, women came to Rich for treatment, hoping that the foreign doctor had some magic pill to help them conceive. He did not. The pressure to become pregnant within the first few months after marriage was intense; one of the women seeking help later committed suicide.

One day I drank tea with a friend of Elisabeth's. I was holding Hannah; the woman asked me her name.

168

I gave her name (clarifying it was "Hannah" not "Henna") then proceeded to tell her the story of her namesake. "Hannah was a very devout woman whose husband had another wife. The other wife kept having children, but Hannah had none. She cried and cried, but her husband asked her, 'Am I not better to you than ten sons?' She finally went to the temple and prayed for a son. And God gave her Samuel, who became a prophet."

The woman listened intently to the story. Later, Elisabeth told me that this Afghan herself had been unable to have children.

Although I would not have described myself as a feminist before living in Afghanistan, it was impossible not to be passionate about women's rights after spending time there. Females labored in difficult circumstances, sacrificing the best food to the men and sometimes being beaten by husbands and sons. It did not always happen (and mothers were usually treated better than other women) but when it did, it was heartbreaking.

Since most villagers did not go out after dark, we were surprised to hear a man calling Rich one night. He opened the window to speak. This villager's wife had complications while delivering her baby, and although Rich made it evident he would be willing to assist, the husband refused. Now, after a day of hemorrhaging, the wife was facing death, and the husband finally decided to seek Rich's help.

My heart almost burst with pride as Rich chastised the man. "You treat your donkeys better than you treat your women!" he said. And then he packed up his medical supplies and went to save this new mother's life.

Being a wife and mother myself, I fit within the Afghan worldview. I was ushered back into the women's area of homes; I was asked questions about sex; I knew and tried to fulfill expectations of the kind of hospitality a wife should provide.

For the single foreign women, I sensed it was different. In order to work with Elisabeth, men seemed to have to view her as an anomaly – a kind of *female* man. Once in Mazar she was working on her car, some local boys sitting on a wall observing. When they asked what she was doing, she told them, "Changing the oil."

"You can't do that," they told her. "You're a girl." She proceeded to prove them wrong.

While no one in the village brought her mechanical problems to solve, apparently the men trusted her with their animals. As a veterinarian, her medical skills were in even more demand than Rich's. Qarya Beykh was a farming community; each morning the cows stomped past our home on the way to pasture and plodded back in at night. The shepherds kept the sheep and goats out in the fields summer nights, and brought them in early in the morning. Often they stopped by and woke Elisabeth for a consultation before heading home. She kept busy with a steady stream of patients.

When village chickens began falling ill, she recommended vaccines. One woman said, "Could you give my chickens the vaccines – but *not* vaccinate the chickens of my neighbor?" Elisabeth was shocked, but later related to me a joke she had heard which summed up the local perspective on such things:

> *God came to a man and told him he'd give him anything he asked for. The only condition, the Lord said, was that whatever he asked for, the man's neighbor would get double. The man thought and thought and thought. Finally the Lord said, "Well? What would you like?" "Could you cut off my left hand?" the man asked.*

Despite the hospitality and kindness we often experienced in Afghanistan, the vaccination incident demonstrated Afghans had adopted the mindset reflected in the Arab proverb, "Me against my brothers, me and my brothers against my cousins, me and my cousins against the world."

❖

Not only was Elisabeth busy with the animals; she also became a center of attraction for the village children. They loved to sit with her, walk with her, and listen to her stories. When she and Nooria started a school – one of the things the village women indicated they desired for their daughters ("so they won't be ignorant like us," they said) – the children were enthusiastic. Elisabeth and Nooria took turns teaching the first class; as the students progressed, Elisabeth took the beginners, Nooria the more advanced students. But sometimes her popularity was too much for her. One Friday morning, she asked me for a favor.

"Do you think you could lock me in my house?" she asked. "That way I can have an hour alone. People will see the lock on the outside and think I'm gone."

"Good idea," I said, and dutifully locked her in.

Not half an hour later, I was walking past her house when I heard a ferocious banging on the door.

"Elisabeth?" I called.

"Let me out!" she cried. "Oh, let me out! I'm sick!" She spent the rest of the afternoon in the outhouse. Despite her otherwise Spartan lifestyle, I am sure she was yearning for a Western sit-down toilet at that point. I was just glad I chanced by her house before she was in a state of total emergency.

In another attempt at finding solitude, she asked if she could borrow our dog Oliver for a hike. We said yes. She returned later to tell us that she had walked up one of the wheat-covered hills. When she was at the top, she looked down and saw a huge wave working its way up the mountain. "A giant snake," she thought, and quickly made a plan. If the cobra (as she suspected it was) should confront her, she would sacrifice Oliver, pushing him at the snake and running away. (Needless to say, we gave her a little flak when we heard about her idea.) However, the snake appeared, took a look at them, and headed back into the wheat.

Snakes appeared several times during our fourteen months in Qarya Beykh. Once, one fell on my head as I pushed aside the privacy curtain to our bathroom. Another time, we found a group of men staring at cracks in the back of Ibrahim and Nooria's house where snakes were slithering in and out. But the most memorable instance was when a villager brought us a snake as thick as a fist and probably six feet long.

"I know you like snakes," he said.

"Where did you find it?" Rich asked.

"In my yard," the man said. "It was all coiled up, so I shot it." He showed us the evenly-spaced holes where the bullet had gone through.

We thought we'd have a little fun with it, since Elisabeth feared snakes. We arranged the snake on her front porch, as though it were coming out from behind her water barrel. But she was too savvy: she walked up to her door, glanced down and said, "Who left this dead snake here?"

While she hated reptiles, Elisabeth was fine with larger animals. She and the men decided that rather than driving to Pul-i-khumri for the weekly grocery run, they would borrow horses and ride across the plain the other direction, to the tiny town of Dahani-ghori. The trip ended up being more challenging than they had anticipated. Ibrahim's horse was uncooperative, so Elisabeth (who was the best equestrian among them) switched animals. Despite her skill, the horse went berserk, bolted down a road, and slammed Elisabeth against a stone wall. The beast then turned on Rich's horse. Rich found himself up in the air as his horse bolted a few times, and then it fell onto its side. Elisabeth and Rich were unhurt, but determined to return the wild horse to its owner. Rich came home with the horse, and Elisabeth and Ibrahim went on to the bazaar. While returning, Ibrahim's horse decided to take a drink while crossing the *joiee* and suddenly dipped, tossing Ibrahim and our bag of flour into the water. The wet flour froze instantly; we were thankful that Ibrahim, while a bit battered and chilled, made it back without major injury.

The next shopping trip, they decided to travel by Land Cruiser.

Splashing in the spring at Dahan-i-ghori, 1994

CHAPTER TWENTY

Holidays

What are a hundred guests in another man's house? (Afghan proverb)

What makes for a perfect childhood? It is a question we have asked ourselves many times. Our children, now adults, have told us over and over how much they appreciate those experiences they had in Afghanistan and India that were alien to the experiences of most American children.

The boys loved the freedom they had to roam the village and visit with Rich. This gave them opportunities to taste dishes we had never seen in Kabul or Mazar. One was rice cooked in milk and sugar. The rice stood heaped on a platter with a large well hollowed out in its center. Into this was poured melted butter; an extra bowl of butter was served alongside.

Rich and the boys managed to eat the rice, but decided there was far too much fat. The host asked Rich, "Are you going to eat your butter?"

When Rich assured him he wasn't, the old man picked up the bowl and drank it down in one gulp.

If we did need butter or eggs, we gave Connor *afs* and sent him door to door to ask if anyone had some to sell. The local women churned the butter themselves in sheepskin they had sewn into bags for this purpose. Connor enjoyed the hunt, and proudly returned with a hand-molded plate of butter or a few eggs for our use.

When we moved into the army fort that became our home, there was still a broken-down military truck in the middle of the yard. Connor and I designed a pirate flag, which he sailed from his new ship. We allowed him freedom to clamber around the old vehicle after we were sure that all the grenades (which he pointed out to us) were removed.

The village children were interested in the outhouse at the end of our property, and the CDP team decided that the new girl's school should have its own restroom. This would not only serve its immediate purpose, but also be a demonstration to the village of what an excellent thing it was to relieve oneself indoors. As the men were busy in the fields, Rich and Ibrahim began digging a pit for the toilet near an outside wall.

One day as Rich was hard at work, a man came by and stood observing him for a while. "You are very *zaieef*," the man said. *Zaieef* means weak – the villager's assessment presumably made because Rich was so thin. Rich looked up. "Well, then, why don't *you* come down and dig?" His offer was declined. But *zaieef* or not, Rich and Ibrahim completed the restroom, which became a hit with the girls.

Kevin came down from Mazar to help with the next project. Since the villagers were now interested in indoor toilets, Kevin designed a mold for a bathroom floor – a concrete slab with a hole in the center that could be rolled into place over a pre-dug pit. (Mud walls would then be built around the floor.) It seemed like a great plan – until the first concrete slab was dried and ready to move. Unexpectedly heavy, it took several men to budge. Kevin revised his plans, and soon many more floor slabs were poured.

But now another obstacle arose. Whereas we would have difficulty relieving ourselves outdoors, the villagers found it impossible to do so inside. The pristine rooms sat unused and the men sheepishly confessed their problem to Rich and Ibrahim. Hopefully the example of their children helped the practice catch on with the fathers.

Not only were piles of human feces a problem in the village; the accompanying flies were worse. Most people did not have screens on their windows, and when we were invited for a meal, the women of the family spent the entire time fanning away swarms of pests so we could eat.

Although our neighbors used dried cow dung to heat their homes, the breeze usually blew away from our end of the village, and we welcomed the arrival of winter and a respite from the flies. We decided to take a break and head to Mazar for Christmas. But first we wanted to introduce some of our customs and beliefs to the villagers.

"I miss the Australian Christmas carols," Elisabeth said. "It's not snowy this time of year at home."

"Australians have their own Christmas carols?" we asked in surprise.

"Yes," she answered wistfully, and then began to sing, "The north wind is tossing the leaves. The red dust is over the town; The sparrows are under the eaves, And the grass in the paddock is brown. . ."

Unfortunately, Australian carols seemed as out of place as the British and American ones we had learned growing up. Instead of caroling, we decided we would just share the Nativity story. Elisabeth translated it into Dari and she and I went around to the various compounds in the village.

There was no difficulty gathering a crowd: all the women and children came out as soon as we entered the yard. As Elisabeth told the story of Jesus' birth, I marveled at the women's response. They understood Mary's shame as an unwed mother (clucking their tongues both in sympathy for Mary and understanding of Joseph's dilemma); they provided words to fill in Elisabeth's description (the "stable" became the *gao khahna,* or cow house). They were appalled that Jesus was born in such a setting. The story seemed even more real to me now that I had seen the raised mud mangers used in the village – with a little bedding, they would be ideal cribs. The shepherds' flutes on summer nights as they serenaded their sheep outside the village have ever since conjured the image in my mind of similar men long before them who were startled by the appearance of angels.

177

In the evening, we stood outside Ibrahim and Nooria's house and – more confident with Rich's voice joining – sang a few Christmas carols.

Snow began falling before we left the village. We made a snowman – the villagers had never seen such a thing – and soon snowmen popped up all over.

We drove to Mazar and Christmas day found us celebrating with a large group of foreign friends. Our meals were even more enjoyable than they had been in the US – the pleasure must have been proportional to the amount of work we took preparing them and the collaborative nature of the cooking. Kevin made his special peanut butter fudge and others brought cookies and meat and salads and fruit. I had spent several days rolling out gingerbread men and cutting them with a tiny cookie cutter, and gave milk cans full of them to friends.

As the afternoon rolled around, I became extraordinarily tired. I decided to lie down on one of the *toshaks*, and finally we went back to the house where we were staying so I could rest. A few days later we headed back to the village.

But I was still weary and dragged around. I did basic work, fed baby Owen, and went to bed. I was glad one day that I had latched our bedroom door; village women heard I was ill and insisted on barging in to see me. Without the energy to descend my elevated bed to tell them to go away, I was glad Rich was there to inform them it was "not our custom" to have visitors when we were sick. We had received a copy of Alfred Lansing's book, *Endurance: Shackleton's Incredible Voyage*, for Christmas, and even though I was thoroughly exhausted, I lay awake late into the night reliving the adventures of the South Pole explorers trapped in ice.

As he had done when Hannah was sick, Rich stayed home from work again – this time to help with the housework. I suspect no one in that village had ever seen a man do laundry, although most of the men claimed they could cook. I later heard the women discussing what a wonderful husband I had, who took care of me like that – not to mention, they added, that he never beat me!

When the whites of my eyes turned yellow, it was apparent that I had contracted hepatitis A. The virus was sweeping through the village, and was too minute for our new water filter to strain out. The children proceeded to get sick and even Owen tested positive for exposure to it, although he was only breastfeeding. Fortunately, none of us got it as severely as Rich had the year before, and by the time Kevin drove down from Mazar to check up on us, we had completely recovered.

Although we had a lot of freedom to walk in the village and surrounding hills, it must have been a lonely place for Elisabeth, living in the middle of our two families without another unmarried foreigner to spend time with. We made friends with an Afghan doctor working with the Halo Trust (a group that clears landmines) and spent time with him and his family in Pul-i-khumri. A handsome young British de-miner was there at the time, and he, too, seemed a bit lonely. He accepted our invitation to come for visits to the village.

On one trip he promised to clear a garden for Elisabeth. Our compound was pockmarked with rocket craters; he methodically searched through the one Elisabeth had chosen to plant in. Cliff found several explosive devices, and carefully moved them to his truck to detonate later.

"I found some stuff in a cave, too," Connor told him. Cliff told him to show where the cave was.

Outside the village, where the road wound toward the mountains, yawned a man-made hole carved into the rise above the rutted dirt track. Cliff peered in and cautioned us while he went inside. The cave, he told us, was stacked with landmines.

"These are particularly nasty anti-personnel mines," he explained. "They spring up and shoot shrapnel outward. Look," he told Rich, "I'll toss them out to you and you put them in the back of my truck."

"Toss them?" Rich repeated. "Isn't that dangerous?"

Cliff laughed. "No. They need a pin to detonate. You can buy the pins in the bazaar in town for less than a dollar a piece, but the mines are safe as is."

They spent the afternoon emptying the cave. Cliff's car was now a well-loaded arsenal, and he told us he would come back sometime and blow everything up.

"Better not do it too near the village," Rich warned him. "There was a lot of fighting here with the Russians, and the villagers are a bit jumpy." Cliff agreed.

He decided to spend the night with us; we set up bedding for him in our shared sitting room. Before turning in he came over and sheepishly admitted, "I took my watch off and looped it over my belt – and then I went to use the toilet. I forgot about it, and as soon as I unbuckled my belt, it slipped into the pit."

We both commiserated with him and then said goodnight. Rich mentioned it to Ibrahim and wondered if it would start beeping when someone was squatting over the hole,

It did. As seven a.m. struck, Nooria heard its musical tones ringing the hour.

She rushed back to their house. "Ibrahim," she said, "I heard the watch. I think we can get it."

He went to the outhouse and began lighting strips of toilet paper, sending them wafting down to illuminate the chamber. Sure enough, he spotted the watch and figured out a way to bend wire to fish it out.

When Cliff arose, Ibrahim approached him proudly.

"We've recovered your watch," he told him. "We washed it and left it on the hood of your car to dry."

Cliff battled disgust and surprise and offered a gracious thank-you – and then exchanged a glance that we knew meant he would be hurling the watch out into a field as he drove from the village.

❖

True to his word, Cliff came back to blow up his stash – this time on Easter weekend. We were very busy – Elisabeth and I had planned a party and invited all the women in the village. We could not do much, we realized, with just the two of us. We planned to serve tea, cookies, and candy, and borrowing a melancholy tune we thought they would like we wrote a Dari song that explained the story of Christ's life.

The afternoon was incredibly chaotic. I rushed up our steep mud staircase to bring trays of tea and scurried down with glasses to wash and trash to discard. There were waves of matching black *kalash,* the loose rubber shoes the women wore, flowing from the steps. With so much noise and coming and going, Elisabeth and I had few chances to sing our song and no opportunity to actually chat with our guests.

At one point, as I passed Rich in the yard, he said, "Have you seen Connor?"

Our eyes met. "I bet he went with Cliff," I said.

At that moment, a terrific explosion rocked the village, and a huge plume of smoke filled the sky behind the hill. I hurried up to our sitting room to reassure the women, who were already in a panic.

"This is how we celebrate Easter," I offered with a smile. They were not amused.

But the party continued for a while before the women began to trickle out. By late afternoon we were left with a bucket of candy wrappers, a carpet embedded with cookie crumbs and dried chickpeas, and one old pair of *kalash* – apparently someone had taken my newer shoes in exchange.

Cliff rumbled into the compound with Connor.

"I thought I told you to detonate those things away from the village!" Rich exclaimed. "You've scared the people half to death. I've already had some complaints from the village elders, and even though they gave us permission to destroy the landmines, they've had second thoughts. And you," he turned to Connor, "are in trouble. I told you not to follow Cliff."

Cliff told us he'd driven for what seemed like a long time (not realizing the road curled around, ending at the top of the nearest hill). He found an old foxhole, arranged the explosives, and then settled in the hole. Just as he was about to detonate the stockpile, he saw Connor walking up the hill. He called him over, they hunkered down together, and then he blew up everything at once.

181

Connor was sent to his room to write out a sentence one hundred times (something like "I promise never to disobey mom and dad again for as long as I live"), but was rescued after he was only half done. The tell-tale cloud of dust that preceded a truck arriving began wafting toward us. We were the only ones who ever got visitors in vehicles, so we sat down and waited to see who was coming.

Our old friends Greg and Mary, with their three children, tumbled out of a car and embraced us all. They brought out a package and unwrapped layer after layer of newspaper to show several frozen juice packs. We all sat down and ate them like ice cream. We rejoiced at having friends to celebrate Easter with.

The next day we drove across the plain to Dahan-i-ghori (not by horse this time) and visited the pool of a fresh-water spring that had recently been renovated by another development organization. The children swung their feet in the cool water and watched giant goldfish swim around. We relished the shade and the beauty and time with Greg and Mary. It was the perfect end to what had been an explosive holiday weekend.

Hannah and Farzia, 1994

Connor and Aidan on their pirate ship, 1993

CHAPTER TWENTY-ONE

Warlords and other visitors

An unexpected guest is like a bolt from the blue. (Afghan proverb)

Life without chocolate may be an oxymoron; at least it's not something I would knowingly choose. We brought a five-pound bag of cocoa powder from the US; with a sigh, I contributed the last of it to a birthday cake for our friend Cliff. It would be three months before we tasted chocolate again.

One *can* survive without chocolate. Coffee, apparently, is a different story. Our Finnish friends guaranteed they would never run out. Despite having a luggage weight limit much lower than for those flying from America, the Finns made packing coffee a priority. They even drank it late at night, claiming they were genetically disposed to consume the ebony liquid without any sleep disturbance. As a tea drinker, I didn't understand the psychological and physical importance of that cup of java.

When a Finnish friend came to visit us in the village, she arrived prepared. She knew how to live simply, so our lack of running water and electricity was no problem. She brought treats from Mazar and then handed me a packet of loose coffee. "Could you keep this for me?" she asked.

I stood on tip-toe to slide the packet on our open shelf, but it slipped from my fingers. We both watched in horror as its contents dispersed through a bucket of water I had sitting on the kitchen floor. With a hysterical cry, she feverishly scooped out the flakes that had not already sunk.

"Three days without coffee!" she gasped. "Three days!"

I expected *her* to survive the village. But a British friend from Kabul, always immaculately dressed – the very personification of poshness – was the last person we anticipated adjusting quickly. One morning, I stumbled from bed to see him outside, humming. In the frosty air he stood, coatless, with our small mirror propped against a wall and a pan of cold water, shaving. He greeted us with a brisk, "Good morning," that shamed me. I always had to bathe in a warm room.

We appreciated the warning when guests arrived by road. One afternoon we saw the cloud and heard the low rumble before a convoy of military vehicles pulled into our yard.

A young man in fatigues jumped out of the first jeep, greeting Rich like a long-lost comrade. I watched from the doorway.

"The governor is here," Rich said. "Could you bring some tea up?"

Elisabeth and I had lived long enough in rural Afghanistan to keep ourselves discreetly attired with guests. We pulled on our headscarves and joined Rich and the governor in our upstairs sitting room. He had lived and attended college in the United States so his English was good.

When we offered tea, he declined. "Do you have any beer?" he asked. We shook our heads. "Wine? Vodka?" We smiled apologetically. "What *do* you do for fun?" he asked in disgust.

His visit was short; apparently disappointed by our quiet lifestyle, he and his guards disappeared in another cloud of dust.

But before leaving, he informed us that his father, Saeed Mansoor, had extended an invitation for us to stay in his guesthouse whenever we chose. As the weather grew warmer, we decided to take the Ismaili leader up on his offer.

We piled in our car with Ibrahim, Nooria, Elisabeth, and all the children, and drove up into the mountains, winding our way through picturesque villages each consisting of a half dozen houses surrounded by fields of wheat. All the people stopped to watch us. But as we descended into the Kayan Valley we noticed a change. Not only did the people along the road stop; they bowed as we went by. We realized they thought we were Saeed Mansoor himself. Even though we viewed him as a feudal landlord, we still marveled that he was treated as royalty by the locals.

We were halted on the road by a teenaged soldier with long, curly hair. He was extremely friendly and told us (in English) that his family lived in Pennsylvania; winters he delivered pizzas, while summers he commanded troops in Afghanistan. (This struck me as a kind of ultimate male fantasy.) He invited Rich to shoot automatic weapons and blow something up with RPGs, but Rich told him we needed to get on to our destination. ("A pity I didn't take him up on the offer," Rich sighed later. "I'll probably never get a chance to do *that* again.")

We continued along the road, pulling over by a stream for a few minutes. The others got out of the car; I stayed seated. The only sounds were the water and the leaves of the trees rustling in the spring breeze. My parched soul had been deprived of such lush beauty for so long that tears sprang to my eyes.

We soon arrived at Saeed Mansoor's house. There were a number of buildings on the property besides his private home, including a museum displaying native musical instruments. White peacocks from India promenaded the grounds; the terraced rose garden was also hung with cages for canaries, parakeets, and other birds. We were shown a waterfall that cascaded down the mountainside near the house at the flip of a switch. One of the servants opened the elegant guesthouse for us and then the cook asked what we desired for dinner. Not wanting to appear greedy, we ordered a modest but delicious dish, *ketchree quroot,* a pilau made with mung beans, rice, and reconstituted dried yogurt. We offered to pay, but were assured it was unnecessary, as we were guests. It was hard to believe a place like this existed in Afghanistan.

In the morning, we were informed the governor had arranged for breakfast with us. We were beckoned into a huge room at the side of the main house; in it was a swimming pool filled with water that looked as black and deep as Loch Ness on an overcast day. Connor mounted the winding stairway to a diving board before we called him back. I shuddered to think what a dip in that pool would be like.

187

A table was already laid by the pool and we were served tea, *naan* and cream, and the delicacy of the meal – a cooked lamb's head. Fortunately, stacks of fresh kabobs were arranged around it. (It was the first time in my life that kabobs sounded like the best breakfast option.) More somber now than when he had hopefully dropped by our compound, the governor joined us briefly. He told us we could stay as long as we liked, but we returned to Qarya Beykh after breakfast.

While most of our visits – and visitors – were welcome, one weekend Elisabeth became a victim of burglary. Somehow the thieves knew she would be gone. One lured our dog Oliver away from the yard with meat while the other broke the padlock off Elisabeth's front door. They managed to get away with the trunk containing her few valuables, including her passport. As soon as she returned and discovered the loss, Rich and Ibrahim began spreading word through the village and looking for the culprits. In such a small place it was not long before they were apprehended and Elisabeth's items returned.

The village elders suggested that the men be whipped as punishment. However, Rich eloquently explained that Elisabeth would want no such thing; she would forgive the men and want mercy to be shown.

Elisabeth, who had not been involved with these negotiations, was miffed. "I think a good whipping would teach them a lesson," she said. But it was too late. We didn't have any more break-ins, though.

We had two more sets of visitors before we were due to leave the country for our six-month break. The first was one of our teammates from Kabul, a former soldier who decided that in the name of security we should have better access to the outside world.

For some time we had been getting news about Afghanistan by listening to the BBC on our shortwave radio. We heard when the Taliban took control of Kandahar in November 1994 and then swept through the country, taking over a third of the provinces. As of spring 1995, they had not conquered Kabul, but our office wanted to be able to contact us if necessary.

Our teammate installed a radio tower and a solar panel which dwarfed our roof. "After accounting for the energy needed for the radio," he told us, "you should have enough to light one bulb."

In the village we had been dependent on kerosene lanterns and the circle of light they provided. To have visibility throughout an entire room seemed luxurious. Once the wiring was connected between the solar-charged battery and our single bulb, we anticipated the moment of illumination. We switched the bulb on – and gasped. Our living space, warm and cozy in the dim light of a lantern, was filthy. Everything was dingy, cloaked in dust.

"Turn it off! Turn it off!" I insisted. *Perhaps*, I thought, *it is better to live without some modern amenities if we don't have others.*

Our final guests also arrived from Kabul. The night before we were due to leave the village, the new IAM director and his wife dropped by to check in with us. We had been in crisis for the last few weeks, but they did not know that when they arrived. Rich was depressed: he was fed up trying to do community development work when everyone for miles around knew he was a doctor. They could only see him in that capacity, and no matter what he was doing, they sought him for his medical skills.

"I think I should retrain as an ophthalmologist," he told me. "That way I can serve in one of the IAM hospitals and have some structure to my work."

"How long would that take?" I asked.

"Oh, probably three or four years," he said. Despite the hardships of our living situation, I had grown to love Afghanistan. *To leave for three or four years. . .* I suggested we move back to Mazar, where he could teach at the medical school with a German doctor who now worked there. Rich shook his head. Our group had started the only eye hospitals in the country, and the sole foreign ophthalmologist had recently left. There was no one to replace him in training local physicians.

"But in three years, surely someone will come and take his place," I protested.

We packed up our personal items, leaving general household goods for other foreigners who would rotate through to keep Elisabeth company. When our IAM director and his wife arrived, we had time to sit and discuss our thinking.

Rich told them his idea about retraining. All the while, I was inwardly thinking, *Tell him it's a bad idea. Tell him someone else is coming to do that work. Tell him it's too long to be gone.* But to my surprise, they wholeheartedly backed his plan.

As we drove up to Mazar, I was weighted with sorrow. I was not the only one. "You are like a brother to me," Ibrahim told Rich. "I am afraid you will never return."

Rich promised him that we would be back. But the thing about a place as volatile as Afghanistan is that you never know if you will be able to return. We would have to wait and see.

The road behind our house, Qarya Beykh 1995

Laurelhurst Park, Portland 1995

CHAPTER TWENTY-TWO

Gardens across the world

No one knows the dawn rituals of a foreign village. (Afghan proverb)

Returning to your own culture is harder than adjusting to a new one. We did not know that. And although we sometimes despaired of ever being Afghan enough to fit in Afghanistan, we now discovered that we had changed in ways that made it challenging to conform to life in the US.

Rich had inadvertently absorbed some of the machismo of the culture we had left. Sometimes I found my opinion or presence in conversations dismissed. We did not realize it was happening for a while.

I had adopted the modest behaviors of an Afghan woman. Once I actually walked into a man in a gas station because I was unconsciously keeping my eyes averted. I could not bring myself to put on shorts. The options at the grocery store overwhelmed me. A friend took me with her the first time so I could start to readjust: *Choose from an entire aisle of cereal. Bag your own groceries. Do not gasp at the prices of meat and fruit.*

Hannah squealed with gleeful shock when she saw a dog inside someone's house – she knew that dogs only belonged *outdoors*.

Everything seemed new and clean. Everyone seemed rich. We brought back our nicest clothes to wear and realized that the whites were gray and everything looked tattered. Our parents, foreseeing this, sent a box of new clothes for us to friends in Pennsylvania, where we were staying first. The clothes we'd brought from overseas were donated to the Salvation Army.

The usual pattern for our organization was three years in Afghanistan and then six months back home. So we continued with our original plan to catch up with donors across the country; Rich also started researching how he could get into an ophthalmology residency.

The good news: he could skip the first year of a program because he had completed a family practice residency. That meant he only needed three more years to qualify as an ophthalmologist. Unfortunately, it was too late to apply for a residency program; usually applications were submitted two years in advance. Someone suggested Rich look to see if there were any openings – sometimes people drop out of their training for various reasons.

There were two openings in the US: one in Cleveland, and one in Madison, Wisconsin. Rich submitted applications to both, and both contacted him; he arranged to fly out and interview with them over a weekend.

The staff in Madison was warm and the program excellent. Rich must have looked like a promising candidate, too. At the end of the interview, Rich told the doctors he had to fly to Cleveland for his interview there. "Wait a few minutes," he was told. The doctors conferred briefly and rejoined him. "We would like to offer you the position here," they said. Rich called and cancelled his Cleveland interview.

Although some medical wives commiserated with me, "Oh, *another* residency?" I knew that Madison on a Spartan salary with a busy husband would be a picnic compared to my last living situation. And while Rich had been on call every third night during his family practice residency, ophthalmologists don't generally have too many emergencies during off hours. We made a down payment on a house with the living allowance we had not spent while in the village. For us, Madison meant four pleasant years of country walks, the children's museum and library, and sledding in the park. We kept our eye on Afghanistan, and former colleagues kept an eye on us. Every few months someone would phone.

"You are coming back, aren't you?" they would ask.

"Of course," Rich would tell them. "That's why we're here – so we can go back *there*."

Our friends the Muellers and the Oswalds visited us, as did other families we had worked with. (We found this amazing, considering Madison was not on any of the main cross-country routes.) They filled us in on what had been happening:

Kabul fell to the Taliban in September 1996.

In the village, all the girls at the school passed their first and second grade exams and they needed an additional teacher to add new classes. Eighty-one pit toilets had been dug; villagers were being trained in veterinary medicine and midwifery; adult women and men had been taking literacy classes. New boys' and girls' schools were built (although at one point, Elisabeth wrote, the foundation of the girls' school was vandalized) and more effort was being made to figure out how to get a hand-pump that would work at the depth of the village's water table. Oliver's leg was broken when a foreigner backed over him in the Land Cruiser. He was taken back to Mazar, where soldiers at a local checkpoint admired him when he was out for his daily walks. One day, our friend Dan Terry informed us later, Oliver disappeared. He heard Oliver bark when he passed the checkpoint, although the soldiers denied holding him. One day, Dan told us sadly, there was no barking when he passed.

Mazar, which had seen years of relative peace and stability, had plunged into warfare. In May 1997 the Taliban captured the city. Refusing to be disarmed, Hazaras and others in the city revolted, for fifteen hours shooting at Taliban militia trapped in trucks negotiating unfamiliar alleyways of the city. This incident left about six hundred Talibs dead and a thousand captured. Mazar had subsequently been looted by another warlord, forcing the UN staff to flee.

In retribution, the Taliban returned in August 1998 and spent days wreaking havoc on Mazar, first targeting anything that moved and then focusing on house-to-house searches for Hazaras to slaughter. According to a Human Rights Watch Report, at least two thousand people were killed in the city and more in aerial bombardments as they fled. Journalist Ahmed Rashid claimed the UN and ICRC estimated five to six thousand people died.

Although ethnic divisions were apparent while we were in Mazar, they were not universal. One of our Hazara friends was saved by a Pushtun hiding him under a wicker mat. People we knew fled the country – some for their lives, some for peace and stability. Foreigners were airlifted out; Ibrahim and Nooria risked their lives to travel overland with Hazara youth to Pakistan. They wrote us and asked for financial assistance. Things settled down again, and some returned to Afghanistan, although many Afghans remained in refugee camps or enclaves in Peshawar.

As refugees in Pakistan, Daoud's parents and siblings had been among many seeking resettlement in Europe or North America. (Daoud was still working in Uzbekistan.) His parents had married off his sister at the age of sixteen when they feared she might be kidnapped by soldiers; she had finished school and now had children of her own. Daoud's mother told her son-in-law that he, too, should apply for refugee status for his family rather than remaining in Pakistan.

"We'll never get refugee status," he said, and did not submit the paperwork. When word came that the rest of the family would be resettled in Europe, Daoud's mother approached her son-in-law.

"Since you are keeping my daughter, I am taking yours," she said. One of her grand-daughters joined her and Daoud's father as they immigrated to Europe. These strange family dynamics bewildered me, and I worried that Daoud's father, the noble statesman, would be lost in a little town in Europe. But he loved people, and we heard from Daoud that he soon learned the language and made connections there.

In early 1999, after Rich's program finished, the IAM sent word that they planned to place our family in Herat, a major city in western Afghanistan near the border with Iran. We were eager to go because Herat was known as the city whose cultural heritage had remained most intact through years of civil war.

Then we received an email from one of the women in the IAM. Did we know about the security situation in Herat? She wrote of burglaries, assault, and even rape of foreigners in the city. Although we had tried to keep up on the news, we had heard of none of these violent incidents. Our excitement withered and apprehension replaced it. We were willing to serve the people of Afghanistan, but at what cost?

A few days later, a representative of the IAM wrote. One of our workers had taken the initiative to inform the officials in Herat that due to the lack of security, and the great love of the American eye doctor for his wife and family, we would not be moving there. We would be located in Kabul. Now that Rich was a medical specialist, it made sense that he would work in a city, and although both Mazar and Herat had functioning eye hospitals, Kabul had the primary facility and resident training program in the country. Needless to say, by that point we were pretty relieved that the capital (rather than Herat) would be our destination.

We flew Washington, D.C. to Islamabad on Pakistan International Airways. As soon as we were seated on the plane, I noticed a row of young people looking at us and talking quietly in Farsi. Finally, one of the women said, "I have seen you before."

I smiled. "I don't think so," I said.

"Yes," she insisted. "You were in a film – at a Christmas party in Mazar."

Suddenly I remembered – one of the American men had filmed us during a get-together. Apparently he had then shown it to a gathering of Afghans in Washington. I found this a little unnerving (the second time films of me were being shown without my permission), but we chatted with this woman and her brothers until we touched down in Pakistan.

After we had de-boarded and gone through the security checkpoints, Rich began looking desperately through his passport pouch, which he had worn around his neck to protect it from theft.

"What's the matter?" I asked.

"The cash and traveler's checks are gone," he said. He immediately notified an airport attendant.

"I need to get back on the plane," he said. "I must have dropped them while getting off."

197

The attendant proceeded to make Rich retrace his steps through all the security checkpoints; he re-entered the plane many minutes later. There were no signs of our money, which included several hundred dollars in American bills. (Fortunately, this time I had kept half of our traveler's checks.) After our previous theft, we knew where the American Express office was, so we were able to get the traveler's checks replaced. It was a rude re-entry to Asia.

Our Afghan visas, harder to acquire under the Taliban, were delayed, so although we spent a few days in the mountains of Pakistan visiting friends, the visas still weren't ready when our planned flight to Kabul departed. A friend in Peshawar encouraged us to go overland. "The road to Kabul has improved," he said. We set out on the three-hundred mile ride (still "the most bone-jarring 10 hour drive I've ever been on," I wrote my parents) and by the end were wondering if our friend in Peshawar had actually *been* on the road.

The house rented for us was not ready when we arrived, so the IAM directed us to another American family's rental to stay for a few weeks while they were out of the country. Kabul had undergone some surprising changes since our previous visit to the city. For one thing, many people had consistent electricity and running water. Parts of town flourished with fancy imports, new street lights and privately-owned cars filling the streets. I listed for my parents what I had been amazed to find in the shops: American mustard and ketchup; Italian olive oil; cheese from Europe; Swiss chocolate; peanut butter; canned mushrooms; and tuna. On the other hand, Karte Seh, where most of our team had lived prior to the Taliban take-over, was like a ghost town. We wrote,

> Buildings where we once shopped or did business sport collapsed roofs; cars peppered with shrapnel are strewn nearby. In the windows of houses still habitable, plastic flutters – is it too expensive to buy glass, or not worth the risk? Elegant walls have been chewed up by rocket fire. Refugees from neighborhoods completely annihilated now wander the lifeless streets.

Our first week back provided opportunities to catch up with friends; there were now twenty-four foreign children in Kabul, so the kids wasted no time in reuniting with those they knew. The families all lived in the same neighborhood, Karte Parwan, so it would be easy to get together once we moved into our new house. But just to remind us we were in Afghanistan, the first days also included a power surge that burned up the water pump and water heater where we were staying, an earthquake, vomiting children, and the nightly sounds of fighting – explosions north of town and jets heading off to attack outside the city.

On top of the physical changes apparent in Kabul since we had last seen it were the social and psychological changes. As the Taliban entered the city (the people willingly turned over power because they were so weary of fighting and lawlessness), stability had been restored. But an oppressive pall hung over the people. When we learned we would be located in Kabul rather than Herat, I wrote to ask Mary Oswald: *What kind of relationships are you able to have in such an atmosphere?* I needed reassurance that moving to Kabul would not mean social isolation. We had been spoiled by the freedom of our lives in Mazar and in the village.

Mary wrote back. She admitted things were more difficult. But, she added, she did not hesitate to push a ladder against the wall, climb up, and chat with her neighbor on the other side. She seemed optimistic. Our new house was next door, she wrote, and there was a door connecting our yards so the children could come and go without appearing on the street. This seemed positive, too.

We walked through the property shortly after arriving in Kabul. The owners had left piles of rubbish inside, and the rooms needed to be painted. (As Greg showed me the dirty kitchen, cockroaches scuttled around and one boldly ran up inside his pants.) We marveled at the jump from the tiny mud dwelling in the village to a mansion in the city. Karte Parwan was a part of Kabul that had many of its original residents. (Other, more affluent areas of town were filled with refugees, both middle-class and poor, as the owners had fled the country years before.) This stability lent a conservative air to the neighborhood. People treated us cautiously, watching for weeks before extending any signs of friendliness. They were not used to having foreigners living among them.

At the back of the huge yard sat the house – a two-story concrete building with two bathrooms and two kitchens. There were five bedrooms upstairs; a living room that opened through French doors into a dining room, a kitchen, bathroom and office on the ground floor; and a basement that consisted of one windowless central room opening onto three rooms illuminated by natural light. The housing director for the IAM said she could not figure out how to split the house for two families, so it would all be ours.

We decided for safety's sake to put the children in the basement, even though it seemed so far up the winding staircase to our bedroom on the second floor. We turned two of the upstairs bedrooms into school rooms, and left the other two for guests.

The property was located on a corner in a commercial area surrounded by shops of various kinds and across from a mosque. Our front gate was inconspicuous, set back between store fronts, and three-story high buildings formed a fortress on two sides: no one could see in. The yard's large grassy area was circumscribed by bushes and trees and a wide paved driveway on the far end. We felt well-hidden in this garden tucked away from view. We were ready, we thought, for life under the Taliban.

The walls surrounding our yard, Karte Parwan 1999

Kabul, 1999

CHAPTER TWENTY-THREE

Bullies in the garden

It's the same donkey but with a new saddle. (Afghan proverb)

For those who grew up in the US, the idea of war on American soil is nearly unimaginable; we can only transfer images from science fiction films or foreign news to conceive what it would be like. Which aspect, we wonder, would be most difficult – the fighting, the new rules, or the psychological effect of being controlled by outsiders?

Although life in Afghanistan was shot through with the effects of constant conflict, we had never experienced it as a day-today reality. Moving into a Kabul already in the grip of the Taliban meant we would taste the war on myriad fronts.

Not long after we returned to the city, the Taliban began a serious offensive to rout Ahmed Shah Massoud's soldiers to the north of Kabul. As we wrote home, "Every day we hear outgoing rockets; the city's crawling with recruits from Pakistan, but we rarely see guns." Arabs were also arriving to help with the battle. UN planes stopped flying into the airport after it was hit by Massoud's rockets; the Taliban went on to seize Bagram airport.

There was some concern that any negative outcome for the Taliban might result in soldiers taking their disappointment out on us. This was before our new rental was renovated, so we decided to abandon our isolated and less-secure living situation and move in with the Oswalds, who kindly made space for us in their finished basement. Meanwhile, I wrote my parents, improvements continued on our house next door:

> Our *chaokidar* has been working very hard, clearing out the weeds and garbage from the yard, which is looking much nicer, and shoveling rubble and rubbish from the basement. Now someone is re-plastering the basement, where the kids will be sleeping, and tomorrow they should paint the upstairs and the basement. Then we can move over while they work on the ground floor.

Summer offensives were the norm; the next year we would wake up to hear tanks and airplanes leaving on moonlit nights to attack outside the city. We also heard other sounds, as I wrote home in August 1999:

> The neighborhood we live in consists mostly of ethnic Tajiks, the same people who have been resisting the T[alib]s this summer. So the Ts have been coming around every day rounding up men to throw in prison. We heard gunshots a couple of mornings ago when a tailor in front of our house was running from the Ts. We hear terrible stories – husbands killed or taken somewhere, all the women and children boarded onto buses and sent to other cities. There was reportedly some fighting between the Pakistanis and Ts because the Pakistanis took young women across the border to marry them.

Hundreds of thousands of Tajiks had fled their homes in the Shomali Valley north of Kabul; it was natural many would end up in Karte Parwan. A month later I wrote my parents that a group of us "prayed by name for the families who are now taking refuge in the Russian embassy compound (there are 1500 children there alone). . . . It's awful, and sometimes we feel impotent to help."

Violence against foreigners was always a possibility, too. In late August we stayed inside for a day to avoid any first anniversary repercussions of President Clinton's authorized missile strikes on Osama bin Laden's training camps in northeastern Afghanistan. We lay low again before the US presidential election in 2000. That summer we also heard nearby explosions and discovered that mobs had attacked the Pakistani embassy. What had once been designed by the British as the most magnificent embassy in Asia – set in a giant park with rolling lawns, snowdrops, and fountains – was assaulted in response to the Taliban's recent attack on Herat. The caretaker allowed us to walk in the gardens on a couple of occasions; while we enjoyed the grounds, we couldn't help but mourn when we saw the skeletons of once elegant structures.

Being a female who was not completely covered in a *chahdri* put me at some risk. As Rich wrote,

> An hour after Melinda and kids passed a mosque where a fiery sermon was being preached, three women on our team were chased and whipped nearby. (Thankfully they were not seriously injured.)

People tried to guess where I was from: some thought I was Iranian or from Tajikistan; others guessed I was German. During the Taliban's rule many of us decided not to offer that we were Americans. Sometimes we would say we were from "near Canada" or "Oregon," knowing that most Afghans weren't very familiar with North American geography. Frank, whose wife was Canadian, told a taxi driver he was from Prince Edward Island, and the man responded, "That's near Sweden, isn't it?"

Occasionally there were incidents involving foreigners. A few weeks before we arrived three foreign women were taken for questioning because one of them (with coloring similar to mine) was thought to be an Afghan. I started carrying a copy of my passport to prove my identity, if necessary.

But physical danger was not our main concern. We were trying to abide by the Taliban's ever-increasing edicts. Some banned behaviors we ignored in the privacy of our homes (for example wearing white socks, listening to music, playing games, and watching DVDs). Even an Afghan friend had rigged up a satellite dish so his family could watch television. Some rules, however, were inescapable. We were told foreign Christians were no longer able to meet at the house, rented since the 1970s, where they had traditionally met. We had to do without fresh bread during Ramazan, since the Taliban closed down our *naan* shop when it was discovered the bakers were cooking during daylight hours. Afghan women who had been allowed to work in our projects had permission rescinded unless they were in the medical field, and then onerous restrictions were put on them. In August 2000, I wrote home:

> Their latest written comment on why women can't work for NGOs is that we are using them for prostitution. Actually, that's probably their only income option now that they can't have legitimate work. The UN and other organizations (including ours) have decided to try to push the women's work issue through more roundabout means, as direct confrontation with this government seems to have exactly the opposite effect desired.

It was impossible to discern what the edict about not having British or American haircuts meant. Rich never got harassed for his hair, and Connor even attracted adulation on the streets. Afghans seemed to have all viewed pirated copies of the movie *Titanic,* and decided Connor resembled Leonardo di Caprio. More than once Rich was stopped while out with him. "Sir," one man said in English, "You have made your son Titanic!" I told Connor he should start signing autographs.

While taxi drivers were theoretically under prohibitions, they managed to avoid trouble in the privacy of their vehicles. They were not supposed to pick up female passengers with exposed faces, but I never had trouble getting a ride (although I always honored the culture and sat in the back seat – this also felt safer, in case I needed to make a quick getaway). Many of the drivers, we discovered, had been professionals in their past lives, and had converted private automobiles into taxis. One told me he had been a girls' gymnastics coach, an idea almost impossible to fathom. While they were banned (like everyone else) from listening to anything but Koranic readings and sung prayers, many times the drivers would ask, "Do you mind?", reach into a glove compartment or under their seat, and extract a cassette of popular Afghan music to play as we drove along.

Taxi drivers were my connection to the world outside my front gate. They explained events that were happening or had happened. One day a driver told me, "If things were different, I would invite your family for a meal. But look at this." He handed me a flyer printed in Dari.

"What does it say?" I asked, scanning the page. I couldn't read fast enough to figure it out.

"It says," he told me, "That if we even spend a half hour with a foreigner, we will become a Christian." That would have been as surprising to us as it was to them, I thought.

Tailors also had restrictions imposed on them. Most Afghans had clothes specially made rather than store-bought; this meant they had to be measured for the correct fit. However, the Taliban ruled that male tailors could not measure women (and of course female tailors were not allowed to work). This was a problem until one of the foreign women discovered that an older man whom she referred to as "the king's tailor" (actually the former queen's tailor) was willing to come to our homes to fit us for clothes.

I had been willing to dress in a manner similar to local women under previous Afghan regimes, but women who had walked freely before were now cloaked in the ubiquitous powder-blue *chahdari*. The only women with exposed faces were the elderly and foreigners. We were now encased in huge scarves that hid everything but our faces and (if we were feeling a bit rebellious, as I was) a little hair. I found it difficult to purchase and carry food and other goods, hold a child's hand, and keep my head covered, so I finally sewed myself two capes – one for summer and one for winter. (This drew hobbit comparisons from the foreign community and comments of interest from local women, who had not seen capes before.) I had to remind myself to smile at and greet females I passed on the street; after a while they became invisible, hidden under their veils, only a hint of humanity visible through the netting that covered their faces.

Our house was surrounded by tiny shops filled with men's tailors. We went out our gate one day to discover the trees along the street draped with cassette tapes glittering like twinkle lights in the sunshine. One of the Tajik tailors had been caught listening to banned music and arrested. He was dragged out of his shop and on the verge of being hauled away by the authorities when a Pushtun friend stood up for him. He was released with a warning and all his music left ornamenting the trees.

There was definitely order under the Taliban, but it was order dictated by fear. The five daily prayer times were not only broadcast from the city's mosques, but enforced; men were sometimes dragged in to participate. Fridays – the holy days in Muslim countries – were deathly still, all signs of commerce gone, every shop locked. The job of seeing all the rules were followed belonged to the Ministry for the Prevention of Vice and Promotion of Virtue (which we referred to merely as "Vice and Virtue"), men who actively sought transgressors of the Taliban's code for righteous living.

Visas, which previously had lasted for years, were more difficult to get, especially for the single women working with the IAM, and those of us who were getting renewals had to appear at the appropriate office every three months. Instead of accepting paperwork from our office staff, the Talib on duty wanted to see each person in our family (the six of us crowded the small waiting room when we showed up). I was surprised when the turbaned official behind the desk leaned close to Rich and said, "Take me to America." Rich could not resist expressing astonishment that the Talib would want to leave the country and pointing out that Afghanistan was the way it was because people like him were in power. Although the man sported a hearty beard, he may well have been a clean-shaven civil servant under the Communist regime and would no doubt transform to a staunch democrat under a later government; for now he appeared the epitome of Taliban orthodoxy. Some Afghans were very good at shifting ideologies for the expediency of a livelihood.

While shuffling the children to the visa office every three months was a hassle, we knew it was worth the trouble. At one point, Rich went to Pakistan for a few days without realizing that his visa might expire while he was gone. By that time our office had established a long-distance phone line, so I called him and had him send copies of passport pages by plane the next day so his visa could be renewed. This was a hot issue, because our friend Dan Terry, who was now working in central Afghanistan, had missed his renewal deadline and spent two weeks "imprisoned" in an office building in Kabul. We took turns sending over hot meals, but Dan was fine.

"You know Dan," Rich laughingly told me when he returned from a visit. "All the soldiers had their guns propped against the wall and they were sitting with him talking and enjoying tea together." Nevertheless, Rich didn't want to repeat Dan's fate.

Because of the difficulty in meeting government requirements, the IAM had full-time local staff to arrange visas and travel, as well as peruse rental agreements and keep abreast of the latest rules. After Rich asked for help getting visas for his parents to visit over Christmas, the office announced that we would now be limited to one visitor per adult per year. In a letter home, I wrote, "Apparently the IAM gets 1000 visa requests a year!" Clearly, many people were interested in seeing what life was like under the Taliban.

Eye camp travels, 1999

CHAPTER TWENTY-FOUR

Duktar Saeb

It's like weighing toads: when you put two on the scales, four jump off.
(Afghan proverb)

Rich started work immediately after returning to Kabul in 1999. Herb Friesen, the retired American ophthalmologist who had talked Rich into specializing in eyes, was visiting and he wanted to orient Rich before he left. Rich's initial impression: overwhelming.

The original NOOR Eye Hospital had been mostly destroyed in the fighting, so care was now spread between three run-down hospitals in Kabul. As medical director, Rich was expected to see patients as well as run a residency program for Afghan physicians, single-handedly overseeing and training nearly a dozen ophthalmologists (including four new ones), a task which would be accomplished by an entire staff of experienced doctors in the US. The local ophthalmologists anticipated the new foreign doctor performing surgical miracles in poorly equipped facilities. In his first letter to donors, Rich asked for such basic "unwanted ophthalmic equipment" as vitrectors (used in cataract surgery), operating microscopes, electrocautery units, slit lamps (an essential for ophthalmologists), and sutures. Besides the hands-on work, Rich was writing and delivering lectures three times a week, eventually creating a cycle that covered all the material every two years.

After a month of lectures, Rich scheduled a test for the residents. The day before, several of the men wrote Rich a note. "Please put off the test because we are not prepared," it read. He gave them additional study time with a warning – he would not defer a test again because they were unprepared. When they finally took it, I wrote my parents,

> they (for the most part) did abysmally. Except one female resident. (He's not allowed to work with them, but he gives them the lecture notes.) He said they didn't seem as distressed as he thought they would. He has no power to throw them out of the program, so he told me he'd just focus on the ones with the most potential and try to do a good job training them.

The women continued to excel, despite being barred from the lectures. The men, however, needed to be taught not only the material, but how to *learn* the material. Afghan schools tended to rely on rote learning. And students sent for medical training were not necessarily those with the most aptitude for being physicians; all applicants took an exam before entering university, with the highest scorers sent to study medicine, the next highest engineering, and so on. This made medicine prestigious but did not account for student interest.

Rich was disheartened by a number of things in his work situation. He wrote his parents in September 1999:

> I have been discouraged the last couple of weeks by some suboptimal surgical results . . . and by several patients with abysmal situations. We are hoping to slowly take back the administrative control over the hospital which the government currently has. The government has proved horribly incompetent in managing health care, and the amount of fraud is really appalling.

Fortunately, he had a number of opportunities to work beyond the confines of the hospital, and this kept his enthusiasm up. NOOR staff often went on "eye camps" to remote areas of Afghanistan to provide ophthalmic care. Although it was demanding, staff enjoyed getting away from the capital to see rural areas and provide critical service to Afghans. The first eye camp was planned for Nuristan, a region most foreigners had never seen but wanted to: "with legendary beautiful valleys and blonde-haired, blue-eyed people," I wrote my parents. Unfortunately, fighting in the area broke out the day before the team was ready to leave, so they headed to the Hazarajat in central Afghanistan, where Dan and others had re-initiated work begun in the 1970s. Over nine days, Rich and the Afghan ophthalmologist with him performed an astonishing ninety-seven surgeries and saw seventeen hundred patients. Unfortunately, there was no way for me to communicate with him.

In October, he left for three weeks on another eye camp. I found these long stints as a single parent wearying; this time we also had two different sets of houseguests and I was sick. Fortunately, I wrote my parents,

> Tom Little [and his wife], who've been here *forever,* look after me. Tom is Rich's boss, so I think they're afraid we're going to disappear. They had me over for dinner a couple of times, and Tom babysat so his wife and I could go [out] one night. That was quite refreshing.

Rich thoroughly enjoyed this second eye camp. He wrote his parents,

> Amazingly, work on the eye camps goes much more smoothly than it does here in the city. . . . On the last one, I was the only foreigner in a team of 18 people, and the people were enjoyable to work with, so it was quite fun. I felt physically great on both trips, so I guess my body responds well to the 50% fat diet. On one Friday (the day

off) we had a local person catch fish with a net in the river for us; unfortunately, the cook boiled them in fat for so long that it appeared the fish had been cooked with napalm! All that was visible was a tangled brown mound with fish tails sticking out. . .

During these two eye camps, the teams performed two hundred and forty-nine surgeries and saw more than three thousand patients. Rich didn't record how many procedures he did at the hospital in Kabul, but he mentioned some of the challenges of the work. In May 2000, he wrote that the eye hospital had been ordered to move "to an unsuitable building (with the recent 'request' to fix it up)" and that they had "constant hassles with the government, constantly broken equipment and missing supplies, and unreliable personnel. Miraculously," he reported with surprise, "some patients do get helped!"

That month he headed to Mazar for nine days to help the residents at the eye hospital there prepare for upcoming ophthalmology exams by giving a lecture series. I told my parents,

The hospital (without government intervention!) is doing so much better there – he gets so many bureaucratic headaches here. It seems like anything that works well, they try to mess up. And the eye hospital isn't even working that well, and they're still trying to mess even more!

A month later, Rich and Tom were given initial approval to move the eye hospital to a facility already nearly ready to use. Meanwhile, another eye camp was in the works – a second attempt to go to Nuristan. Not only did medical staff want to go – other teammates signed up as well. I wasn't too interested in joining the group, especially after a Scottish woman recounted a previous trip she'd gone on:

. . . drive two days, and then hike one long day. . . .she spent the last day of driving "crying and praying" because

214

the road is terrible and winds along a steep cliff edge. It was enough to convince me to settle for photos!

This time, Mary – who loved the outdoors – signed on, so Greg took time off work to stay with the children. Again, there would be no contact with the group until they returned.

Homeschooling filled much of my time while Rich was traveling. Connor, Aidan, and Hannah – now twelve, ten, and eight, respectively – were focused in their studies. Each child had a desk in one of the two dedicated "schoolrooms" in our upstairs. Owen, at age six, had started first grade, and completed his lessons in the mornings. He had always been our most mischievous child – the one (I told people) for whom warning labels were written. With his father away again, he seemed to sense that more opportunities for trouble waited.

And so one afternoon when I heard Greg's deep voice bellowing over the wall between our yards, "Who has done this?" I instinctively cringed, edging over to see what crime had been committed. I pushed the wooden door open between our yards and entered. There, at Greg's feet, lay their family pet. Simba was a large, black dog with a reputation for biting anyone looking Afghan. The Oswalds' *chaokidar* had developed a mutual respect pact, but we heard that even some foreigners had been bitten.

Simba was not dead or injured, to my relief, but he was trussed. Somehow Owen had managed to tie his four legs together, and the poor beast squirmed on his back. Owen reluctantly appeared when I called.

"Why did you do this?" Greg asked, untying the dog.

"I wanted to stop him from biting people," Owen offered altruistically. I was mystified as to how he had accomplished this feat, but filled with some admiration that he had conquered the dragon. At the same time, I felt a little emotionally worn down and again sensed my total inadequacy as a single mother.

Rich returned, whipping out a description of his experience:

> It took two days of hard driving (at the extreme limits of 4wheel drive) followed by a rigorous eight-hour hike, with

much of our gear being hauled by donkeys. Most of the patients spoke a local language which none of us are familiar with, so we required translators. . . . Our team is hoping to establish a permanent work (probably a general surgical center) in this area.

To his parents, he wrote:

The people have been Muslims only for the past 120 years, and the culture is unique in that the women do all the farming and the men do much of the child care. What a gorgeous place – very much like Yosemite or other places in the high Sierra Nevada mountains, with the only real forests I have seen in this country, and sparkling water everywhere. The eye work only occupied us until about noon each day, so we had plenty of time for hiking.

He amused us all with a story of walking around the bend of a trail to see a man bouncing along with an enormous mushroom perched like a hat on his head. He then confessed that he and one of the Afghan staff foolishly climbed late in the day without water; after watching the sunset, night fell suddenly and they found themselves scrambling down "an extremely precipitous canyon in the dark." To this day, although he recounts the danger of that climb, it is the raging thirst he most recalls. Yet, he cheerily followed this story in a letter to his parents with the comment, "If there is a next time I may take Connor along."

Because of the security situation in Kabul, the IAM instituted a nightly call-around on our hand-held radios. This provided an opportunity to make sure we were all home and safe, to deliver any announcements, and to interject humorous remarks. We all knew when to expect the call; we would often lie in bed just waiting to say, "We're fine, good night," before switching the radio off.

The night the Nuristan team returned, we were all happy to turn in early – after all, they had been gone for two weeks. We snapped off the radio as soon as we had signed out.

But the Oswalds were still listening as Kevin's family was repeatedly called without response. Finally, Greg volunteered to walk several blocks to their house to make sure they were okay. Celebrating a birthday, they swung open their door to Greg, and laughing, apologized for making him walk over.

"I can't believe it," he grumbled the next day. "Too bad you guys didn't leave *your* radio on."

But we had to make up for lost time; Rich wasn't done traveling for the year. He made another trip to Mazar in October and then headed by road to Peshawar to book air tickets to the US for his ophthalmology Board exams. He was in the States for most of November to take a review course and then the exam itself. Even before that trip, we calculated he had been away from home twenty-five percent of the time since we had arrived in Afghanistan the year before.

Before that last trip, however, he had one more visit to Peshawar. This one was unplanned. Rich described the situation to our donors:

> A 5-year-old boy, the only son of a man from a very remote area in the central mountains, walked into the eye clinic with his father one day. His left eye had been bulging out more and more over the previous two months. Suspecting a malignancy, I biopsied the tumor behind the eye the following day, but had to wait an agonizing three weeks for the result from Pakistan.

> Suspicions confirmed [he had rhabdomyosarcoma], we briefly considered our options. . . 90% of these tumors, when caught early, are cured in the West with radiation and chemotherapy – but in *our* country, neither is available, and surgery alone would almost certainly fail to cure the disease.

> I sent the patient and his father (who speak a difficult dialect and are completely without funds or connections) to

217

Pakistan with one of our hospital pharmacists and a large amount of money.

Days later, they returned; the pharmacist informed Rich that all the money had been spent and the boy needed to return to Peshawar in ten days. The father told Rich, "There's no way we could have spent all that money." Rich, distressed, wondered how the pharmacist could be so heartless, knowing that the rapidly growing tumor would kill the boy. He decided to accompany the family himself. His account continues:

> I returned over 10 hours of bumpy roads to Pakistan with the boy and his father. We first contacted a "Mission Hospital" which showed a distressing lack of compassion. After looking at two more places, we arrived at a radiotherapy center. Although the staff expressed some frustration that so many of the patients came from our country and could pay nothing, they also expressed a touching amount of concern and agreed to give the necessary two month course of treatment at greatly reduced cost.
>
> A watchman at our office in Pakistan has agreed to check up on the patient every few days; the cook at our office helped write a letter which we will try to direct (without a postal system!) to the boy's remote village, in order to let his mother know what's going on.

Despite this care, the boy died two years later while undergoing chemotherapy. Once again Rich's heart was broken by the suffering of a child resulting from a primitive medical system.

Aidan and Hannah in The Ordinary Princess, *2000*

CHAPTER TWENTY-FIVE

Daisy chains

A porcupine says of its own baby, "My child of velvet." (Afghan proverb)

Many people are haunted by their childhoods. Mine was a happy one: my family loved me; I could walk to school and church and a small locally-owned store; I knew the perimeter of the neighborhood where I was allowed to bike with impunity. But elements that made my own childhood rich – the freedom to move around without adults and the relative safety of my environment – were lacking for our children. We had to find ways to create the best possible space for the next generation.

There was an IAM school in Kabul but I still doubted the stability of the country enough to trust that our kids could start a school year and end it without an evacuation. So we hauled boxes of books, art supplies, music, and materials for science experiments to Afghanistan and each child did grade-appropriate lessons.

Although I told people we were homeschooling, the non-Americans seemed mystified and one of the teachers even implied there might be actual *cruelty* involved in this system. Nevertheless, I had taken to heart the advice given to me by Dan's wife years before: "It is *your* responsibility to make sure your children are educated."

The kids joined others for some learning experiences. Greg taught a drawing class on Thursdays (our Saturday); Kevin's brother-in-law directed them in a carpentry class over a winter break

(Connor and Aidan made a sword and shield for Owen and then, perhaps unwisely, painted a red cross as a coat of arms); the fiancé of one of the short-term workers taught physics and helped the children create egg parachutes. They performed at the British and Italian embassies in a children's choir at Christmas and Easter. And they swam in the UN pool.

Although the pool was intended for UN staff, there were so few in Kabul that families were allowed to join during the summers. This provided a mental-health break for mothers who threw off their scarves and sat under the boughs of the grape arbor chatting or reading while children splashed in the water. Some even ordered cans of Coca Cola or French fries as a treat. Our progeny would go as often as we would take them.

Because we were the main clientele for a few years, the staff running the guesthouse, restaurant, and pool decided to bring in a swing set – clearly not useful to the UN employees, whose own children were not allowed to accompany them to Kabul. Many times we would talk with men who sat wistfully watching the children play Marco Polo or have diving contests. "I wish my kids were here," they would say with a sigh.

Life at home got more appealing when the Muellers moved into the newly-rented house behind ours. A door was installed leading to their yard; this meant the children now had a degree of freedom, running between three connecting properties. The Oswalds installed a tree fort and the Muellers a giant climbing structure; our yard had the largest grassy area. All of us had huge houses, so when it was dinner time we would swing the cow bells I brought from India and hope the children could figure out who was ringing them home.

Between our families were eleven children, which meant everyone had someone to play with (except the Oswalds' youngest son, who followed whoever was available). And when invited, they would go play with Kevin's five children or the Finnish sons of the latest IAM director. There were Germans and Koreans and Americans . . . a large enough foreign community to meet any child's needs.

I warned Connor when we returned to Afghanistan in 1999 that few new families would come with children his age; we had been

222

advised that kids over eleven had a hard time adjusting to a foreign culture. So we were surprised one afternoon to arrive at the pool and see two older boys sitting on the swing set, conversing.

"Hi," I said, stopping as the children went into the bathhouse to change into their swimsuits. "I don't think I've seen you before."

"I'm Dirk," the elder said. "We just moved here."

They explained: their parents, who were Germans, had been working in Pakistan and couldn't get their visas renewed. The boys were homeschooling – one was fourteen, the other twelve (Connor's age). It was a blessing to have Dirk and Matthias around. Dirk was gentle, artistic, interested in animals; Matthias quiet and athletic. Both became Connor's friends. They adopted Aidan into their circle, and the four boys spent alternate Thursdays hanging out at their house or ours.

Since most of the middle and high-school aged foreigners went to boarding school in Pakistan, families took summer vacations. (It was also a great time to avoid the heat and military conflict which invariably increased with the temperature.) We, however, preferred winter breaks: that way we could escape the cold and head to south India to play on the beaches or explore the ruins of ancient civilizations. While this made for great vacations, it meant that ours were among the few children left in Kabul all summer.

As a solution to what looked like an interminable march of hot, lonely days in 2000, I adapted *The Ordinary Princess,* a book by M.M. Kaye, into a play, providing roles for the Oswald girls and our three older children. This kept them busy for a couple of months; I reported the results to my parents:

> Our play was FANTASTIC! Speaking not only as parent, director and writer. . . almost everyone on our team came, and a few others, so we had about 60 people. We slated it as an open-air dinner theater, so people brought their blankets and food and we used our driveway (which goes along the entire length of a side of our yard) as the stage. Although I wasn't sure Hannah would be able to memorize everything in time (she certainly put on a few diva-like tantrums before showtime!), she did great –

223

actually *improved* before a live audience. Aidan, surprisingly, is a natural, and told me later he wanted to be an actor when he grows up(!). Connor did a good job as the grumpy king. The audience cheered when Aidan gave Hannah a hug (instead of a kiss) when she accepted his marriage proposal. R and K were excellent as hysterical queen and crotchety fairy godmother

(respectively). I think most of the people came to see the show as a courtesy but they all seemed so impressed that we got requests to do more plays! It took a lot more work than I expected, but it was definitely a good experience for the kids.

By that autumn, we had a routine down. We did school in the mornings. On Sunday afternoons, the children took Dari lessons; on Mondays, we had youth group meetings at our house; on Tuesdays we attended IAM team meetings, during which the children played games and hung out; on Thursdays the boys spent time with Dirk and Matthias. Fridays and Saturdays were days off for everyone.

I was thankful the children were able to continue learning the language. We studied under the same teacher – Mr. Bashir – but he took the children slowly through the Long Course book, which I had already completed. The building we met in was shared with English classes taught through the IAM. But one day in May, about five minutes after the children had finished their weekly session and we were hailing a taxi back to Karte Parwan, men from Vice and Virtue raided the school. I wrote my parents:

> . . . the students and staff were arrested. The reason: two foreign women were teaching English. (All the students are men.) Although our group had permission to have women teaching, the government has now said they must keep the school closed until they reopen without women. Our director negotiated the release of all those taken (the foreigners, by the way, weren't arrested) and is now trying

to get the gov't to reverse its decision. One of the women told me, "I was SO glad your kids were gone!" Me, too. And I'm glad that it was the first week I'd arranged to have my lesson a day separate from the kids, because no doubt they would have arrested my language teacher if they'd walked in on us alone together!

Although the children had lost the freedom which they had when we lived in the village to wander around and interact in Dari, they were able to practice speaking with the *chaokidars,* Farid and Amin.

Farid worked for the Oswalds. In his early twenties, he was friendly and a quick learner. He told me the story of his life to that point.

"I agreed that I would work and put my brother through college," he said. "Then my brother would work and put *me* through school. But," he added sadly, "my brother wants to get married now, and that will take more money. Then he will have to use his wages to provide for his family."

Recognizing the unfairness of this situation and Farid's potential, Greg and Mary paid for him to take accounting classes part time. When he was finished, Greg hired him to work in his project.

Amin, our *chaokidar,* was probably in his early thirties (Afghans often looked weathered and older than they were, so it was hard to be sure) and married with children. While Farid was energetic, Amin always seemed tired. He preferred reading to working, although he would shop when asked. He was also the one who had to clean up after the dog and kill the turkey at Thanksgiving. (Rich was happy to delegate the slaughter of the birds to Amin after the children peeked in the bathroom and saw their father covered with blood. Shocking as that was, they were all attentive when we performed a science experiment demonstrating how pulling the muscles of a foot forced the claws to move.) There was a fair distance between Amin's room and the front gate, so when someone rang the bell, he usually ran down the walk to answer it. He was a reliable *chaokidar* who did the requisite work and got paid for it.

One day I sent Amin out for groceries. Then I waited hours for him to return. I was getting irritated; *What is he out doing so long – sipping tea with his friends?* He finally stumbled into the yard, pulling his mangled bicycle. Amin sat down on the porch and told me a story that made me repent my annoyance.

He had found himself walking in the bazaar behind a young man with shoulder-length hair. Although the Taliban allowed *themselves* long hair, they did not permit it on any other males. So the young man was stopped by a Talib.

"Get your hair cut," he was ordered.

"I'll get my hair cut when you fix the streets and open the schools," the young man responded.

The Talib and his associates dashed the young man to the ground and began kicking and beating him. Seeing Amin nearby, they grabbed him and started beating him, too. They hurled his bicycle down, bending it out of shape. Then both men (and Amin's bike) were thrown in the back of a truck and driven to Pul-i-charki prison on the far side of Kabul.

The young man was unconscious, blood running from his ear. Amin was questioned about his connection to the stranger and forced to show his identification card to the prison authorities. He told the officer that he did not know the man and had only been walking near him. After some time, Amin was released and forced to return to Karte Parwan by foot, since his bicycle was unusable.

The most humiliating aspect of his mistreatment was that he was given a quick haircut – his thin comb-over mercilessly chopped off at the roots. And he was told to grow a beard. We knew that Hazara can only grow wispy goatees. Feeling bad for him, we gave Amin time off and money to get his bicycle repaired.

In the fall of 2000, Amin came to me in tears and told me his younger sister had married three years before and moved to Pakistan. He'd just gotten word about her. I wrote my parents,

> ... she'd had a premature baby who'd died, and she'd been bleeding ever since (10 days). He wrote and told her to have her husband take her to the doctor, but she wrote back and said he'd starting taking drugs (cocaine maybe?

some form of opium) and wasn't able. Amin was afraid she'd die, and she's his favorite sister. (It's one of the redeeming values in this culture – brother/sister relationships.) So he wanted to know if he could have time off to go get her and her husband to try to help them both. We gave him some money for that. I told Rich it's a weird sensation to know that you can make a difference between people living and dying – it's not something that came up much in my experience in the US.

Our children did not know all the details about Amin and Farid and their lives, but they knew enough to love them. Their relationships with them were part of the mosaic that made up their formative years, years far different in experience from my own insulated childhood.

When my brother and sister-in-law invited Connor to come stay with them the following summer to get an opportunity to have the American experience, we thanked them:

> Although [Connor] loves you and your kids, he's not eager yet to leave the nest. And I think Rich and I have come to grips with the fact that our kids are not going to be "normal" American kids, and we're not going to make a huge effort to try to conform them to that mold.

No doubt some have criticized us for that choice; like many who grew up outside their "passport country," our children have had their share of adjusting to the way Americans do things. (Imagine our daughter's horror when she heard there was such a thing as a "strip mall" – "They have *malls* for that?" she asked, aghast.) But considering how and where they grew up, they have become lovely adults. And I'm not just saying that because I'm their mom.

Owen taking a swim break at the UN pool, 2000

The Kabul bird bazaar

CHAPTER TWENTY-SIX

Kabulis

Why are you blocking the bazaar when you don't buy or sell?
(Afghan proverb)

Afghans, despite the crumbling of their societal norms during years of war, continued to value hospitality.

In Mazar, we had frequent visitors; in the village, people dropped by daily to chat or see the *duktar saeb*. Under the Taliban, friendly visits ground to a halt. We were being watched, so our guests were, too; most people determined the risk of being seen at a foreigner's house was too great. Ibrahim and Nooria had made their way from Pakistan to Kabul and now worked for the IAM – at least, Ibrahim did. Despite cautions from us, he visited each week; but in deference to the authorities he now sported a robust, Taliban-worthy beard. Another friend of Rich's came by periodically – an ophthalmic technician who secretly longed to be a movie star. (In those days we thought it a quixotic dream, although he later did have a bit part in a Hindi film.) Most days the only Afghans in our yard were *chaokidars*.

One day while I was in the bazaar, a veiled woman started chatting with me. "Come to my house," she said.

"No, you come to *my* house," I urged her. She followed me home, and once inside threw off her *chahdari* and began beseeching me for work. My heart sank; I longed for friendship but was viewed as a lifeline. "I am so sorry," I told her, "but I don't have any work to offer." I never saw her again.

While there are always beggars in developing countries, during the Taliban's rule Kabul was replete with them. Women sat in the street, between lanes of traffic, babies in their arms. We could not see their faces through the netting, but the patched *chahdari*s – and the fact that they would risk their lives in such a precarious position – were telling.

Women came to the gate as well. It was hard as an American to know how to deal with the begging; we had grown up being told people should "go out and get a job." But these women no longer had the option to work, and there were thousands of them – both widows and those whose husbands were languishing far from home in Taliban-run prisons. I finally decided the best thing to do was provide food. I bagged rice and mung beans together and kept these parcels ready for beggars who appeared at our door. Usually the women were grateful, although once I was chided. "How can I eat this without *roghan*?" the recipient demanded. (*Roghan*, palm kernel oil, sold in cans in the bazaar.) "Give me *roghan*!" The main source of calories in these poor Afghans' lives seemed to be fat.

As well as women, children swarmed the streets of Kabul – partly because the schools were closed, but also because they were the ones allowed to make a living, even if their mothers couldn't. When they begged, I didn't give money, but looked for a way to feed them. A whole generation of Afghans seemed diminutive, probably because of malnutrition; I figured Afghan children never got enough food. Usually roasted chickpeas or raisins were available from nearby shops and I gladly purchased bags for them.

Families suffered such economic hardship that some parents sent their children to live at the orphanage just so they could get meals. We heard of one family where the children were determined to stay together after both parents died; a neighbor tried to help as much as she could and finally contacted one of our foreign friends for assistance. We marveled at the tenacity of these people in the face of the difficulties they endured.

The expatriate community impressed on us the idea that providing work for locals was a moral obligation – a way to satisfy their needs while meeting ours. We hired a wonderful woman to clean for us; our house was too big for me, I knew, especially since I now had four children to homeschool. Our cleaning lady worked diligently until the day she was stopped outside our gate and told that if she returned, she would be arrested and beaten. One of her male relatives sent word that she would not be back.

My solution, as Connor informed his grandparents, involved bribing the children to help me:

> [Mom] has created a reward system by which we get "Chicken Street points." (Chicken Street is the street in Kabul where shopkeepers sell foreign goods and expensive Afghan things, i.e. marble chess sets or lapis boxes.) Each point is worth 10,000 Afghanis. The exchange rate is around 55,000 Afghanis to the dollar. We get points by sweeping, mopping, dusting, or anything else Mom offers us. . . Our cleaning lady was threatened so she can't come to work, so a lot of what she used to do goes to us.

Periodically we would take trips to Chicken Street and Flower Street. The latter sold foreign foods. Chicken Street, where once the thousands of Americans and others who worked in the capital had bought trinkets and carpets as souvenirs, now stretched lifeless and empty. We wandered freely (beset only by a few children who had learned enough English to charm us and ask for dollars), able to bargain for the best deals. We sighed years later over the low prices we had paid for lapis lazuli, malachite, and silver. Even though chess was outlawed by the Taliban, Rich bought a board to play in private with Ibrahim. We fingered relics of the Soviet invasion, and Connor began collecting swords.

We employed a mother to cook for us once a week; but with the crackdown on women working, I told her she had better stop coming. We then hired the son of a man who had worked for foreigners for years. I asked him what he had learned; he told me he could prepare lasagna. The result was a biscuit crust buried in spaghetti sauce. The few other dishes he made were similarly unrecognizable. When our cleaning lady was forced to quit, I asked this man to keep house for us instead of cooking. He was great at cleaning, although I know it was a drop in status for him. He was perky and the children all liked him.

One day, he paused while washing the dishes to ask me a question that had been bothering him.

"*Malia-jon,*" he began (Malia being my Afghan name, and *jon* a suffix attached to show familiarity or endearment), "I have not grown at all in about five years. Could there be something wrong with me?" (He probably stood about five foot five.) "How old are you?" I asked.

"Twenty-five," he answered.

He had recently married, and I wondered if the parents had tried to assure his bride that her groom would be taller as time passed.

"I'm afraid you're done growing," I told him. He looked crestfallen for a moment, and then returned cheerfully to the dishes.

Since we now had no cook, our Finnish friend Hilkka recommended a man she had taught who still had time for part-time work. Hilkka, fantastic in the kitchen herself, had a knack for training staff, so I eagerly took her up on the offer. She warned me that the man had spent a lot of time in prison and she thought it had done something to his mind; consequently, he sometimes made mistakes. Many Afghans had spent time incarcerated by the various governing powers, so we weren't too concerned about his past from a security standpoint. I told her I would give him a try.

Ayub was a reserved and somber middle-aged man. He showed up in the afternoon, quietly setting to work. Every dish he prepared was delicious. As time went by, I sometimes stood in the kitchen and talked with him as he worked. He told me about his children – his daughter had been the top student in her class before the Taliban came to power and banned children from school. When pressed, he told me that he had been tortured in prison, and showed me his gnarled fingernails, the remnants of beatings he had endured. He was a gentle man and eager to add new recipes to a notebook he

234

kept. I taught him how to make my favorite chocolate cake. He laughed delightedly as I dubbed it *Cake-i-neem-shao ("cake of the middle of the night"),* and immediately penned it into his notebook.

I was so pleased with his work I recommended him to the Oswalds; Mary decided to employ him once a week. But during one of his mental lapses, he replaced cinnamon with cumin in an apple pie, so she let him go.

However, she frequently and discreetly hired women to do jobs for her. She had someone take clothes home and press them. She also had a young woman come to cook once whose face was horribly disfigured by an exploding pressure cooker. (We found out this was common, so I stopped using my Afghan one and asked my mother to buy a new overpressure plug for our American-made cooker. "Our meat is pretty much shoe-leather texture right now," I wrote while awaiting the new plug. "One of Connor's molars fell out during dinner the other night while we were eating stroganoff; our dinner guests immediately began feeling their own mouths!") Mary scoured the second-hand bazaar and found an old German pressure cooker to protect herself and anyone working in her kitchen. She also made friends with a brave single woman who held classes in her home for girls. There were, we discovered, a number of women in prison for doing that very thing.

❖

While living in Mazar and in the village, we had plenty of invitations to dine in peoples' homes, but from 1999 to 2001, we only ate out a handful of times. We took a taxi to Ibrahim and Nooria's, asking to be dropped off some distance from their house so the taxi driver could not report us, and visited after their twin boy and girl were born. Nooria's mother, whose legs had been injured in an explosion, was immobile, and Nooria (who could no longer work) spent her days caring for her and for their four children. The only other home we visited during that time belonged to one of the doctors Rich worked with. We missed the joy of intermingling with Afghans. Frequently we were told, "I'd love to have you over, but it's too dangerous."

We were invited on one picnic, another part of Afghan culture we rarely experienced. Rich's friend owned an orchard outside Kabul. As I wrote my parents,

> The kids had fun collecting bullet shells and I enjoyed sitting under the trees and listening to the breeze. It's easy to get claustrophobic here; there aren't too many places to go where one isn't under scrutiny. So it was nice to get out.

People in our neighborhood, initially wary of foreigners, had warmed up to us, so we relished the interactions we had with shopkeepers. We made occasional trips to a little store across the street for yogurt or eggs or onions. One evening at twilight, we stood in line behind a little girl. Most eggs were kept unrefrigerated and after discovering fresh eggs would sink, I brought a bowl of water with me to test them. Perhaps it was that strange custom – or maybe the Afghans had been using us in place of bogeymen in the stories they told their children. At any rate, when the girl turned after making her purchase, she caught a glimpse of us and let out a shriek. "Eeek! *Kharijee!* (Foreigners!)" she cried before scurrying off.

A nearby junk shop was run by an elderly man, Kaka Khan. The boys loved to rummage through his collection in search of treasures. Kaka Khan became friends with Greg and Mary. Once, in need of cash, he brought them a small packet. Carefully unfolding it, he displayed cut gems of various sizes. "Emeralds," he told them. He wanted Mary's father, who was visiting, to send them to a friend of his in the US who could appraise and sell them. Weeks later, Mary had to report the sad news: they were not emeralds at all; they were glass. The old man shrugged philosophically. "Oh well," he said, "send them back. I'll sell them to somebody else."

Around the corner was a shop the Oswalds dubbed The Wide Store because it was twice as long as the usual shops, and had doors at both ends. This was the place to find not only food, but all kinds of useful items and gifts. (Once we even spotted a bobbing hula-dancer doll on the counter.) This shop was close enough to our front gate so that we would occasionally let the children go as a group and buy candy.

A soft-ice cream seller set up on our corner, and Rich tried it a few times (every time they ate it, the children got sick). My bout with hepatitis convinced me to stay away from this treat and its consequences. But at least it offered an opportunity to greet the man behind the counter.

Each of the shopkeepers, tailors, taxi drivers, and beggars we encountered provided us with a brief connection to Kabulis during this difficult period in the life of the capital. I don't think I could have stood living there if we had not had those associations.

Hiking outside Kabul with foreign friends, 1999

CHAPTER TWENTY-SEVEN

Expats and pets

There is a road from heart to heart. (Afghan proverb)

We think little about our nationality until we step off American soil. Then, suddenly, we realize we are adrift in an ocean of non-Americans; some desire our friendship and help in reaching the Land of Promise while others scoff at – or even hate – us. Whatever else happens, we tend to migrate toward our own kind, even if they are not necessarily the same people we would seek out while in the US. And we found that anyone who spoke English felt suddenly connected.

Our isolation from Afghans brought the foreign community together. Without the usual American outlets for entertainment – sports, music, movies, the mall – we were compelled to create our own diversions. At our weekly meetings, the children played group games like capture the flag. We held a talent show. The mothers who played the piano gave lessons to children (some of whom became surprisingly accomplished). On their weekly afternoon off, fathers took sons and daughters to the university gym to play soccer or hockey. When Board members arrived for meetings they competed against team members in heated volleyball matches, passing the trophy back and forth as the years went by.

Sometimes we rented vans from the office and loaded our families to drive to Qarga Lake (once a delicious retreat, complete with a golf course, outside Kabul) or to other places where we could go for long walks without pestering crowds. Since we had a self-imposed curfew (earlier than the government-mandated one), we sometimes invited individuals or whole families to sleep over so we could play games and talk late into the evening. Tom Little and his wife hosted a pancake night every Friday, where a cross-section of the foreign community converged, each contributing a topping or side dish. We relished the interaction with our international friends which we lacked with Afghans during this period.

Our Thanksgiving celebrations continued as they had, even in the village. In 1999, I wrote my parents that we hosted the feast for all the Americans in Kabul except five people – a total of twenty-seven. Like most of our big meals, it was a potluck with three turkeys. "If we got two cups of meat off of ours, it would be a miracle," I wrote, noting that Afghan turkeys seemed to be composed primarily of feathers. Rich wrote that, "The kids were both fascinated and grossed out by the various organs that came out of the thing. None of them resisted the meat."

Christmas was another opportunity to celebrate, and some Afghans even bought us cards (although they usually thought that New Year was our big holiday). One of the IAM teachers arranged the Christmas service. I related the fiasco to my parents:

> . . .[O]n Christmas day, the children had the entire program. Unfortunately, influenza has got much of our team down, and at that point the Oswalds were completely wiped out. So half of the music they weren't able to do; the other school kids forgot to bring their musical instruments; "baby Jesus" shrieked and had to be taken out (I quickly swaddled a doll lying nearby that I realized later was Humpty Dumpty); and all the youngest children, who were supposed to quickly put on animal masks for one of the songs, wandered aimlessly in front of the congregation.

Owen was also a shepherd, but the way Rich had tied his scarf, he looked like a very small Mother Teresa. I haven't laughed so hard in weeks. The poor school teacher, who was in charge of the production, was fit to be tied. She said she's never doing a Christmas program again.

My oldest brother, a computer programmer, suggested we head back to the US for New Year 2000 because the anticipated computer disaster known as Y2K could cause global chaos. I pointed out to him that we were scarcely affected by technology, so we might be in the safest place in the world. Instead of hunkering down, we invited Kevin's family and the Oswalds for a celebration. Since we were under a nine p.m. curfew, our guests spent the night; although the children were pretty excited about New Year's, the parents all just wanted to go to bed. There were no fireworks.

For my birthday, I told Rich I wanted to go to the Intercontinental Hotel in western Kabul. Opened for business in 1969, the hotel had seen better days; although the view over the city was spectacular, and the hotel boasted a swimming pool and restaurant, it suffered after fighting in the 1990s. I shared a little of our experience with my family:

> We invited [Kevin's family] to go with us. Between us (including various guests staying with us) there were 15 people. . . I can't decide which is more tragic – the bedraggled poor on the streets, or the fading elegance that is maintained where possible. The manager of the hotel was gracious as he led us into the one heated room (formerly the bar) – bedecked with ornately carved pillars etc. and overlooking the city. Of course, without electricity in the houses below, the view was a bit weak. . .

Since three of our children have summer birthdays, I planned a party for them before boarding school started, as I wrote home:

Even hot dogs and hamburgers are a challenge here – it took two days of cooking and cleaning to get the house ready. We had about 28 people for dinner (parents were invited) and celebrated Hannah's and Owen's birthdays, as well as two other kids on the team. . . Hannah and one of the older girls sneaked into the boys' room while they were sleeping and painted the toenails of one of the 16-year-olds. That gave everyone a good laugh in the morning.

One of the perks of our lifestyle was that age seemed almost irrelevant. If something fun was happening, everyone wanted to be included.

Our "compound" – the houses of the Oswalds and Muellers joined to our own – provided much of the social life we needed. We took turns hosting weekly dinners. One of us would often drop by – day or night – with questions or concerns. Greg came over in the middle of the night to ask what our voltage was; his had shot up and the surge set his desk on fire. Rich was summoned during dinner when the Oswalds' older son fell off his chair, ripping his ear partially from his head. (Rich stitched it back on.) We were like an extended family.

One afternoon I saw Greg standing on his porch, absorbed in gazing at something. I asked what it was.

"Look over at the Mueller's house," he said. "There's a monkey on the roof!"

We had never seen or heard of a monkey in Kabul, and we all rushed over to James and Ann's yard to see the creature frolic on the roof. He descended with a stopover on the balcony. Two Afghan men had come into the yard to catch him – we guessed they had bought him elsewhere and were using him as live street entertainment when he escaped.

Rich brought a pole over with the intention of helping the men corner the animal. The monkey watched intently, and when Rich extended the pole toward him, instead of running away, he grabbed it. They yanked the pole back and forth a few minutes before the monkey ran away and was captured in a blanket by his owners.

The monkey was not the only animal to provide amusement. Rich wrote his folks,

> Our zoo now includes a rapidly growing puppy the kids named "Clifford," two small rabbits which Hannah named Gabriel and Michael (though we've no idea of the sexes), and a canary. We plan on having a couple fish as soon as the silicone glue holding the fish tank together dries completely – the first two lived only a day in it when the glue was fresh!

One of the neighbor girls decided to experiment with our rabbits (which had been safely ensconced in separate cages) and put them together while we were on vacation. When we returned, we greeted a whole litter of bunnies, and discovered to our horror that rabbits kill and eat their young.

We had anticipated that Clifford would grow large, but he settled into a standard mid-sized dog. Usually he lounged on our front porch, but whenever we returned from an outing, he dashed furiously around the walls of the compound barking at birds, an exhibition of his usefulness before he settled back on the porch. One night he accidentally slipped out the gate and hobbled back the next morning with slightly chewed ears as a result of a tangle with the more savvy street dogs. He never ventured out again after that.

Our *chaokidar* urged us to tie up the dog because he wrought havoc on the garden. We put up fencing, but Clifford managed to jump over it (sometimes landing in the middle of the flowers), so we gave up. We figured a happy dog was better than a manicured garden.

The Oswalds' dog Simba acted as a snooze alarm each morning. Something about the resonance of the call to prayer set Simba howling. Afghans consider this very bad luck (not to mention bad form) so each day we awoke anticipating the routine: the first notes of the call to prayer, then Simba's accompaniment followed by the slam of a screen door, and finally Greg's cry of, "Simba, shut up!"

❖

We resisted purchasing a car; it was easy and cheap to catch a taxi in front of our gate and Rich often rode his bicycle. Foreigners were able to get Afghan driver's licenses, but I decided not to. Sometimes Mary drove to the bazaar on the other side of town or to the swimming pool, and I watched from the passenger seat as astonished men stopped, gaping, or swerved their bicycles off the road in wonder.

One day Mary began backing her car out of the yard only to discover that someone had parked a taxi across her driveway. She got out of the car and began asking whose taxi it was. People on the street told her there was a man visiting nearby, but no one seemed motivated to find him. Mary tried the back hatch and found it unlocked, so she crawled in, putting the car in neutral. We pushed it out of the way before she returned it to park.

"You can't do that!" the men on the street protested.

"I just did," she said as she got back into her car and drove away.

Mary was a great shopper and often came back telling of an amazing purchase she had made. One day, she announced that she had found root beer for sale. Root beer is a purely American drink, and we discovered the Afghan shopkeepers misunderstood it. When I asked, "Do you sell root beer?" one shopkeeper smiled slyly and pulled a box out from under the counter. (We heard this was also the technique used for alcohol, although we never bought any.) He declared a price double that of other soft drinks.

"That's expensive," I protested.

"But it's root *beer,*" he emphasized.

"It's not beer," I told him. "It's like Coke or Pepsi." He remained unconvinced, so I decided to skip it.

But Mary bought some and served it on special occasions. When she discovered one of the diamonds from her wedding ring was missing, she rounded up the children in our compound and told them whoever found the diamond could have a whole can of root beer. They spent several minutes scouring the yard unsuccessfully. But, too tenderhearted to deny them the pleasure, she ended up giving them each a can.

Mary seemed especially gifted in hospitality. One day I went over to find a young foreign mother dressed in Afghan clothes visiting with her children. When she left, Mary related her story.

"They are Austrians," she told me. "They became Muslims while in Europe, but her husband wanted them to live somewhere where they could really understand Islam. So they moved to Afghanistan." At one point, the husband toyed with the idea of taking a second wife, and the young mother came to Mary in her unhappiness. Apparently she had not wanted to adapt to culture *that* much.

We met other foreigners: pilots, aid workers, a man who spent three months seeking a genuine Afghan hound (he did not find one). The Western expatriate community was so small that it was rare to see someone we did not recognize. Sometimes the foreign church gathered in our living room, the windows closed to hide our singing from the Taliban. We were bound together by a strange camaraderie during a strange time.

Rich training local physicians

CHAPTER TWENTY-EIGHT

Kindling

If a forest catches fire, both the dry and wet will burn. (Afghan proverb)

We grew so used to things not working – or not working properly – in Afghanistan, we were surprised to rediscover it happens in the US, too. But the stresses of daily life here are different from the kind we experienced living under the Taliban. The psychological and emotional pressure was like nausea: I kept sensing that something was going to happen and almost wished it would, to relieve the tension.

Rumors swept in waves over the capital, and it required effort to ferret out which were true and which were not. While Rich was visiting Mazar, Greg told me he'd heard that the Russians were planning airstrikes there. (They didn't attack.) We heard rumors that Osama bin Laden had a house in our neighborhood. (He did.) At our weekly meetings, we heard rumors about atrocities outside the city.

Afghans pressured us to help them. Everyone seemed to be entering a lottery to receive asylum in the US; they thought we might have clout to put in a good word for them but we were just ordinary citizens. People confessed they were saving money to be smuggled out of the country.

"Please don't try it," we urged them. "It's expensive and dangerous. You might not survive the trip."

In February of 2000, an enterprising group of Afghans hijacked an internal flight. Instead of landing in Mazar, the plane from Kabul continued on to Tashkent, Uzbekistan and then made other fueling stops before landing in Britain. Most of the people on board sought asylum, and for weeks afterward our friends said wistfully, "If only I had been on that Mazar flight! For only $20, I could be in England now!" We sympathized with our friends, knowing that unlike them, we could leave at any time.

I wrote my parents about the hijacked plane:

> It's probably the first time in history where the hostages were *happy* to end up in a location other than the one intended. . . . Among the foreigners, the airline was already known as "scariana" because of the security and maintenance. [Its alleged motto – "Scariana. . . three frights a week."] The last time James Mueller came down, he said the whole plane was filled with T.s who wanted to keep their guns on board. Fortunately the pilot wouldn't have *that*. (James said the T.s went on to fight over who got to sit next to the windows!)

PACTEC, a charity providing air service to aid organizations, set up an office in Kabul and began offering safe transport between cities and to remote areas. Although India had begun operating Ariana, the Afghan national airline, we were warned we should not travel on commercial flights; the planes were not being maintained adequately. Sometimes this added to our stress: the PACTEC planes were few, and for awhile there was nothing large enough to transport our entire family.

Having armed men everywhere was also anxiety-producing. At check posts around town we were stopped, our taxis or cars perfunctorily searched by men who appeared to be farmers with machine guns. Sometimes Rich tried to lighten the mood of the moment by saying in English, as he rolled down his window to answer questions, "Yeah, we'll have the burger, fries, everything" or "Hey – you lookin' at my woman?" I was grateful none of them spoke English, or we probably would have been pulled out and shot right there.

Rich's father and stepmother, who had unsuccessfully tried to visit us when we lived in Qarya Beykh, traveled in with Rich after his Board exam. Unfortunately, they had to face some of the challenges of life in Kabul, including an illness exacerbated by the dry mountain air and a ban by the Taliban on foreigners leaving the city. Mary's parents visited at the same time, so we had a temporarily grandparent-rich compound.

Along with keeping the family going and hosting visitors, I had to make sure that homeschooling didn't turn into nonschooling. As Rich wrote,

> It should be a challenging year with interruptions by Dad's visit in November-December, and by a family holiday in India in January-February. Can these enriching and delightful experiences really substitute for the study of early civilizations and long division? We will likely not have the chance to find that out, since the headmistress of our school (known to her students as "Mom") is a strict discipline and by-the-book sort of person, and there may be postponements in the school schedule, but no omissions!

Afghanistan was undergoing troubles not directly related to the Taliban. The country had not had a good snow since the Taliban came to power (some claimed it was divine commentary on the current government), and many of my letters in the year 2000 noted the results:

> (May 19) It's really hot and dry here. Kabul's not so bad off, since we're in the mountains, but we hear down south rumors about a half-glass of water selling for a dollar. We prayed that the poppy crops would die, but now we're

praying that God would have mercy on this miserable place and send rain. The rivers should be gushing now, but they're down to trickles. Every afternoon clouds roll in, but not a drop of rain falls. We expect our electricity will run out before the summer does.

(May 21) The government is pretty much financed by opium revenue. Someone told me a quarter of this year's crop has died because of the drought.

(June 3) We still have well water, but it is very salty, and our trees and plants are starting to turn yellow. We have a new gal on our team who is a civil engineer and is giving talks to our watchmen and to the rest of us about how to conserve water, and how to make the water we have drinkable.

(June 11) In Kabul we've had no rain for a couple of months, and the winter was not great in the way of precipitation. Peoples' wells around town are already going dry, and the water table will not rise until next winter.

(October 1) The drought conditions seem to be easing up a bit in town here – at least the water level in our well has gone up, and it's rained a couple of times recently. (You should hear the kids rejoice!)

(October 5) [I reported we had some rain but the crops had been affected.] And even if food becomes scarce and expensive there is always (sigh) enough for the foreigners. We try to give bread and fruit to the street kids when we see them.

Our electricity was unreliable, but not merely because of reduced water flow through the generators. In the fall of 1999 I reported,

250

Right now we usually get electricity every other day from 7 p.m. to 5 a.m. It's funny how one runs around, pumping water into the tanks, vacuuming, bathing the kids, and using the computer while it's possible. I told Rich I'm about ready to unplug the fridge, because it kind of loses its effectiveness when it's off half the time!

Rich installed solar panels, which eased the difficulty a bit: we were able to have lights at night on the days when we had no electrical power. We tried to rely on solar power as much as possible, especially after receiving a huge bill one month:

We were rather shocked to get our last electricity bill. Our previous bill (they're figured every two months) was $37.50. This one was $220! And we were gone one of the months. Several families complained to our representative, and she said they had started charging foreign homes at the same rate they charged offices for power. She is in the process of negotiating so that we can be charged at the Afghan home rate. But even if we were charged at what she says is the office rate, there is no way our bill would be that high, so we think our neighborhood might be tapping into our line.

Our next bill was down to $12. "Someone told me," I wrote home, "the high bill was a kind of retroactive surcharge (the Taliban needed money for something) but I suspect someone in the billing office had to pay for a wedding." Fortunately, the bills never reached into the triple digits again.

Our team's children had very few major accidents or illnesses – the occasional broken arm or bout of chicken pox – but Hilkka's second son, a friend of Aidan's, was reaching for a thermos of hot water when the lid came off, spilling boiling liquid across his lap. His mother, a nurse, cared for him at home while we all waited and wondered if he should be evacuated. Eventually he was flown back to Finland, where he received professional help. Years later I saw the streaky scars running down his legs and was thankful that he had survived the terrible incident.

Probably the most stressful and anguishing situation involved a friend in early January 2000. I recounted the incident to my parents:

> X was loading things into his car on Sunday to go to work, and checked around the car as one usually would before driving off, but he didn't see that as he was going back and forth from his house, a 1 1/2 –year-old boy sneaked out and crouched right in front of his tire. The mother wouldn't let X take the boy to the hospital, and he died shortly after he was run over. Needless to say, this would be a tragic and traumatizing event in any country, but here it's got nightmarish consequences. Under normal circumstances, X would be in prison. As it is, his passport's been taken away. Our director and Afghan staff members have tried to negotiate with the family. (It's normal in this culture to make some kind of financial reward to the surviving family members.) To make things worse, the father of the boy works for the department of defense, and all their neighbors are Taliban. Although the father seemed sane initially about what happened, his neighbors, including a particularly malicious guy from Kuwait (I'm not sure why he's here – some kind of military advisor?) have pressured the family to go for a huge financial settlement ($50,000) since X's a foreigner. The neighborhood, who did like [X and his wife], have been turned against them, so finally they moved out of their house. (Of course they can't leave the country, since X has no passport.) And although our office tried to do normal negotiations, the extended family wants to go through the Shariah (Islamic law) court.

We all grieved for the child's family and for our friend, who avoided the foreign community for some time as he wrestled with his own emotions. Several weeks later I wrote the outcome:

Instead of $50,000, they resolved on $5,000. Our group here decided to cover the whole thing. The neighbors asked [the couple] to move out of their house, so they did. I guess they didn't want constant reminders of what had happened. Also, there were other neighbors who were kind of out to get them. A lot of people here say that X got a better settlement than many locals have in similar situations. One deciding factor seems to have been that his daughter called the Taliban representative in New York to complain. That got back to officials here, who didn't want some kind of international crisis!

Among all the other burdens of this time were the ever-increasing restrictions on our movements. We began wondering if it was worthwhile to be in Afghanistan. Rich was doing good work, training Afghan physicians and treating patients. But one day a Welsh colleague shared at our group meeting that he and his family would be leaving the country.

"We no longer feel that we can continue to work here and support an evil government," he said.

This gave us pause. Were we, by providing aid under the Taliban, in fact prolonging its rule? We all supported our Welsh friends in their decision. But for most of us it seemed the plight of the poor would only degenerate and their suffering increase if we left. And so we stayed.

CHAPTER TWENTY-NINE

Garden afire

When water goes over your head, what
difference if it's one fathom or a hundred?
(Afghan proverb)

2001 was the year that broke my heart.

We couldn't anticipate at the beginning of the year what awaited us; we were lulled by good news and good times. We took our annual vacation – several weeks in India – exploring mountains and gardens and beaches and ancient cities. We returned to Kabul to find that something extraordinary had happened that would improve Rich's work situation.

While we had been away, Tom Little, Rich's boss and the man who dealt with the administrative side of the NOOR Eye Hospital, had figured out a way to get around the Ministry of Public Health's constant attempts to thwart their work. He signed a new protocol, this time with the Ministry of Higher Education, to create a teaching hospital near Kabul University. Secretly, Tom and Rich moved their equipment to a temporary clinic (to avoid having it seized by the MoPH) and set to work while most of the ministers were on pilgrimage to Mecca.

Rich and Connor spent an afternoon measuring the building. It needed about twenty-five thousand dollars' worth of repairs, including a new roof. I wrote my parents,

> Fortunately one of our dinner guests is a big potential donor, and Rich had made a beautiful floor plan on the computer.

Not only did the building need repairs; there were changes to be made outside as well. During fighting, trenches had been dug around the walls, and Rich discovered mounds in the courtyard were full of bodies from the morgue next door. The NOOR staff also wanted to test a new idea – installing composting pit toilets. These were especially useful since many of the rural patients, inexperienced with flushing toilets, repeatedly clogged the pipes by tossing rocks (their toilet paper) down the drain.

A number of our teammates planned home leaves over the summer, including the Oswalds, the Executive Director and his family, and Tom and his wife, who planned to take a year away. That meant that Rich would be responsible for his own job as well as negotiating, planning, and managing staff necessary to get the new teaching hospital functioning.

James would step in as the temporary Executive Director. We teased him about this: disaster seemed to follow him wherever he went. Besides the fainting episodes in Mazar, the blizzard in the Solang Pass, and an incident on one of the PACTEC planes where hydrogen peroxide shot into his nose when he had to use the oxygen mask, James seemed to have chronic aches and pains, remnants of high school football. That meant that the Executive Director (who was also a trained physical therapist) came by periodically to give him excruciating back treatments. If something bad was going to happen, we joked, it would happen under James' watch.

But even before the regular director left, two explosions occurred. The first was hours from us, in Bamiyan, where the Taliban elected to destroy two massive Buddhas carved into the mountainside, one of which was supposedly the tallest standing Buddha in the world. The other took place two blocks from our house, a street we often crossed in taking our children to Kevin's or Hilkka's house, when a car rigged with a remote-control bomb blew up. I was in the schoolroom reading to one of the children; the others were playing outside. Shrapnel flew across the yard, but none of the children were injured. More miraculously, the Oswald's *chaokidar,* Farid, who had been balancing on the grape arbor trimming vines, was unscathed.

I quickly ushered the children inside. On the radio, I heard an Argentinean friend whose house was a block from the blast.

"My window has blown out," she said.

I told the children to stay in and that I would return soon.

Mary and I headed over to Sofia's house. She and her three- and one-year-olds had been in a bedroom when the plateglass window shattered from the blast. I wrote my parents,

> Fortunately she had nailed up cloth over the window recently because someone had thrown a rock through and broken it. So all the glass fell inside the cloth. None of them were hurt. Then we went next door, to the house of Owen's German-Korean friend. The room they often play in had a plate glass window blow out, too. Thankfully they weren't even home, and arrived as we were cleaning up the glass.

Usually we knew which areas of town to avoid or which dates to lie low. A car bomb in a residential area at that time in Kabul was not part of our experience. I thanked God for protecting our children.

Despite this shock, in the same letter home I managed more prosaic topics.

> Last week we planted the seeds you sent and the seed we gleaned last year from our locally available plants – snapdragons, hollyhocks, bachelor's buttons, and daisies.

Hopefully the *chaokidar* can do a better job watering this year, so we don't have to stare at brown, dead grass all summer!

I also mentioned how busy I was homeschooling, overseeing the children's program in our little expatriate church, and giving piano lessons. The car bomb was just a loud blip on the screen of our life that spring. Another came when the Oswald's youngest son found and consumed twenty tablets of children's Tylenol, thinking they were candy. I sat with Mary as she settled him into the bath tub and spooned an entire bottle of Ipecac into his mouth so that he would vomit up the toxic dose. There was no ER to head to; as a pediatric nurse, Mary provided the best care available. Her son did fine.

Rich had begun studying Pushtu, realizing that the Taliban was not going away soon; he wanted to work better with his Pushtu-language patients. One day, while we were shopping on Chicken Street for a gift, we saw three black-turbaned men gazing into a shop window. When they saw us, they stared at us, scowling. Rich, unabashed, greeted them in Pushtu. They broke into smiles and immediately tried engaging Rich in conversation. He confessed he couldn't communicate much. But the incident put a personal face on the force behind the government.

Pushtuns from southern Afghanistan were not the only newcomers to Kabul. The Oswald's *chaokidar* Farid told us he had met Arabs at the gym where he lifted weights. Money from Saudi Arabia was pouring into the country – at least into mosques. New, elegant structures sprung up around town. We wondered if a few mullahs would be sent as well. The call to prayer broadcast from the mosque across the street from our house was sometimes painful to listen to, the local mullah even having coughing fits in the middle of prayers.

"Why are you in Afghanistan?" Farid asked his fellow weight-lifter.

"We were told that infidels were taking over," he complained. "It's not true, and now we can't get back home."

In June I wrote my parents with ominous news regarding the thousands of Hindus and Sikhs in Afghanistan:

You might have heard about the edict issued last week saying Hindu women had to be veiled and all of their community had to be identified somehow (like the Jews with armbands in WWII).

We discussed this with the foreign community: should we voluntarily wear the identity label, too, to show support for religious minorities? Although we rarely saw the Sikhs, there was a temple in Karte Parwan. According to Mohammed Wali, the head of Vice &Virtue, there were no Jews or Christians in Afghanistan, so they didn't need to be labeled. Although there may have been few members of these groups in the country, Rich at one point met Kabul's last two Jewish rabbis, one as a patient. While living on the same street, they remained enemies, arguing over who should have control over the Torah in Kabul.

In the end, the identity label edict did not become law and there was no effort to mark the non-Muslims in the country.

The government continued to put pressure on us as an organization and individuals. At the beginning of the summer, I wrote:

> The Vice and Virtue guys (it's supposed to be the Prevention of Vice and the Promotion of Virtue, but we often wonder at the word order) declared that foreign women could no longer drive – an edict no one protested but the IAM. (We have a lot of single women and we don't have professional drivers like the other groups.) Then came this rumor that foreign women had to be veiled. I agonized over that one for a couple of days, until I found out it was just a rumor.

> The V & V guys seem to be running the country. Despite having a government-signed protocol, our physiotherapy school was forced to discontinue classes for women. (It was the only school in the country which had

259

permission to teach women.) None of the other ministries (e.g., education, public health, etc.) are willing to stand up to them, because they have the ring of divine authority. And whenever the Taliban suffers in battle, they come down hard on innocent people. Last week they were beating people on our street, including a tailor in a wheelchair! (He had been listening to music, which is against the law.) Sometimes I wonder that the populace doesn't rise up and do something.

Before our first stint in Afghanistan, I had spoken with an American who had worked for years in Pakistan. She was adamant that veiling was an oppressive practice that would chisel away my self-confidence. Perhaps for that reason I had decided that donning the *chahdari* was something I would not submit to. When that possibility was mentioned, I told Rich I wasn't willing to do it. We were glad that the story about forced veiling of foreigners turned out to be false.

June and July continued with weekly proclamations of what had been outlawed. The Taliban's prohibitions seemed increasingly outlandish – from white socks to brassieres to make-up to lobsters.

"Lobsters?" I asked Rich when we heard this one. "They have *lobsters* here?" This ban seemed particularly ludicrous, since Afghanistan was under trade embargoes and had no ocean access to acquire seafood.

August was the month when things began to fall to pieces for us. On Friday, August 2, two young American women in Kabul took their computer to an Afghan house and allegedly showed a DVD about Jesus, which the local family indicated an interest in seeing. However, they soon discovered this was a set-up: both women were arrested by Vice & Virtue and taken away. (Their story is told in their book, *Prisoners of Hope.*)

Authorities waited as others arrived for work at the office of Shelter Now International, the German charity the two women were affiliated with. The father of Connor and Aidan's friends Dirk and Matthias, as head of the group, was arrested that day, along with five other foreigners and sixteen Afghans. In a letter to my parents I wrote that sixty-four street children who had contact with them were also taken; the others working with SNI left the country.

When our house helper arrived that day to work, I discovered that he had also been employed part-time by one of the American women taken.

"I'm going to her house this afternoon," he told me. "I need to pick up my pay."

I panicked. "No," I insisted, "You must not go back there. Someone might be watching her house." I looked at him thoughtfully – he had always been good-natured and hardworking. Slowly, I said, "It would probably be safer if you didn't come to our house for a while." I gave him his pay with an extra month's salary and watched sadly as he disappeared.

I had now let two house helpers go out of concern for their well-being. As I left the yard that day to pick up our children at Kevin's house, I passed people on the street with the feeling that I carried the plague. I was afraid to greet anyone, afraid that by being seen with me – talking to me – they would be questioned, arrested, imprisoned. I brushed off the pestering throngs of street boys and hurried to get my children and whisk them into seclusion behind our walls.

On the nightly radio call, we were told there would be a meeting the following afternoon to discuss the situation. We all knew the arrest of two Christians would have repercussions for the rest of us.

Rich planned to bicycle to the meeting from work, so I hailed a taxi to carry us to Karte Seh. One of our regular drivers, who had become a family friend, picked us up.

This man had lived through a difficult few months. His wife accidentally filled their kerosene lamps with diesel, and when she lit one, it exploded in her face, setting her on fire. In an attempt to rescue her, our friend was burned and his beard singed off. Despite his best efforts at getting care for his wife, she died. The taxi driver was picked up a few days later by the Taliban and thrown in jail for having his beard too short. Although he tried to explain what had happened, there was no mercy, and he stayed in prison until Vice & Virtue deemed his beard long enough.

We drove along our usual route, a curving street that fed into the main road leading to Karte Seh. As we approached the intersection, I could see from the left a black Toyota Hi-Lux barreling towards us. Apparently (I was told later) I had the forethought to cry out a warning to our driver, but he did not look left before pulling into the road. The truck slammed into our taxi, sending it flipping over and over. I remember the crystalline beauty of the shattering windshield, the plea of one of the children ("Jesus, save us!") and desperately clutching Owen, who was on my lap. None of the vehicles in Afghanistan had seatbelts, let alone child safety seats. The taxi landed, after a one-and-a-quarter flip, onto the passenger side. Every window was broken. Aidan, who had been sitting on the opposite end of the back seat, and Hannah, who had been in the middle, tumbled with Owen and me onto the pavement.

Somehow we were able to climb through the back window and I helped the children onto a traffic island nearby. Hannah hit the pavement head first, but had not lost consciousness. Her forehead was already swelling. Aidan, who had been sitting in the back seat behind the driver, the side of the car which received the impact, walked away with only a scratch on his face. Owen's right arm was bleeding, lacerated by broken glass. His tee-shirt looked like it had been shredded by shrapnel, but other than his arm, he was unharmed. Connor, who had been the front-seat passenger, was covered with blood. It was not his own.

"He flew past me out the window," Connor told me, in a daze. "I think he's dead." He had seen the taxi driver face down on the pavement, his head partially covered by the vehicle.

One of the amazing phenomena of life in Afghanistan is that no matter how empty streets are before a crisis, they immediately fill up with crowds as soon as something happens. We were surrounded by people trying to help us up, to take the children, to get us to the hospital.

"No, no," I said, "we'll go home. But the driver needs to be taken to the hospital." They assured me they would take care of him. I flagged down the next taxi that appeared; the driver took us the few blocks home without charging us. We offered up a quick prayer for our friend, and when we were dropped off, I went into

262

The Wide Store. (Our driver was a friend of the family who owned it.) I told them that he had been in an accident and taken to a hospital, but that I didn't know which one.

We staggered into our yard and were met by our cook Ayub, who had agreed to work until the end of the month. (Since he was not connected with SNI in any way, I thought his association with us would not be a problem.) He tenderly helped me wash blood and dirt off the children. As I checked them quickly, they seemed all right, although I was worried that Hannah might have a concussion.

I got on my radio and began calling around, trying to reach Rich. My voice trembled as I told the office staff that we had been in a car accident, and asked if they could send Rich home.

But no one could reach him. He had decided instead of heading straight to the meeting by bicycle to ride home in hopes of taking a taxi with us. When he strolled up to the front gate, one of our teammates met him. "There's been an accident," he said. Rich rushed in.

It was a miracle we had survived. Rich examined us, and finding us okay, set off in search of our friend the taxi driver. With no idea where he had been taken, Rich traveled from hospital to hospital until he located him. A few days later the taxi driver was let out (or escaped, as he told us – he was afraid the hospital care would kill him). Battered and bruised, he sat on our front porch and apologized for risking our lives.

I gazed into his face, now covered in scabs and purple bruises. "We have nothing to forgive," I told him. "I'm just glad you're alive."

The taxi driver's father had come by the evening of the accident. The Taliban impounded the vehicle, and were bringing charges against his son for being at fault.

"But the other car was going the wrong way on a one-way street," I protested. "He was careless not to look – but he wasn't at fault."

With help from Farid, Rich used my account to write out an explanation of what had happened, and went the next day to the hearing to speak on our friend's behalf.

"The driver of the Toyota Hi-lux was a sixteen-year-old Talib," Rich told me later. "He had no driver's license. But instead of punishing him, the authorities decided to fine our friend." We gave him money to help fix his vehicle so he could continue working once he recovered.

It was shaping up to be a rough month – already our friends had been arrested, our house help let go, our family taking a "direct hit" by a Taliban vehicle, and our taxi-driver friend injured and unjustly accused of wrongdoing. But August was not yet over.

The IAM's sandbagged headquarters, Karte Seh

Our last smiling family photo of 2001- on an Indian train, January

CHAPTER THIRTY

Fleeing the garden

A broken hand can work but a broken heart cannot. (Afghan proverb)

Kevin drove over after the IAM team meeting to check on us and fill us in on what we had missed.

"We need to destroy any Dari-language printed matter we have," Kevin told us. "The Taliban have warned that we are next on their watch list and our houses and offices will most likely be searched. They already stormed the IOM office, probably thinking it was the IAM." We all laughed at this mistake; the IOM was the International Organization for Migration, which assisted returning Afghans.

But our mirth was short-lived. I spent the evening standing over an old barrel in our driveway burning papers, photos of friends, even the English-language Sunday school material I had been using with expatriate children. We did not want to keep anything that might seem suspicious to the authorities. The IAM leadership also told us that those who wanted to leave the country should feel free to do so.

That night, I cried myself to sleep.

We got up the next day with external bruising and muscle aches from head to toe. Some of Rich's co-workers were afraid that they would be arrested if they came to work. Although each day more foreigners were leaving the country, Rich assured his staff he would not go.

We were not prepared for emergencies. From our first days in Afghanistan in 1992 we had been told to store two weeks' food for potential lockdowns, but we never had. We also did not keep many cash dollars on hand. James and Ann, however, sensing the increasing instability, had saved a large amount of money for a potential evacuation. As we discussed our plans to leave, James went into his office and opened the cabinet where he kept their money.

It was gone.

They were flabbergasted. Besides their family, no one had access to their house – except their *chaokidar,* who had been doing double-duty as a cleaner. Even though James always locked his office, he realized now that the *chaokidar* had gotten a matching key and not only stolen the dollars, but also pilfered a few *af* notes from each stack of local currency.

"I thought we were burning through money a little faster than usual," he said grimly.

Ann sent the *chaokidar* to the bazaar for some groceries. While he was gone, I suggested we search his room. I went in and lifted his mattress. Underneath was a child's cassette tape taken from the house, but no money. James set a trap for the man, placing a small piece of paper above the door so that if it was opened, the paper would flutter to the ground. He found it on the ground the next day, and more money missing. We discussed the next step.

"I'm concerned that if I report him to the police, he'll either find some pretext to get us into trouble, or he'll get an unfair conviction," James said. (Four men had been hanged on August 8 for allegedly setting off bombs; some doubted their guilt.) Instead, the Muellers swallowed their losses and asked the office to transfer their *chaokidar* to guard an empty house.

We went ahead and arranged to rent a small bus and packed up school books (just in case we were delayed in returning) and clothes to take to Pakistan. I sat down with the children.

"I want you to pack like you might not be able to come back," I said. "Take what is most important to you, and leave a stack of things that could be sent out if we can't return."

All the boys were avid Lego fans, and Aidan had finished constructing some elaborate space ships. He was unwilling to dismantle them, despite my urging, so he left them behind and took a few loose toys. The others packed their favorite items.

On Friday, what was left of the foreign Christian community met in our living room. Emotions ran high; many people were departing besides Ann and me, so we said goodbye with heavy hearts.

"Ann and I are leaving by road tomorrow for Peshawar," I announced. "If anyone wants us to carry their computer out, bring it to our house by tonight, and I'll leave it at the guesthouse in Peshawar for you." Since the American women from SNI were arrested with a computer, the Taliban were especially interested in getting access to ours. As the afternoon wore on, several people came by, entrusting us with their laptops.

The Toyota Coaster waited outside our gate at four the morning of August 11, a little over a week since our friends from SNI had been arrested. The air was still cool and the street barely light. Most of the small bus – which could seat seventeen passengers – was full of our boxes and suitcases. The laptops we stowed as best we could so that they were neither visible nor crushed. Rich and James watched us drive off. Who knew what might happen in our absence?

With us on our ride to Pakistan was a South African, a friend of the two seized American women. There was some concern he might be arrested because of his association with them. We piled him in the backseat with the children and our lunches, the stacks of luggage behind them. There were ten of us, plus the driver, and no spare room.

Like most cities, Kabul looked pristine in the dark. As we turned through the quiet streets of Karte Nao along the Jalalabad road, I couldn't stop thinking about Rich and James standing outside the gates waving us goodbye. We would be back in a couple of weeks, but August 2001 had already been physically and emotionally traumatizing. I wanted the government scrutiny to be over so we could return home.

A half hour from Kabul we began descending the winding mountain road that led to Peshawar. Suddenly we stopped. I didn't remember there being a checkpoint here. A black-turbaned Talib spoke with the taxi driver. "Get out," he told us.

We spilled from the vehicle, our blond offspring blinking in the morning light. The Talib boarded the Coaster.

"Where are you going?" he asked. "Are you moving?"

"No," I said. "We're just going on vacation."

He opened a box wedged behind the back seat and pulled out a handwriting primer. Flipping through the inverted booklet, he asked, "What are these?"

"School books," I told him. If we were delayed, I figured, we could start the new academic year while waiting to return.

He pointed to my backpack. "What's in there?"

"Our lunch," I said, pulling back the flap so he could see.

He glanced around another minute and then waved his hand. "You can go."

We re-boarded wordlessly. Ann and I were thinking the same thing: if he had discovered the computers, we would have been arrested like our friends. If we had been imprisoned, what would have become of us? What would have happened to the children?

After that search of our vehicle, I could not wait to get out of the country. We made a quick stop in a forest outside of Jalalabad for the children to use the bathroom, but not long after we returned to the highway, one of the boys said, "I need to go." We stopped again. Our driver swerved around the pothole-studded road like a maniac. We pulled the curtains across the windows as we went through Jalalabad, the major city halfway between Kabul and the border where we had previously stopped for restaurant meals. This time we opted to keep going. We arrived at Torkham, the border crossing into Pakistan, and passed over with little trouble.

Although those traveling through the famous Khyber Pass to Peshawar were required to hire an armed guard to accompany them through the winding mountains, we already felt safer being on Pakistani soil. The children were anxious to settle into the

270

guesthouse; they had access to a television, a refrigerator full of pop bottles, and a small, lush garden around the building where they could watch snails and play games. We were usually on vacation when we passed through Peshawar. This time Ann and I were each given a bedroom big enough to accommodate our entire families.

The team counselor stopped me in the kitchen as I was getting a drink of water. "We are having a debriefing session tomorrow with those who have been evacuated," she said. "I want you to join us."

"But I wasn't evacuated," I said, surprised. "We came out by choice."

The counselor was insistent; I felt defensive. I was fine. I did not need to be debriefed. But I showed up for the meeting anyway.

I listened as each person told his or her story of leaving Afghanistan. The arrest of our friends, worry about Afghan staff, the car accident – any one of those would have been stressful and disturbing. But to have them happen within a week was so disorienting, that as I shared my story, I realized I could not even put events in chronological order.

Later, I thanked our counselor for making me talk through what had happened.

We spoke in shrouded language about those arrested in Kabul. We had all heard too many stories about rape and abuse; what hope did our friends have of coming out of captivity unscathed? Every morning as I gazed at my bruises in the mirror, remnants of the car crash, I thought of the women being held.

But we were mothers, and we had to protect the children from as much trauma as possible. We did our favorite Peshawar activities – buying ice cream bars, going to a nearby club where we could swim and eat American food, and watching whatever DVDs had been left behind by others in the guesthouse. The building had two stories. On the ground floor was an office, kitchen, dining room, lounge, and a number of guest rooms; upstairs was the bigger lounge with the television and a few more guest rooms, including ours. I arranged the six twin beds so that there was room to walk from the door to the bathroom, but there was space for little else. The children preferred to roam freely through the entire building, which was quickly filling with evacuees.

271

Classes were starting at the small international school close to the guesthouse; Ann enrolled her children. Since I had brought a semester's worth of books for each child, I began homeschooling. In a bedroom in a guesthouse in Peshawar, Connor began his eighth-grade year, Aidan sixth grade, Hannah fourth grade, and Owen second grade.

At least our children saw many of their friends in Peshawar. Dirk and Matthias were staying in a rental house with their mother. I watched these teens with concern. One seemed worried about his imprisoned father; the other appeared at peace. Their mother not surprisingly seemed a bit scattered, but had good support from others in their organization who were in Peshawar.

The kids also made friends with children of the PACTEC pilots, who were based in Peshawar. Unfortunately, the Pakistani government shut down their office on August 15 and they were told that the pilots' security passes had been cancelled; they weren't even allowed to go to the airfield to work on their plane. This was worrying for us, too: if PACTEC was not flying to Kabul, how would Rich and James and others get out quickly if they needed to?

Day by day more people arrived. By August 17, there were only eighteen IAM foreign staff left in country – down from about fifty. Whenever anyone arrived at the guesthouse, I asked them about Rich and how he seemed. Although he and James called from the satellite phone they were keeping in our compound, we could not speak long. At one point, I said to a man, "Rich doesn't seem to think things are so bad, yet everyone keeps leaving."

Our friend smiled gently and said, "He's like a frog in a pot of water. As the water heats up, he doesn't notice." I knew Rich was committed to the hospital and his staff, but it was hard not to fret about him.

American diplomats arrived in Kabul hoping to secure the release of the two women being held by the Taliban. None of us were sure if they would receive a prison term and deportation, or execution; there seemed to be uncertainty even about what they were charged with. After meeting one of the diplomats, Rich and James invited him to dinner (they were sharing meals while we were away).

272

"You know," he told them, "It would make things a lot easier for our government if there were not so many Americans in the country." He must have been pleased to hear that few were left from the IAM in Kabul.

While Rich and James dined with a diplomat in our house, I went with Kevin to meet the American ambassador in Peshawar. Having never met an ambassador, I had no idea what the meal would be like. There were so many things to say, but within the confines of the formal dining room, they evaporated. She said she wanted to know about the situation in Afghanistan. Each NGO representative gave a one-sentence assessment: they monitored the work from Peshawar and entirely trusted their Afghan staff; things were going well. As the only ones living inside the country, we told the ambassador a different story: we had trouble finding workers we could whole-heartedly put confidence in; we had to be close to keep them accountable. She received our brief updates, cheerfully discussed her daughters, and bid us goodbye as though we had been at a cocktail party.

Meanwhile the IAM office was informed that – like Scrooge – it should expect three visitors: inspectors from the ministries of Security, Vice & Virtue, and Intelligence.

On August 25, while talking to Rich on the satellite phone, I asked, "Can we come back yet?" Two weeks had passed since Ann and I had left Kabul.

"You better not," he said. "I'm thinking that next weekend I'll come out for Aidan's birthday and then fly back."

The next day, the Taliban banned international organizations from using the Internet. Rich packed a backpack with some clothes, his laptop, and a few pieces of medical equipment and on Thursday, August 30 flew to Peshawar on a Red Cross flight. He gave multiple reassurances to his colleagues that he would be back on Saturday. They feared he was fleeing the country.

That was the last he saw of Afghanistan in 2001.

Kabul River Gorge, 1993

Trying to enjoy an evacuation, Bangkok 2001

CHAPTER THIRTY-ONE

Ashes

The dust sought refuge with the ashes and the wind carried the ashes away.
(Afghan proverb)

Birthdays were important in our family. Even if the children could not remember the celebration, I had photos to prove that cake had been served and gifts bestowed. I'm not sure why I latched on to that marker as particularly significant; maybe I just like parties. Anyway, I determined that come hell or high water, we would have a party in Peshawar for Aidan's eleventh birthday.

We invited the kids from SNI – whose minds no doubt were on their incarcerated father – and a couple of other boys for pizza, ice cream, and a sleepover complete with a rented copy of *The Phantom Menace,* which had recently been released. The toy shops were disappointing, but we found a dartboard for Aidan. We got permission to have a Friday evening party and sleepover in the upstairs lounge of the guesthouse.

Aidan once wrote an essay entitled, "My Worst Birthday Ever." He tried to put a good face on it, but his party was overshadowed by news that arrived that morning.

The evening of August 30th (the day Rich had left), James was asked to meet with Taliban officials, who escorted him to the IAM office, sealed it, and took his keys. They then drove him around the

277

city with an armed convoy, insisting he point out IAM projects and team member homes, all of which were sealed. He was returned home in the early hours of August 31 and told he would need to reappear at the Ministry of Foreign Affairs office at eight a.m. James had time to call Ann on the satellite phone and contact team members. A guard was posted at his house.

The next morning James was handed a letter informing him that IAM expatriates had seventy-two hours to leave the country or face the consequences. "The IAM," he was told, "no longer exists."

After attempting to persuade the authorities to negotiate and hitting a dead end, James began calling team members around the country. Five of the Kabul team had left by road early that morning; the other four (including James) left the following day. The four expatriates in Mazar flew out on a Red Cross flight; the five in Herat chartered a UN flight. That left three in the center of the country and two in Jalalabad – the latter were under house arrest, and James had to convince the Ministry of Foreign Affairs to release them.

On Saturday, September 1, PACTEC pulled its staff out of Afghanistan, claiming they relied on the IAM for logistic and ground support. Peshawar was overflowing with NGO workers. The last of the IAM team arrived before the seventy-two hour Taliban deadline had passed.

To both inform the press and remind the Taliban what they had lost by our expulsion, the IAM released a statement:

> IAM consists of 117 professionals (some with families) from 17 countries. Approximately 300 Afghans were employed by the IAM.

> IAM's work consists of 10 programmes: National Organisation for Ophthalmic Rehabilitation (NOOR), the primary provider of medical and surgical eye care in Afghanistan; the Physiotherapy School in Kabul (PSK), which has been teaching physiotherapy for the last 15 years; English as a Foreign Language (EFL) schools; Skills Development; Maternal Child Health Care Clinics and

278

community based health training programmes; school for blind children and adults; Community Development; Primary Mental Health Care; and renewable energy source development.

Afghanistan was in the third year of the worst drought it had experienced in decades; this was another reason we all regretted being kicked out:

> The Disaster Management Program began in April this year with a 2.5 million dollar budget to assist people in drought affected areas of the country.

How would the Taliban provide relief to the suffering of the country without the presence of NGOs?

Hilkka's husband, the Executive Director of the IAM, had been on home leave, but he flew to Pakistan. He and James immediately began negotiations with the government for permission to work with Afghan refugees. There were already established camps around Peshawar; now IAM employees joined their displaced countrymen. I wrote my parents on September 7:

> So far about 50 of our employees have come here; they say they were being looked for. Someone says all employees have moved from their previous homes. Tonight we heard that the radio announced all IAM employees were to report to the Ministry of Planning to receive their final salaries and that 31 did – nine were detained. [It was a trap.]

By the end of September, about a third of our Afghan staff had arrived in Peshawar to collect September salaries, severance pay, and gifts from the IAM's benevolence fund.

The guesthouse became the hub of activity. Each morning, team members showed up with their computers to sit in the lounge outside our room, recording capital losses and trying to balance accounts without the materials now in our sealed office in Kabul.

Ironically, Rich received word that he was approved to buy a YAG laser and continue repairs on the new teaching hospital.

He was busy downstairs with exiles seeking financial help and assistance in obtaining refugee status. Many looked at this as their opportunity to relocate to a third country, preferably somewhere in Europe or in Canada or the United States. My heart sank when I stepped into the lounge and saw our language teacher, no longer looking regal and dignified, but shaken and lost.

At one point a BBC cameraman arrived and began filming Afghans as they approached the gate of the guesthouse. Rich went out to speak to him. "Please turn the camera off," he said. Then, thinking the photographer had complied, Rich said, "These people are fleeing for their lives, so please do not film them." Naturally that night we saw Rich on the BBC news, giving his statement "off camera."

Many of our colleagues decided to take a home leave or vacation and departed from Pakistan. Rich and I spoke uncertainly about our own future. Should we rent a house in Peshawar, and try to work with refugees? We spoke with the head of PACTEC. "There aren't any houses to be had here," he told us.

The children and I continued homeschooling as best we could. A German counselor flew in to help families deal with the stress of our situation. She arranged for the children to meet at the small school nearby for a day of fun and talk. We had already sat the children down and told them that we would not be able to return to Afghanistan; we cried about losing our dog and our material goods. (The only items I really wished I had brought were Owen's tattered t-shirt, the reminder of how God had protected us all in the car crash, and the Christmas ornament my mother had sent with us in mind: the cross of peace.) I wrote my parents:

> I was gratified to hear both Hannah and Aidan express a few days ago that, "I now realize that possessions aren't that important." Some people spend their whole lives without figuring that out.

280

We decided to hold a service to provide some closure for our team as we began to disperse. On September 9 we held a memorial for the IAM. Each person brought a stone to drop into a pot to signify the people who loved and had served Afghanistan. We then went to a hotel and ate dinner together to celebrate thirty-five years of work in the country. I was touched to see the teenage son of Filipino friends there to represent his family. He had been in boarding school in the mountains, and when refused permission to join us, had come of his own accord.

On the evening of September 11, we had a brief team meeting. One of our families had just returned from the mountains after welcoming a baby, and the mother was introducing their new son when Carol, who managed the guesthouse and office, stuck her head in the dining room.

"I just got a call from the travel agent," she said. "A plane crashed into the World Trade Center." We all murmured in shock, finished our meeting, and went upstairs to turn on the TV just in time to see footage of the second tower being hit. It didn't take long to figure out what was going on.

"Osama bin Laden's going to get blamed for this," Rich said.

We spent most of the night watching the BBC. Our heads whirled – we knew it meant war between two countries we loved: America and Afghanistan. We were caught up, we felt, in the middle of it.

Naturally, Pakistan seemed like one of the worst places to be at the time. The next morning we were told that everyone had to get out of the country as quickly as possible – everyone except the Muellers and a handful of other people who would stay to help our local staff. The friend who had told us a few days before that no houses were available to rent in Peshawar wryly informed us he could get us a great deal now.

The German counselor who had met with the children took Rich and me aside and showed us pictures they had drawn. Everything in Hannah's was black and frightening. I was also worried about our thirteen-year-old, who refused to express any emotions about what was going on.

"Your children have had a very dark time," the counselor told us. "They need to see that there's still some light in the world. Why don't you take a vacation before heading back to the US?"

The last thing we felt like was a vacation, but there was really no option anyway. All the other Americans in Asia were trying to get back to the States, and flights everywhere were full. We asked the children: did they want to go west, and stop in Ireland, or east, and visit Thailand? They chose Thailand. We flew out the evening of September 13.

I felt jittery at the Lahore airport. "Look at the people on our flight," I whispered to Rich, pointing to the dark-clad men in turbans.

"This is Pakistan," he reminded me. "That's the way people dress here."

On our flight to Bangkok, we picked up the newspaper. The headline screamed that Al-Qaeda operatives had been found staying at a hotel in Bangkok. "I feel like they're following me everywhere," Aidan told me.

We checked into a hotel for the night and the next day visited a travel agent to book a flight to the US. "I'm sorry," she told us, "all the flights are full for the next three weeks."

We bought the earliest tickets available, then made plans to head north to Chiang Mai for a visit, since we had friends there. The hotel had a spacious pool, so we all went for a relaxing swim. A pair of Middle-Eastern looking men arrived shortly after us and sat down at a table nearby, apparently watching us. I got more and more uncomfortable (in light of the newspaper headline we had seen on the plane) and mentioned it to Rich.

"Look," Rich told me, "We can't go on living like this." He walked over to the two men at the table and said hello.

"Where are you guys from?" Rich asked.

"Iran," one of them answered. "Where are you from?"

"America," Rich responded.

And then the man said something that brought tears to our eyes. "I am so sorry about what has happened to your country," he said.

This was the side of the story that most Americans were not getting. Even though the TV kept flashing the same images over and over of people dancing with glee at destruction in the US, there were many Muslims who did not share their feelings.

We had as much fun as we could in Chiang Mai, taking the children to the zoo and riding elephants and strolling through a modern mall (ironically called the World Trade Center). Our hearts were heavy, and we were frustrated to find that every hotel we stayed in had just discontinued its subscription to CNN or the BBC. The best we could do for tracking news was to watch the financial channel. Sometimes in the corner of the screen we could see a tiny image of President George W. Bush or Mayor Rudolph Giuliani of New York, but as the stations had Thai voice-over, we could not hear what was going on.

We went south to the beach. Other friends from Afghanistan were there, and we walked together, commiserating over our loss. Despite the beauty, it was the most wretched vacation we have ever had.

The year to follow was no better. Although we arrived safely in the US, we were wounded. Our children spent months in counseling and Rich and I were on hold as we waited to see what was next.

In November, our SNI friends were rescued by American forces and the IAM invited to return to Afghanistan. Teammates began to trickle back. By late 2002 our family seemed recovered; we all agreed we had grown individually and in our relationships with one another. When we asked the children, "Do you want to go back to Afghanistan?" We were greeted with a unanimous and unqualified, "Yes!"

Miserable vacation in a beautiful place – Thailand, 2001

Connor outside Mussoorie, 2005

CHAPTER THIRTY-TWO

Replanted

In a ditch where water has flowed, it will flow again. (Afghan proverb)

In a conversation with several homeschooling mothers about living overseas, one of the women turned to me and said, "I bet you found that stuff isn't that important to you." I had to laugh. I told her we had lost so many possessions that she was right – material things weren't that important to us.

Nevertheless, we were curious: which of our household goods would turn up again and which were gone forever? We heard horror stories about the situation when our teammates returned after the fall of the Taliban. The Talibs had collected things from every IAM house and stacked them in the backyards of the two buildings we used as offices. Every item was caked with dust from months outdoors. Those that weren't reclaimed were hauled into an IAM warehouse. Greg and Mary managed to recover most of our belongings. Fortunately, we had written our name on our furniture and other items. (At one point, I had even initialed every

Duplo in our toy basket.) Some things we retrieved later (from other peoples' houses) and some things never reappeared (like our books). We made one foray into the warehouse ourselves. The floor was buried in piles of junk – children's half-used workbooks, toys, sheet music. A mouse scurried by as we gingerly dug through one stack of papers. It must have been overwhelming for those who returned first, and we were grateful that someone else had done our dirty work for us.

The Oswalds had not only collected our possessions but also persuaded the office to rent a house for us above the allowed rate. In the interest of getting us in quickly, Mary assured the office that rather than painting all rooms a neutral color, as was usually done with a newly leased property, we would be happy with the house as it was. We found a candy shop of hues: the hallway a shiny mint green; the living/dining room robin's egg blue; the kitchen and nook pink. Upstairs was a small blue central room with golden stars splashed across the ceiling. We had a lavender bedroom; Connor's was salmon; Hannah's pink; and Owen and Aidan's pale green.

We mourned the loss of our old compound (and our solar panels). Our house in Karte Parwan had leased for an exorbitant one hundred and eighty dollars per month during the Taliban times; with the influx of NGOs after 2001, it rented for fifteen hundred dollars. James and Ann retrieved many of their things when they returned to Kabul, but Greg and Mary, who were already in the US when we evacuated in 2001, discovered their landlord had seized some of their furnishings before the Taliban got to them. On scouring the bazaars, James located many of his books, muddy and bent; when we were out to dinner at one of the newly opened restaurants, Mary pointed out her beautiful brass coffee table hanging on the wall. I tried to cheer myself with images of Osama bin Laden working his way through our eighth grade reading books in some cave in Tora Bora.

Although we missed our previous home and neighborhood, there were many perks to being back in Karte Seh. For one thing, we no longer appeared the wealthiest people around. (I had wearied of explaining to Afghans that we were not rich – by American standards, we owned little, but from an Afghan perspective we

288

appeared part of the financial elite.) What had been ruins in the neighborhood sprang back to life as elegant homes, reconstructed by people who had sojourned in Pakistan or Dubai or Iran. The buildings began to emulate the grand houses we had seen in Islamabad, with columns and marble and even glittering outdoor chandeliers. It was an odd contrast seeing a house whose outer walls were clad in marble with windows of green one-way glass next to a house where the roof had partially collapsed, the whitewash dissolved, and plastic tarp flapped over window frames. Our house was neither as flashy as the updates nor as battered as those waiting to be fixed.

Window panes were the initial sign of optimism we observed in Karte Seh. There had been so many rocket attacks and so much street fighting that it had seemed a futile effort to reinstall glass before. We also saw little shops opening on side streets, fashionable imports from other Central Asian countries and India, and people driving new cars, motorcycles, and scooters. (We felt environmentally virtuous with our bicycles.)

Another plus to living in Karte Seh was that many foreigners were now within walking distance. Some families spread out to other parts of town, but over time everyone migrated back. The children could walk or bike to their friends' houses – usually with an adult (parent or *chaokidar*), but sometimes alone. There was a field at the place we met each week, and the kids could play soccer or basketball and even held a carnival. We had ceildhs (Scottish folk dancing evenings) and the children performed at piano recitals. It was nearly a normal life for them.

Before returning to Afghanistan, we had talked to Connor about the possibility of going to boarding school. It was something we had always dreaded, but almost all the high school students had either gone to Pakistan or India to finish their education. Since the boarding school in Pakistan had been attacked by gunmen in August 2002, we ruled that one out. The daughters of our friends Dan Terry and Tom Little had attended Woodstock School, an international school in the northern part of India, nestled in the Himalayas. Connor and Rich took an exploratory trip, and Connor came back excited to go to India in the summer.

Our lives became structured around boarding school. Rich and I took turns accompanying Connor to Woodstock the first semester of each year. The trip meant a flight to Delhi, a train trip to the city of Dehra Dun in the Doon Valley, and then an hour's taxi ride up a narrow, winding mountain road to the school.

Alternatively, we could travel overland, crossing Pakistan and India by car and railway. Rich visited during Connor's fall break, and I went out in the spring. We continued taking vacations during the long winter breaks and returned Connor – and then Aidan, who begged to join him the following year – to school in February.

The other children continued homeschooling, although we did allow Hannah to attend the IAM school for a semester. Not all children appreciate having their mother as a teacher, and Hannah was happy to escape me for a time. But in the end we decided to stick to the boarding school schedule so all the children could enjoy breaks together. Hannah counted the years until she could join her brothers in India.

Rich set back to work at NOOR. He developed written exams for the doctors, and arranged for ophthalmologists to come from abroad to administer both the written and oral exams. It was a huge challenge for the Afghan physicians, since the tests were an evaluation of their medical knowledge given in English. Passing meant the doctors received a certificate acknowledging their success (and later, an increase in their stipends). They also had opportunities to take internationally-recognized ophthalmology exams, and the IAM offered to pay for those. Fear of failure was so great that although thirteen doctors signed up for the first test, only three ended up taking the exam. The next year Rich instituted a system whereby the doctors had to make a hundred-dollar deposit to assure that they would show up. (The deposit was returned when they took the test.) Even with this incentive, some of them still did not appear on test day.

Keeping the eye program functioning required constant vigilance. Despite its growing capacity to reach across Afghanistan through hospitals, clinics, and mobile eye camps, it was always at risk of losing funding. Staff kept busy writing grant proposals, and it seemed like every fiscal year there was a threat the hospital would close for the last few months if emergency funding did not appear. (At the last minute, money always came.) For donors, there was apparently something less satisfying in covering day-to-day operating costs than in buying a new piece of machinery or building a clinic. Rich was thankful for the first ophthalmic laser donated, although maintenance was a problem.

Despite allotted vacation time and sick days, staff always had funerals (and it was shocking how often people had relatives dying) and weddings to attend. Even the arrival of out-of-town guests pulled workers from the clinic. Sometimes the resident physicians would go home for a holiday and not return for weeks.

It was also difficult to handle the patients. They sat in waiting areas separated by gender, but when one person was called forward to be seen, a crowd encircled Rich to see what he was doing. One positive cultural practice was that patients often brought a relative or friend with them to appointments, so Rich could give instructions to their advocate if the patient seemed confused. The relatives were also responsible for picking up medicines in the bazaar and bringing in food to those hospitalized.

As the country-wide medical director of the eye hospitals, Rich not only trained residents in Kabul, but also continued traveling to the other eye facilities. He went to Mazar several times. Once, during the Taliban time, someone had inadvertently cancelled his PACTEC airline ticket, so he rented a seat in a van going north with Afghans. At one point, the van was stopped, and Rich questioned by the Talib who was searching the group.

"Why is your beard so short?" he asked.

"Because I am a foreigner," Rich answered.

The Talib eyed him dubiously. "You don't *sound* like a foreigner," he said. The group in the van assured the soldier of the truth, and they were allowed to continue the journey.

In post-Taliban Afghanistan, we both had mobile phones, so I could keep tabs on Rich's travels. One morning he called me from Mazar.

"What are you doing?" I asked.

"Oh, I'm on the way to the hospital for a meeting," he told me cheerfully. "But I should be home by dinnertime."

Our *chaokidar* Yusuf let him in the front gate at dusk and as soon as he was out of view, I gave Rich a welcoming kiss. As we walked toward the house, I looked more closely at his face.

"What happened?" I asked, tracing lines across his forehead where he had been bleeding.

"Well," he said, "after I spoke on the phone with you, I arrived at the hospital. I'd been out to dinner the night before at an Afghan's home, and was feeling a bit queasy this morning, but thought I'd be better. I sat down at this meeting, but as it went on, my stomach began roiling. Finally, I rushed out of the room.

"I hurried down the hallway and asked someone where there was a restroom. A nurse pointed it out to me. I went to the door, but it was locked. I rushed back and begged someone to unlock it. As soon as the door was unlocked, I ran into a stall. And then –" he looked at me – "I fainted head-first into the toilet. I hit my head on the rim, breaking my new glasses. Fortunately the toilet was dry, or I might have drowned."

I listened to this story in horror, and then wiped my mouth. "I wish you'd told me that *before* you kissed me," I said. "But I'm glad you're okay."

As Afghanistan worked its way into the consciousness of North America, both aid and opportunities for Afghans to study abroad increased. Doctors affiliated with the Rotary Club offered to host two Afghan physicians for the Academy's fall meeting and allow them to stay in their homes. The night before the two men were due to fly out of Kabul, we had them over for dinner. They were full of questions: *Was there a restaurant on the plane?* (We explained that on international flights, food would be served without any charge.) *Would they be given enough tea in America?* (We assured them most hotel rooms had coffee makers where they could brew their own tea or they could order tea at the meetings.) *What should they buy?* (I suggested children's books and toys; other than that, it seemed like everything could now be found in Kabul, which had from ancient times been a crossroads of world trade.)

We expected them to return from the US discouraged about the disparity between medical facilities in both countries. But to our surprise, one of the doctors merely said to Rich, "Your country has a lot of problems."

I have often contemplated: what was it that struck him? In what ways was Afghanistan doing *better* than the US? Perhaps the less permanent nature of family ties in the US and the consequent social implications shocked those from a culture so people-oriented that it was considered rude to leave guests alone for even a moment. His comment still haunts me.

Nova, 2003

CHAPTER THIRTY-THREE

Nova and the chaokidars

A new servant can catch a running deer. (Afghan proverb)

We are constantly calculating which we value more: privacy or security. I tend to choose privacy. For that reason, when we returned to Kabul in 2002, I was happy to be free of cooks and house helpers.

Our house was much smaller than the Karte Parwan mansion. We bought a generator and stored it in a back shed to mute its sound so we could pump water and use a vacuum cleaner, washing machine, and iron when the electricity was out. Like all of the Kabul houses we lived in, the walls seemed to consist mostly of windows. (The glass was not double-paned, either; the children burst through one playing blind man's bluff the first week we were there.) In the interest of privacy, I hung lace to obscure the view of our curious *chaokidars,* who circled the house on their frequent walks around the property.

Our former employees reappeared shortly after our return. The young man who had cleaned for us dropped by to ask if I would write him a letter of recommendation so he could get a job as a *chaokidar;* I did so gladly. Ayub, the cook, pulled up one day in his own car. I would have hired him back, but he told me he had gotten a job as a car salesman. He had gained a lot of weight, a sure sign that he had found a path to prosperity. I thought it interesting that both men decided the rigors of housework too much and eagerly entered other occupations.

Our gentle day *chaokidar* showed up while Rich was meeting with someone, so I ushered Amin into another room and sat down to talk. I asked about his family. He told me that his wife had another baby now, bringing their total number of children to five. Somehow the way he told me made it clear the child was not *his*. I tried to grasp the shocking implications of this, but he went on to explain.

"One day my wife went to the clinic where she works," he began. "There was a baby on the porch that had been abandoned. They tried to find out who the parents were, but since no one came forward, my wife offered to bring the baby home, and we adopted it."

This was a pleasant turn. "Is it a boy, or a girl?" I asked.

"A girl," he said.

To most Americans, that might be a warm – but not amazing – story. However, this man already had three girls and only one son. And in Afghanistan, boys are much more prized than girls; they represent economic stability for a couple in their old age, and daughter-in-laws do the housework, since married couples usually live with the groom's parents. I was astonished that Amin, on his low wage, would take on the additional financial burden of a female – and one that was not even blood-related. Afghans continued to astonish me.

Since Clifford had never reappeared, we searched for another dog. (This would be dog number five, more than I had owned in my entire life on American soil.) One day Rich saw some boys with a puppy and asked them if they knew where he could get one. They showed up at our house not long after with a darling black-and-white pup. It was so small it could curl up in its food bowl. Rich ordered a proper dog house built which Aidan (who looked after the dog as his own special pet) painted. Aidan had done some reading in the US about how to rear dogs, and was determined that this time we would not have one who was vicious toward our guests.

Whether it was something genetic – being born from generations of street dogs – or the persistent taunting of children who poked things under the gate or banged on the gate and ran away – our new dog, Nova, became even more dangerous than Clifford. She was gentle in some ways, and clever – she would eat the apricots that fell to the ground around her house, even breaking open the pit to get the edible nut inside. We had several scorpions on our new property, and watched in amazement as Nova danced around each, barking, until someone killed it.

She probably would have been a good dog, especially since Aidan tried hard to train her right, but one of our *chaokidars* began to tease her. As he swept the sidewalk that lined our yard, Yusuf would take her chunk of dry *naan* and hold it away from her, batting her with his broom when she tried to retrieve it. After that, no one dared to take or touch her food, because in her eyes anyone who laid hands on her *naan* was a mortal enemy. I often fed her; she always watched me, askance, until I was out of view, before she would eat. Whenever she saw someone with a broom she eyed him or her suspiciously and picked up her bread, carrying it around and around the yard, sometimes burying it in a big sand pile at the back of the house. Only Aidan was considered trustworthy. Sometimes Nova would bring her *naan* and drop it at his feet.

The boys who brought us Nova came back later, deciding they wanted to profit from their gift. Rich gave them some money and a table we did not want. We were startled several months later when they appeared on an afternoon during the weekly IAM meeting. For some reason I had not gone that day. I heard the doorbell ring, and glanced outside to see our back-up *chaokidar* (who covered for our regular man on his day off) letting one of the boys in the yard. He had a leash in his hand. I rushed outside to see what was happening.

The boy greeted me nervously. I asked, "What are you doing?"

"I'm going to take your dog to show the man I got him from," he said. "He just wants to see her. And then I will bring her back."

"No," I told him, obviously doubting whether I would ever see Nova again.

The boy then explained his dilemma: the man had not actually *given* the dog to them; they had stolen it. I was not sure of the veracity of this story, but decided that after having Nova so long, it was too late.

"I'm sorry," I said, ushering him out of the yard. "If you stole the dog, that's your problem, not mine."

For some reason, our office had decided that instead of hiring one watchman for the day and one for the night, we would have two men at night, each of whom would work half-time. The idea seemed sound – except we had never known a chaokidar to stay awake at night. Sure enough, they both slept. Yusuf was an older man with a grim face. At first I was afraid of him as his eyes followed me narrowly from the warmth of his woolen pattu, the long cloth men wrapped around them in the winter. The younger man, the handsome son of one of the office workers, had promising English and a dignified manner. He seemed likeable.

As the months went by, my impressions reversed. Yusuf was conscientious, watching over us zealously; the younger *chaokidar* seemed to take his responsibilities lightly. Yusuf had a wonderful sense of humor; he was bright, an excellent innovator and problem solver. As we got to know him better, I realized that if he had been raised in a different place, he would have been a college-educated leader. But in Afghanistan he lived as a half-time watchman.

One night I woke to a banging sound outside. I looked out the window and saw Nova rolling an empty plastic pop bottle across the pavement. Apparently the *chaokidars,* whose room was toward the back of the house, could not hear it. I went down, retrieved the bottle, and went back to bed.

After a couple of minutes, the sound repeated. I looked out – there was Nova again, frolicking playfully with an empty bottle. I marched down the stairs, grabbed the bottle, and returned to bed.

Someone told me once that if you have an anger problem, Afghanistan is not the place to be. I didn't realize how angry I could get until moving there. The Night of the Plastic Bottles, alas, demonstrated this to me.

The third time Nova began his one-dog soccer game, I went ballistic. I grabbed the pop bottle and stomped to the *chaokidars'* room. I could see them both curled up on their *toshaks,* sound asleep. I hurled the bottle at the window.

From inside came a voice. "Did you hear something?" one asked the other.

Before he could answer, I jumped into the conversation.

"Yes, he heard something," I said. "*Finally.* It's the third time the dog has been dragging bottles around the yard." They both hurried outside and sheepishly gathered the rest of the bottles that they had been lining up in their outhouse. I went back to bed and finished the night without interruption.

Our day-time watchman was an easygoing teenager who swaggered in each morning modeling his latest fashion find – sometimes purple velour pants and a tee-shirt with an Indian pop star's picture on it, sometimes sporting colored glasses, always looking as though he was on top of the world. He was so amiable and apparently helpful that it was hard not to like him. Since our return I had decided to dress in a black coat and scarf (as many of the returning Afghans were doing – a custom they picked up in the Arab countries) and one day asked Hafizullah to go with me to the fabric bazaar. I told him I would indicate what I wanted, and he could bargain for it. Since I had been told more than once that I could pass as an Afghan, I hoped it meant savings in the bazaar.

We walked around the maze of shops and perused the cloth. At last I found some I liked. A crowd of small boys had been following us, hanging on the few words I spoke as I questioned shopkeepers about their supplies. Finally one of them turned to the others and announced, "She's a foreigner."

The other boys picked this up, chanting, *"Kharijee! Kharijee!"* I tried to hush them, afraid the quoted price would rise, but in the end we got enough cloth for our curtains at a reasonable cost.

Hafizullah was a good shopper and got along with our children. But he began hanging out on the street to chat with *chaokidars* from houses nearby. It was annoying to have to look for him to answer the gate or run errands.

Finally, I asked the office if I could switch Hafizullah to night duty and move our older *chaokidar,* Yusuf, to days. This was a big benefit to him, since Yusuf would receive full-time pay; he had four children to feed, and his only son had a mental disability and was unable to work. It also benefitted us, because Yusuf was not only excellent around the yard and with the family, but also at selecting groceries. Plus he could read the simple scrawl of my Dari shopping lists.

Now that the responsible *chaokidar* worked days, the younger two began to slack off even more. They arrived later and later, and Yusuf insisted on waiting around until one of them showed up. One night, when they knew Rich was in India with the boys, they both sauntered in about thirty minutes late. I had already sent Yusuf home for the day.

I was in a bad mood again, distressed at having to part from Connor and Aidan. (Despite their enjoyment of boarding school, goodbyes never got easier.) As soon as the *chaokidars* walked in, I said, "You're late."

They smiled, and one said, "Just a *little* late."

"You are half-hour late," I corrected him. If they had apologized at that point, all would have been well.

But the handsome one began complaining. "Well, I hardly get paid," he said. "I'm only getting paid to work half-time."

I knew his heart was really in academics – he always carried English books with him and studied hard hoping to get accepted into the journalism program at the university. I could appreciate the value of that. But his attitude irked me.

"Well, why don't you just go home?" I said. "Go home, and don't come back."

He stood on the porch, uncertainly. I looked at Hafizullah as well. "You go, too," I said.

They both left. One came back a few minutes later to argue with me, but I was adamant now. I bolted the door and trusted that Nova, who was the best watchman we had, would keep an eye on the children and me.

The next morning I told the office I had fired them and that I wanted to hire the man who came once a week to cover their night off. He seemed quiet and responsible. They agreed.

Hafizullah's father, who had worked with the IAM for a number of years as a watchman, showed up at the gate the next day. He tried to sweet-talk me into taking his son back. That didn't work, so his words turned poison. "You know, Yusuf is a rich man," he said. "He drives a car around town and has all kinds of money."

This fabrication was so ridiculous that I had to restrain myself. "Well," I said, "whether he's rich or not, he's a good worker, and your son is not. So I'm going to keep him." I did – and never regretted it. Yusuf became indispensable to me.

Things seemed to be working out with the *chaokidars* and Nova; they all kept safe distances from one another. Yusuf, despite previously teasing the dog, became good friends with Nova. Sometimes I would look out to see them on the porch together, thoughtfully contemplating their domain.

But our night *chaokidar* apparently had not learned a proper respect for Nova's power. One of the houses next to ours was undergoing a beautification project which meant that men stood for hours on ladders, carefully sculpting scrolls of concrete around the windows. Nova had always barked at anything – or anyone – that could be seen on or above the gate. (One of the neighbor cats seemed to relish this, and frequently paraded slowly across the wall.) Nova went berserk, barking and barking at the workers. Finally Assef could stand it no longer. He came out of his room with his broom in hand.

"Quiet!" he yelled at the dog, waving his broom. (We got the story the following day from the workers next door.)

Nova continued barking, so Assef reached out and whacked her on the muzzle with the broom. Nova turned on him and bit his thigh. Panicking, Assef thrashed out at her, and she gave him such a chomp that he ran out of the yard and down the street to our office.

Rich was pulled aside at our meeting. "Your *chaokidar* is at the office," he was told. "He's been attacked by your dog."

We were all in shock. Nova had been known to bare her teeth or nip a hand shot into her face, but not to seriously injure someone. I took the kids home and waited until Rich returned from the office.

"I showed up and found Assef covered in blood," he told me. "I asked him where he'd gotten bitten and he pointed." Rich imitated with a grimace, indicating his crotch. "I told him he'd better let me have a look, since I am a doctor." He shook his head in sympathy. "He'll be all right, but Nova bit him right on the tip."

We all squirmed. And worried. But after a few days, Assef was back – keeping his distance from Nova. She seemed to have gotten over the trauma, and apparently Assef did, too, as he went on to father more children. But we got serious about tying Nova up when visitors came into the yard. (Elisabeth had told us that dogs should be put down after biting a human, but considering one of Nova's main functions was to guard us, we decided we would keep her and try to protect people from *her*.) The positive outcome of this unfortunate incident was that word spread around the neighborhood about our vicious dog, and we felt more confident we would not be targeted for any burglaries.

And like our *chaokidar,* we learned a little more restraint when feeling angry with others.

The cause of the altercation between Nova and the chaokidar

Tom Sawyer, *Kabul, 2004*

CHAPTER THIRTY-FOUR

Dahkheli and kharijee

(natives and foreigners)

Our first term in Afghanistan, a European woman told me that she had no Afghan friends. I remember being shocked – this woman had lived in Kabul for years; how could she not have friends? But later, as we came to see that many people only sought relationships for what they could glean from us, I understood her comment. We had very few real Afghan friends. But the connections we had survived the changes in circumstances through various regimes.

Ibrahim was still working for the IAM and now that the Taliban was out of power Nooria was employed, too. They sought our help in building a house on their family property; we visited and enjoyed seeing them ensconced in a newly-painted home with a proper kitchen and bathroom, a hallway large enough to hold parties, and an elegant sitting room complete with a television. Watching Persian music videos in a clean, carpeted room was a far cry from our days together in the village. Ibrahim proudly showed us their new well and the trees he had planted in their tiny yard. His oldest son now attended a private English-medium school.

Ibrahim's brother, who had spent years in Pakistan during the conflicts in Kabul, returned, setting up house away from the rest of the family. He and his wife were both educated and NGO-employed; their daughters all spoke English well and were trying to brush up on their Dari language skills so they could finish high school. The family also had a teenage son with cerebral palsy. It was precious to watch how lovingly they treated him – many families apparently kept their children with disabilities hidden away.

During the summer the other boy in the family, a seventeen-year-old, drowned. We knew that families who had lost a member during the year celebrated *Eid* differently, but this was our first evidence of it. When we went to their house, instead of the usually festive atmosphere, Rich and I were ushered quietly into separate rooms. None of the family was out visiting; according to custom they were compelled to stay home. Friends and family came to them, and although they ate cookies and drank tea, their purpose was to mourn the loss of the son.

I entered the room where the mother of the boy waited, and kissed her on both cheeks (the usual greeting) and sat down. I said the traditional blessing for those who have lost a family member (*zendagi sar-e shuma bahsha* – life be on your head); she asked about our children and I responded.

After a few minutes, more guests came in. They, too, kissed our hostess and sat down and were served tea. They chatted briefly, and then the women began to rock and sigh. They cried and spoke about the youth's untimely death. His mother also dabbed her eyes while everyone wept.

I dropped my head. Even though I knew that the loss of a son would be an unbearable tragedy – I contemplated my own seventeen-year-old, Connor – I could not *force* myself to cry.

The weeping stopped as suddenly as it had begun. Now the ladies chit-chatted about various pleasant things. After a few minutes, they suddenly reverted back to mourning. I was as surprised by the happy conversation as I was by the outbursts of grief. I could not understand their ability to bounce emotionally back and forth at such a rate.

❖

One old friend I thought we might not see again in Afghanistan was Daoud, our early language teacher. We had last said goodbye to him in Tashkent, Uzbekistan, after Owen was born. But he was back in Mazar working, and Rich connected with him on a trip north. He was on his way to Kabul to meet his mother, who had secretly entered the country to attend Daoud's wedding. (As an asylum-seeker, she was not supposed to return to Afghanistan until she received official citizenship papers from the country she had immigrated to.) Daoud and Rich rented a taxi in Mazar and got all the way to the Salang Pass before they were forced to stop. The tunnel had been undergoing renovation work, and the Turkish employees doing the labor strictly controlled traffic, allowing northbound and southbound vehicles only on alternate dates. Rich and Daoud had arrived on the wrong day.

Daoud, always the negotiator, spoke politely to the men in Dari, then Pushtu, and then in Turkish. They were adamant: no one would be allowed through the pass. If they wanted to go to Kabul, they would have to drive back to Mazar and do a detour that would take two days.

Rich and Daoud noticed other travelers trekking up the hillside that covered the tunnel. "Why don't we just walk over the tunnel and get a taxi on the other side?" Rich suggested. Daoud agreed. They got their luggage, and – both in blazers and dress shoes – began to ascend.

The Salang Pass had been the location of fighting for years, and as Rich and Daoud followed someone up the hillside, they began to notice rocks painted white or red. The white rocks meant landmines had been cleared; the red meant that the area was still mined. At one point, they both stopped and looked around. They were encircled by red rocks.

It took four hours to accomplish what should have been a half-hour walk. They scrambled down on the south side of the tunnel, swearing that they would never try anything so stupid again.

Rich called to tell me that he and Daoud would be arriving for dinner. When I saw our former teacher, he was changed: no longer the youth eager to learn idioms, he greeted me with the demeanor of a diplomat.

Daoud's mother had grown impatient waiting for her son to marry. Since he had not chosen a wife for himself (and was now nearing thirty), he told his mother she could find him a bride. "But," he insisted, "she has to be a Pushtun, and she has to be willing to return to Afghanistan to live in Mazar." Afghans have amazing networks around the world, and soon his mother had found the perfect wife – a woman whose family had moved to Vancouver, British Columbia. This woman had met Daoud when she was a young teenager and remembered him. She was willing to come back to Afghanistan.

Not only did we marvel that our friend would be willing to marry a woman outside either of his ethnicities (since he was half Tajik, half Uzbek) but we also thought it amazing that anyone who had seen Mazar would be willing to leave Vancouver, arguably one of the most beautiful cities in the world, to return there. Daoud's mother spent a couple of nights with us and delighted us by telling how the family had adapted to life in Europe. We missed them but were relieved to find that they had settled well.

With the fall of the Taliban the number of foreigners now in Kabul swelled – soldiers, aid workers, and even those who had grown up in the country back for a visit. One of the latter was a woman whose parents, both doctors, had worked for the American embassy and then come back with the IAM. She showed up at the beginning of summer with a stage version of *Tom Sawyer* in hand. Most of the foreign children in town got involved; Aidan won the role of Tom and Hannah was Becky. At the end of the play, Tom was supposed to give Becky a little kiss, but Hannah got flustered and pulled away. Aidan ended up grabbing her and giving a smack on the cheek anyway, much to the audience's amusement. He complained later, "Next time I do a play, I don't want my sister to be my romantic opposite!" Owen stepped in to take the role of the slave Jim when another child dropped out. He stole the show.

When Connor and Aidan left for boarding school, bedroom space was freed up for guests, and we were happy to host a number – Board members coming from abroad for the semi-annual meetings; teammates from other parts of the country; and people involved with medical or other short-term projects. We enjoyed the stimulating conversations with them. But we made it a policy never to change the sheets until their airplanes actually left the ground, because flights were often cancelled at the last minute. Many times we saw a taxi pull up at the gate to return guests we had already sent away.

During the Taliban time we had known almost every foreigner in Kabul; now we went to Flower Street (where imported delicacies were found) and saw people we did not recognize. Sometimes they were military men and women looking for DVDs, sometimes workers with the multitude of NGOs that flooded the country. The IAM found a special role by offering an orientation course to these newcomers; after so many decades of cultural experience, staff could help others avoid mistakes that would offend the people they were trying to assist.

With the increase in foreigners, the cost of everything went up. We got savvier in the bazaars, and prided ourselves on any purchasing coups. One day while Connor and I were in a shop, he spotted a stack of Kraft Macaroni and Cheese boxes, a favorite of our kids. He pointed them out to me.

"How much?" I asked the shopkeeper.

"A dollar each," he said. Each large container held several smaller boxes. Trying to look nonchalant, I said, "We'll take them all." The shopkeeper realized he had underpriced his merchandise, but it was too late to back down.

The arrival of the American military meant we could also now buy MREs (meals ready to eat). After consuming one, I decided they must have been designed to encourage soldiers to get their military service over as quickly as possible. But the kids liked opening them to find packets of candy or gum or little boxes of cereal inside. We could buy squeezable jams and cheap salsa, things I had never seen before in Kabul, at low prices. Some of the foods had passed their expiry dates, but most were in good condition. Occasionally we went to the "Bush bazaar" (formerly the "Gorbachev bazaar") to find whatever cast-offs filtered down from the military. (Once we spotted a box of fresh pancakes, apparently carted off after that morning's breakfast.) James and Ann's younger son set up a business selling American snacks at our weekly team meetings.

Compared to the well-regulated quality of foreign foods, we still had to deal with the more questionable standard of local goods. James and Ann beneficently bought us a barrel of the finest rice from northern Afghanistan only to find that if one skimmed away the top grains, poorer quality rice was hidden beneath. Mary found glass ground into her hamburger, and one day her daughter bit into a meatball I had made and informed me there was a tiny nail inside. A friend who had moved to Kabul from Pakistan shared her concerns that the butchers were generously lubricating the meat grinders – and spraying the sides of beef – with Tar-o-Mar, an insecticide made of DDT. I usually asked our c*haokidar* to buy *surkhi,* which was boneless beef; sometimes I found chunks of liver thrown in (which I suppose made sense, in a way). Hannah complained about her meat and upon examination we decided it was a bull testicle. Even our dog, we discovered, would not consume *those.*

Without reliable electricity, we decided to use a nonfunctioning refrigerator from the warehouse (studded with bullet holes) as an old-fashioned icebox. The *chaokidar* rode his bike to the bazaar a couple of times each week and brought back a huge block of ice; we kept this in the freezer compartment with perishable items. Since the only floor with a drain was in the bathroom, we kept the fridge there.

We still had the problem of disposing of food that had gone bad; now we did not even know anyone with a cow to feed it to. We knew we couldn't throw it away without raising the ire of our neighbors. When the *chaokidar* brought home a mushy watermelon, I was not sure how to get rid of it. Finally, I came up with what seemed the perfect plan. I chopped the melon into small pieces and flushed them down the toilet.

The next day, our toilet was backed up.

The IAM used a plumber with legendary qualities. He was tall, broad, and always wore a distinctive karakul hat (made of fetal sheepskin). His hearty greeting of, *"Salaam, Khanom-e-Duktar-Saeb* ("Hello, wife of the doctor"),*"* always brought a smile. The children joked that wherever they were around town, they would glimpse the plumber and his karakul hat.

I ushered him into the bathroom and explained that we were having trouble with our toilet. After about a half hour with the plumbing snake, he called me in.

"Khanom-e-Duktar Saeb," he began, looking at me with an expression of incredulity, "there was *watermelon* in your toilet!"

My mind quickly shot back to the *naan*-burning debacle in Mazar. I tried to match the plumber's look of disbelief. *"Rahstee?"* I responded. ("Really?") I decided it was better not to say anything more. The plumber got our toilet working; I posted a sign on the refrigerator side (facing the toilet) with the instructions that guests could "flush everything except watermelon."

We found it challenging now to use the UN's swimming pool; there were so many actual UN staff members who wanted to swim, we were restricted to mornings. But the children discovered other places to go – school playgrounds (an international K-12 school had opened) or a coffee shop where they could play ping pong and listen to music. Hannah created her own weekly newspaper, Owen joined a youth group for middle-schoolers, and Connor and his friends made a video of a fictional story about terrorists that was filmed in and around destroyed buildings at the edge of town. They played badminton with an older Scottish friend, skate-boarded around the yard, and had water fights in the backyard while neighbor children peered over the wall in curiosity. We ate pizza with Italian troops and sorted through donated boxes of books from the Americans. We were able to get most of the latest movies, and as a family we often read aloud in the evenings. When volunteers were sought to create a skit for our annual Christmas party, Hannah raised her hand – as did an older British gentleman. He graciously came to our house in the evenings to help Hannah write the script.

Aidan, who had always been artistic, helped us with an elaborate prank. Because Nova had alerted us to so many scorpions in the yard, I persuaded Aidan to construct a giant one out of bakeable dough. He painted it brown and put a rose thorn in the tail as a stinger. It looked fairly realistic, if somewhat large. One evening the family went out on the front porch at twilight as planned, and engaged our night *chaokidars* in conversation.

As arranged, Aidan came running around from the back and said, "Everybody come quick! There's a huge scorpion back here."

We all rushed around to the back and Aidan pointed.

There, on the steps leading into the c*haokidars'* outhouse, was the massive scorpion.

The two men froze for a minute, and then the older man went and got his flashlight. As he shone it on the scorpion, its shadow sprang up behind it, covering the wall. Yusuf moved closer carefully and then said, "Hey – it's *plastiki!*" He turned and had a good laugh, and we explained the trick. The younger man assured us after the fact that he, too, had known it was not real. "The color wasn't quite right," he said smoothly.

For adolescent girls and women there was an increasing problem with harassment by males along the streets. (This may have been a result of a new access to explicit films and Internet pornography.) Although we were now allowing Connor to go out alone, and Connor and Aidan out together, we escorted Hannah everywhere, or had the *chaokidar* take her.

The pre-adolescent and adolescent girls took an almost wicked delight in seeing bothersome boys on bicycles veer off the road or be batted at by some elderly man on the street when they irked the girls. Many of the girls and women (Hannah and myself included) had begun riding bicycles. Not only did we have to keep from falling on the rutted roads and avoid crazy drivers; we had to keep our massive scarves covering us discreetly. We also contended with boys taunting us by driving in circles around us or trying to force us off the road. I had a hard time resisting a snicker as a teenager would drive up close and fold his arms and ride hands-free to show me his amazing skill. Sometimes when a boy circled me dangerously, I would say, "Oh, you're doing so well! Did you just learn to ride?" It was not gracious, but it did relieve some of my frustration.

While walking I accidentally discovered two ways to avoid being bothered. During a dust storm I pulled my scarf over my nose and mouth and continued down a familiar street, but this time I noticed the men did not call out to me. I began doing this whenever I was walking alone and feeling uncomfortable. A similar technique was carrying an umbrella as a parasol. Whenever someone rode up beside me on a bicycle, I would lower the umbrella enough to hide my face. This was pretty effective, although once I heard an Afghan ask me in English, "Why are you hungry at me?" And once I almost whacked Connor when he rode by and slurred, "Hello, beautiful lady," with just the right intonation.

❖

We felt fairly free in Kabul for the first couple of years after returning. We had to stay home a few times to avoid potential conflicts – for the first election day (our *chaokidars* showed us their inked thumbs, evidence of having participated, and told us proudly, "I voted!") and for some religious and national holidays. But mostly we could travel where we wanted with impunity. For the first time ever our curfew was extended until ten p.m. There was some talk of giving up our nightly radio calls, especially since we had phones. But every time someone suggested this, he or she was hushed. For the single people on the team dealing with social isolation, those calls were a signal that somebody cared. We kept up the routine.

One of our American friends worked with an Afghan whose wife had given birth to five daughters. That by itself might have been considered a disaster in Afghanistan; in the fall of 2004 she delivered twins, and they, too were girls. The mother began hemorrhaging, and our friend's wife, a nurse, rushed her around from hospital to hospital to get aid. Neither the new foreign-run hospital nor the military hospitals were equipped to help this mother, and she died.

Sandra immediately asked the family what would become of the infants. "Let them die," the grandmother said. "There is no one to feed them now."

Appalled, Sandra asked for permission to take the babies home and feed them herself. The distraught woman shooed her away, and Sandra left the house with both babies.

They were small and too weak to suck, so Sandra and Mary put tubes in to get them enough milk. Sandra stood up at church, announced the situation, and a rotation of volunteers began. People spent the night, waking to feed the babies every two hours, so that Sandra could sleep. She had four children herself, and the situation would have been impossible without help from the community. Hannah and some of the other teenage girls spent one night with the babies; she was ecstatic afterward. The infants became stronger by the day.

Events unfolded that exposed us to a fascinating side of Afghan life. The father wanted his girls back, but he was told by family elders that he could not cope with the five girls (all under ten years old) that he already had. They decided that various family members would help. Two distant relatives, after interviews with Sandra (who wanted to make sure they had good motives for adopting baby girls), were allowed to take the infants. One couple had no daughters; the other had not been able to have children at all. After the babies could suck on their own and seemed able to thrive, Sandra gladly handed them over to their new parents. She checked back on them periodically and was happy to see that they were doing well. When Sandra left the country years later, these girls were at the airport to see her off.

Despite the devastation that years of war had wrought on the country, we were glad to see some social systems still worked.

Karte Seh mosque, Kabul, 2005

CHAPTER THIRTY-FIVE

Death, taxes, and the man next door

If you don't recognize God, at least know Him by His power.
(Afghan proverb)

Certainties in life are an illusion. We put our hope in people, institutions, and structures that won't sustain us. This was all too apparent in Afghanistan, a country whose infrastructure and social organization had been weakened by repeated attacks. It is true in America, too, but we don't realize it until the uncertainty becomes painfully personal.

However, there are some certainties we agree on: death and taxes come to us all.

Kabul felt safer *before* 2001. Now the city crawled with tanks and troops; nothing made me more nervous than being stuck in traffic next to an American tank with a gunner on top, scanning constantly. There were private security guards posted outside homes and offices. The neighbors behind our back wall had guards standing at the intersection nearest their front gate. The young man who lived there was in danger both because he was the Minister of Tourism and Aviation, and because his father was a powerful governor and former warlord – Ismail Khan of Herat.

317

Only rarely did we see our neighbor Mirwais Sadiq with his wife and young children, but Connor and Aidan became friends with his guards. They would often call out greetings as we passed; they also served as impromptu protectors of the children. When a pack of wild dogs encircled Connor, the guards chased them away. They understood the importance of looking after a sister's honor, so one day they helped Aidan, too.

Aidan and Hannah were walking home from a friend's house when a young man on a bicycle slowed beside her, reaching out to brush his fingers through her long blonde hair.

Both Aidan and Connor had developed an acute sense of chivalry. Aidan immediately began chasing the young man, who took off on his bicycle. Aidan yelled, and one of Sadiq's guards stepped out of his booth.

"What's wrong?" he asked.

"That man touched my sister!" Aidan cried. He slowed to a stop as the guard took over. Hannah's honor was defended.

Sadiq, who went home to visit family in Herat for Persian New Year in 2004, was killed in an ambush. Despite his robust security presence in Kabul, he had been too vulnerable in his hometown. Our neighborhood security guards disappeared shortly thereafter.

❖

Sadiq was not the only Afghan with enemies. In early 2006, Abdul Rahman's name splashed across world headlines. He had been arrested, turned in by his own family, for being a Christian. Since he worked with one of the other Christian aid organizations, we all watched to see what would happen.

At first it looked likely that he would be martyred for his faith and we waited to see how our government – so intimately involved with Afghan politics by now – would deal with something clearly contrary to our national value of religious liberty. But before the US was forced to make a statement, the Italian government stepped in and offered to grant Rahman asylum. One of our friends told us walking down the street he was stopped by a little boy who said, "I'm a Christian, too! Take me to America!"

We were a little concerned that our own worship services would be targeted for violence. In our congregation were those who had suffered in the bombing of a church in Islamabad in 2002. Journalists began coming with questions, and the *chaokidars* at the building we rented referred them to Rich. But the only response reporters got was quoted in the German *Der Spiegel* magazine: "Rich Lewis declined to comment."

Expatriate Christians had met together for self-run worship services for years. Our group had shrunk or grown, depending on the political situation. During the Taliban time we had broken into smaller groups and met in private homes for times of quiet singing and prayer. With their departure in 2001, we felt free to join together as a large group again. One week during the Abdul Rahman affair, however, we decided to stay home. We heard that some of the mullahs were planning sermons to rail against Christians in Afghanistan, and thought it better to lie low for the day. We were pleased when, just as the Friday services ended at the mosques, a heavy rainstorm swept through the capital, clearing the air in more ways than one.

Earthquakes occurred almost as often as the rain, an average of one each week across the country. We had developed different ways of coping with them. Rich, who had grown up in California, was initially in favor of standing in doorways and hiding under tables; but eventually we both felt that getting outside was the best bet. We had heard too many stories from India and Iran of massive loss of life as mud and brick buildings collapsed.

The children had honed their response time to such a degree that one night when I closed the glass door to their balcony, Owen leaped over Aidan's bed in an attempt to escape what he thought was a tremor. I appreciated their speed. But while I was in India with Connor, they were awoken by a shaker. Again, they jumped out of bed and ran for the stairwell. Rich stepped out of our bedroom and stopped the children to give them a mini-lesson on the dangers of rushing headlong down the steps. I shivered with them in terror as they recounted that minute standing and swaying by the top railing. Hannah told me she didn't know which was worse – being lectured during an earthquake, or having to stand looking at her brothers and dad in their underwear.

On a fall morning in 2005, we had a huge quake. As I was in the kitchen, I bolted outside. The children, who were in their rooms upstairs listening to music, persuaded themselves that the force making their furniture move was a sibling on the other side of the wall. I called them to come outside, afraid to go back in myself, but they couldn't hear me. The house swayed, the tops of the trees bent toward the ground, water in the dog's dish sloshed over the side. Finally everything came to a rest. The thirty to forty-five second quake seemed much longer. The children, unperturbed, were surprised by my reports of what had happened.

Later we heard that the quake was centered in northern Pakistan. Parents in Kabul began getting text messages from children in the boarding school about twenty miles from the quake's epicenter. (Connor, who was taking his SAT exam that morning, even felt it in India.) The loss of housing and life was so great that some of our friends in Afghanistan headed to Pakistan to help with the relief effort. One of them chided me later for leaving our back door locked when we got a shake during dinner and he couldn't get outside quickly.

In Kabul, earthquakes affected us less than the pinch of government regulations. While IAM staff had served for decades on free visas, the authorities now decided we must pay a dollar a day per person. For a large family this was burdensome: since most of us lived on money donated from people in our home countries, it meant we had to raise even more. We also had to start paying taxes, not only on our living allowance, but also on our Social Security tax. (I.e., we were paying a tax on a tax.) Retirees who had come to volunteer at their own expense were not exempt from the tax and visa requirements.

We were also supposed to start keeping track of our staff earnings and hold back a tax for those who earned over a certain amount each month. (Fortunately our *chaokidars* did not qualify for this.) Since paying taxes was voluntary (but with stiff penalties for noncompliance), it seemed that only NGO workers were targeted with the expanding list of financial obligations. We could not tell if the government was merely trying to gain revenue or also trying to send a message that foreigners were not welcome. At the same time we were dealing with increased visa and tax payments, the government commenced sweeping evaluations of NGOs to make sure that they were really working on behalf of the Afghan people, as some businesses had entered the country under the guise of aid and development work. The IAM came through this scrutiny well.

One night while we were guests at a friend's house, a New Zealander commented on how passionate Americans were about contesting the taxes on us all.

"You forget," I told her. "We fought an entire war over taxes." For our part, we were surprised at the response of our European and other friends: those who were used to paying high taxes at home were content to pay taxes in Afghanistan as well. I wondered if the money would even end up where it was supposed to go.

Rental properties were harder to find as more aid workers settled in Kabul and landlords took advantage of the opportunity to raise rents. Our office had a staff member who negotiated with the home owners and wrote contracts. I contacted him when our landlord stopped by to tell us that he had decided to reclaim our property.

"Don't worry," he assured me.

Days passed without any sign that a new house was being arranged for us. Finally, I walked to his home one afternoon.

"Our landlord is moving in tomorrow and we have nowhere to go," I told him.

Calmly, he said, "You should have let me talk to him. You would not have to go." Nevertheless, he arranged for men from the office to help move our furniture into an empty house the following day.

This house had not been inhabited over the winter, but we were assured everything was okay. After our furniture was in, we were informed that the office wanted to paint inside before we took possession. So we stayed at the house of friends who were on vacation.

Daily I walked over to check on progress. On the first visit we noticed that a leak in the roof had sent water and whitewash running down both upstairs and downstairs walls. The office assured me workers would get up on the roof to fix the leak. They filled the water tanks on the roof. The next time I dropped by I discovered it was not merely the roof that was leaking; the water tank and pipes had cracks as well. Our furniture was drenched. But eventually we were able to move into our new house.

Although in many ways I liked this house less than our previous one, it did have a lush, grassy backyard and friendly neighbors. I suspected that at least one of our former neighbors was glad to see us go.

Mohammedullah was patriarch of a large and affluent family. It was not clear where their money came from; none of them had outside jobs. Mohammedullah showed us a photo of a little shop in a town in the south of the country, claiming it as their source of income, but that didn't seem to account for their evident wealth. (There was some talk that opium profits made their way through family networks to those in the city.) He had a booming voice and when we went for visits, his family sat in quiet respect – or fear – whenever he spoke.

This family, like ours, had a generator to pump water. But while we put our generator in a shed to deaden the noise, they put theirs outside – right next to the wall beside our bedroom window. We woke up many nights when the beast fired up and began chugging away. Exhaust wafted up to our room, forcing us to close the window on summer evenings. One night when the machine kept dying, I leaned out and asked, "Excuse me, do you *have* to run the generator in the middle of the night?"

The son shrugged. "We're out of water," he said. He pulled the starter cord again until the motor caught.

Another night I lay in bed listening to the roar of the motor, and thought, *Okay, I'm not going to get mad. Lord, you know we need sleep.*

Suddenly, the generator sputtered and came to a complete stop. After a few tries at getting it going again, the son gave up and went inside.

The next day was a holiday, and we went over to visit. As we were sitting in the living room with Mohammedullah, he said in his loud voice, "*Duktar Saeb*, I have a terrible cough – it sounds like a generator."

Rich could not resist. "I thought that *was* your generator," he said with a smile. There was an almost audible gasp in the family at Rich's effrontery.

The man leaned forward. "Has your wife been praying?" he asked. "Our generator stopped working last night." Rich laughed, denying it.

I told him the truth when we got home. Unlike death and taxes, humor is one of the certainties in life I can appreciate.

Rich on the road to Kandahar

CHAPTER THIRTY-SIX

Quicksand

*When the floodwater reaches your mouth, you put your son under your feet.
(Afghan proverb)*

We had a friend whose wife died of a brain tumor. While visiting his home, I couldn't help but notice the cobwebs and dust in the family room, which had transformed into a shrine in the months since her death. When our friend went to sit down, he kicked a cardboard tube out of his way.

"You know what that is?" he asked with a sad smile. "That is the five-year plan we developed before she was diagnosed with cancer. All of the plans," he told us, tapping the tube, "involved my wife and I doing things together. It's completely useless now."

You cannot predict the twists and turns your life will take.

Rich's work was going as well as could be hoped. Foreign ophthalmologists delivered exams; all five of his trainees passed, two with distinction. Brothers in Kandahar, thriving businessmen who wanted to invest in their own country by constructing an eye hospital, offered an interim building for the IAM to use while the permanent facility was being erected.

Because security on the road from Kabul to Kandahar was worsening (people being pulled from cars and beheaded, or explosive devices detonated to destroy convoys and those in them), when Rich and a colleague decided on a trip south, I expressed concern.

"Don't worry," Rich reassured me. He dressed in his Afghan clothes. Their driver, who was nervous about hauling foreigners on that road, insisted they stop and buy plaid scarves to wind into turbans. Rich told me that the drive was uneventful – except that we both had picked up a stomach bug before he left. While I was violently ill in Kabul, he also got sick in the car. Their driver refused to stop on that road, so Rich had to get out and wash his clothes when they arrived in Kandahar.

Nevertheless, he had a wonderful time visiting friends working there, and he took photos of what looked a peaceful and developed place. I reiterated that Kandahar held no draw for me; the challenge of living in a blazing hot city completely enveloped in a *chahdari* and unable to speak a single word of the difficult Pushtu language took a special kind of woman. (Not me.) But Rich was enthusiastic about the new project.

A few days after he returned, he was phoned by an Afghan working for the American Embassy. Sahlem, who had represented the US at the embassy for years when we had no American staff, knew Rich personally. They had first met in 2001, when Rich received a call: *Sahlem was terribly sick; could he go see him?* Rich examined Sahlem and suspected he was poisoned. Sahlem was airlifted to a hospital in Pakistan, where Rich's diagnosis was confirmed.

So he and Rich became friends; Sahlem introduced Rich to others as "the doctor who saved my life."

"I was wondering if you knew anything about this," Sahlem said over the phone. "We heard that there is an American doctor working in Kandahar."

"No, not that I know of," Rich told him. "But *I* was in Kandahar last week."

Sahlem exploded. "What, are you crazy? Don't you know it's dangerous down there? How did you get there?"

"We went by road," Rich answered.

Sahlem was even more upset. "The consul wants to know if you can come in and speak with her."

Rich thought he was in trouble, but he arranged his schedule so he could visit the embassy. The consul was friendly and told him the real reason for his visit.

"I just wanted to know what it's like out there," she said. "What is it like to live here? What are people saying?"

Rich spoke with her at some length and then came home, amazed that the embassy staff, insulated by their barbed wire fence and sandbags, were checking in with "normal" Americans to get a gauge on the situation.

❖

Since we had been in Afghanistan for three and a half years, we were due for a six-month break in the US. An American ophthalmologist offered to come and cover for Rich during our home leave. Rich spent a couple of days showing him around the hospital.

"I hope he survives here," Rich told me. "He's a vegan."

We thought about all the foods Afghans love most – meat and dairy products – and wondered if this doctor would get enough calories. We later learned he introduced Tofurky to the hospital staff at Thanksgiving.

"What did they think of that?" Rich asked him.

"They loved it!" his replacement responded.

When Rich asked the Afghans, they made it clear that the synthetic meat was awful. Rich wasn't surprised; when he'd offered to take all the doctors out to lunch and they chose a Chinese restaurant, their response to the food delivered was dismay. "Where's the meat?" they complained. Real meat, and sizeable chunks of it, was what they really enjoyed.

Two days before we were set to leave Kabul, while Rich was orienting the new doctor, rioting broke out across the city. The brakes of a military cargo truck had failed that morning, plunging it into twelve civilian vehicles, killing and injuring people. The rumor quickly spread that the Americans were shooting people; angry Afghans took to the streets in protest, targeting aid organizations for looting.

I had gotten used to leaving my hand-held radio on and heard the directive that we should all stay inside or get home as quickly as possible. I listened as people called in that they were shuttling children from the IAM school to their homes; as a boy called his father to tell him he had been dropped off at home but his mother was still at work; and as other people, one by one, answered that they were safely in their residences. Hannah, Owen, and I sat on the floor by our couch as the sound of gunfire rang through nearby streets. (The house had no rooms without windows; some panes still bore bullet holes from previous periods of unrest.) Everyone had called the office to confirm that they were safe – everyone, that is, except Rich.

Calls were not going through on the phone; I tried repeatedly. Finally I sent him a text message, and for some reason that worked. *Where are you?* I messaged. He wrote back that he was at the hospital and was fine. When he got home after the chaos dissipated, he told me they had seen smoke and heard the rioting at nearby Kabul University, but no one had come to disturb the eye hospital. We discovered that one of the few places where we ate out, a pizza restaurant a few blocks away, had been torched.

The next day we were told to stay home, so we missed our usual opportunities to say goodbye to friends before heading to the US.

❖

We had a couple of months with the family before I escorted Aidan and Hannah back to Asia. Our daughter, beginning high school, had opted to follow her brothers to the oldest international school in India rather than joining the new American-curriculum school in Kabul with her friends. Connor started his first year of college in southern California, and Owen, Rich, and I visited supporters across the US until December. I continued homeschooling Owen in a variety of locales (from the backseat of the minivan to a casino in Las Vegas).

The cost of living in Kabul had shot up with the change of government, and we found it difficult to get increased donations to return. What would we do, we wondered, if we didn't make it back in time to pick up Aidan and Hannah? They would effectively be stuck in India for the two-month winter break. Fortunately it was not an issue: our support came in at the end of November. We met the children at school and boarded the train to the beach in south India, waiting for Connor to complete his semester and join us.

Considering the smoothness with which the six of us had traversed the globe over the years, it was inevitable at some point there would be a hitch in our plans. It came that December. Connor had sent his passport to the Afghan embassy in Washington, D.C. for a visa, and it had not returned.

From a tiny communications office in Goa, Rich called the Afghan embassy in the US. They had already mailed out the passport, they told him. He called the US Postal Service; they traced the passport to Baltimore, but then lost record of it. The central post office informed us that after a package had been missing a week, their responsibility ceased. (This was a shock, since we had paid to have the passport returned registered mail.)

It was final exam week for Connor. He was stranded, penniless, in America – and we were half a world away. I confess to crying helplessly as we bicycled back to our guesthouse after our fruitless phone calls.

Connor handled the situation adeptly, especially for an eighteen-year-old. Between studies, he found a place where he could get a new passport with an Indian visa in twenty-four hours. He would barely make it in time for a midnight flight from LAX on the Friday before Christmas (which was the following Wednesday). Before heading to downtown Los Angeles to turn in his passport application and photos, he went once more to check his college mailbox. There, in a slightly battered mailer, was his passport.

Because Connor had been to boarding school and traveled multiple times between India and Afghanistan, we figured the transition to college in the US would go seamlessly. I tried not to think about my own first semester (at one point I called my mom and told her I wanted to drop out and become a waitress). Why did we think we could drop our son off without any tangible support in a "new" culture, a thousand miles from grandparents and over seven thousand miles from his parents? There was a crack in my confidence when we left him to fly to India to meet his siblings; that crack widened with the passport incident.

We spent Christmas together. Our entry into Kabul met with another hiccup: our flight was cancelled due to snow and then the airline rescheduled us onto an Ariana (the "scariana" airline) flight. We debated whether we should risk it, but decided to go ahead rather than spending Christmas in Delhi.

As we settled into our seats, I whipped open the in-flight magazine. Rich had developed a fear of flying in college, although he never let it interfere with his travel plans (except that road trip to Kandahar, when he opted out of going by air). I couldn't resist teasing him by passing the magazine. Instead of the usual glamorous photos and fluffy feature articles, this issue contained a letter from the new head of Ariana descrying the terrible maintenance and safety issues of the airline. The centerfold consisted of photos of the mangled wreckage of various planes at the Kabul airport that had been destroyed during fighting over the years.

Needless to say, we never traveled by Ariana again.

The winter of 2006-2007 was bitterly cold. We had a brilliant, film-worthy snowfall on Christmas and as we trudged back from Greg and Mary's house after the holiday dinner, I told Rich something that had been on my mind.

"I feel like this is going to be our last term in Afghanistan," I said.

He stopped in the street. "What do you mean? Why didn't you mention this in America?"

I couldn't explain, really. Usually I had been happy to come back, but this time it seemed like a weight on me. Maybe it was having our family so spread out (and the prospect of not seeing Connor for another year) and not having any real work to do. But whatever it was, I asked Rich to tell his colleagues that when we left after Aidan's high school graduation eighteen months in the future, we probably would not be coming back.

This was painful for Rich, but he did it. Of course his staff was disappointed and Rich really did not have any reasonable explanation; we had always said we had no plans to resettle in the States. We had discussed coming home for a year at some point so that I could get certified to teach; now we did not know what we would do after that.

In preparation for my teacher training, I had made a special request of the testing company administering education program qualifying exams to take both two-hour tests in Delhi the following August. Permission was granted, so I brought back a pile of books to study. While Owen ploughed through eighth grade work, I read college textbooks on economics, psychology, and history.

Winter turned to spring. But the external brightness was not matched by corresponding lightness of spirit. Increasingly, we worried about Connor. He had been hired to work in Alaska for the summer, but he knew no one there and sounded down during our phone calls. The crack in my parental confidence about our separation grew into a fissure. The semester was nearly over and he would be checking out of the dorm and flying away from all support. My motherly instincts told me that our son should not get on that flight to Alaska.

There are times in marriage when I have been nearly speechless with love and appreciation for Rich. That was one of those times. The morning after our last call with Connor, Rich took a taxi to the airport, bought a ticket to Delhi, and headed to California. He didn't even have time to say goodbye to his coworkers.

Rich phoned Hannah and Aidan from the airport in Delhi to tell them he would not be in Kabul when they returned the following week for their summer break. He hoped to stay a few weeks with Connor before returning to Afghanistan, he told them. The weeks stretched on just as they had when we had left Rich behind in 2001. This was our younger three children's last summer in Kabul, one way or another (since we planned to leave the following May). I knew they would need closure, no matter what lay ahead.

We went to ceilidhs, ate home-made ice cream at Greg and Mary's, enjoyed dinner several times a week at James and Ann's, and hung out with many of the other youth and their parents at a coffee house. Every night boys biked by and invited the kids to play capture the flag.

For Hannah's birthday, I planned a surprise breakfast party. Mary dropped in with her daughters. While we were playing games, she got a call. After listening with concern, she told me that a busload of Koreans had been kidnapped on the road from Kandahar to Kabul.

This cast a pall over the foreign community. By now none of us were using that road because of kidnapping concerns. And now a group, mostly people who had come for a short aid trip, had been taken (and two, found later, were murdered).

The South Korean government told their people that those working for NGOs would have to return to Korea, and that if they did not do so immediately, they would be jailed and heavily fined when they did.

All of us grieved this news. The Koreans had been involved with health and education projects not only in the capital, but also in places that were considered too dangerous for most of us to go. It would be a huge loss for the Afghan people.

Owen's birthday was three days after Hannah's, but a lot of his friends were still gone for the summer, so we decided to have a party when they got back. Meanwhile, I kept in touch with Rich by Skype and phone.

Two comments from others shaped the following months. One was from a counselor, who told us, "You can question your calling to be in Afghanistan, but you cannot question your calling to be good parents." It became clear over the summer that we needed to ease our children back into our home country, to offer moral support so they could thrive in the US.

Someone else told me, "You know, if your children are in boarding school, *you* can be anywhere." It was true: our high school students had friends and support in India. Aidan was entering his last year; to pull him out would be more traumatic than having us continue our normal schedule. Rich and I decided that Owen and I should take Aidan and Hannah to school and then come back to America.

All three of the kids sorted through the stuff in their rooms. Connor had left little behind; Aidan was not a hoarder, and his things were easy to pack. Owen had all sorts of odds and ends – Legos, action figures, bottles of "potions" (experimental mixtures he had concocted from various household liquids) and notebooks full of lyrics to songs he and his friends hoped to one-day record. As we picked through these things, junk piles expanded in their rooms and in the hallway.

For Hannah, the sorting was especially hard. One Christmas we had given her a trunk with several small pots of paint. She created an ornate design on the lid with elephants and Mogul designs, and had locked in this trunk many of her treasures. She also kept art supplies and stories she had written – sometimes on lined paper, sometimes on napkins, sometimes typed on an old typewriter we had borrowed. It was a challenge to pull apart her childhood and decide which memories deserved to be carried back to America and which left behind.

As we waited for our taxi to the airport, Aidan and Hannah went to the backyard to say goodbye to Nova. Aidan could not resist gazing into her brown eyes and tenderly ruffling her fur. She was blissfully ignorant that she would not see them again.

Nova was the first dog to outlast us in Afghanistan.

Owen (top) at his going-away party, 2007

CHAPTER THIRTY-SEVEN

Heroes in the garden

The world lives in hope. (Afghan proverb)

I was once asked to speak to a group of single mothers. As I looked around at these women, my own inadequacy welled up.

What could be a more difficult job than being a single parent? During the few stints when Rich and I had been apart for medical training or trips, I sorely missed his part of the equation. To be alone raising children sounded more challenging than anything I had ever done. In my mind, I added single mothers to my list of heroes.

My idea of heroic behavior had altered over time in Afghanistan. Coming from a culture that exalts the showy rescue or grand act of celebrity generosity, I was startled by the realization of who I now admired: The award-winning scientist who gave up honor and prestige to work in an Afghan hospital. The farmer who loved nothing better than the rich soil of his own field, but left it to assist poor villagers high in the barren mountains. The woman who turned down two marriage proposals to help people with disabilities gain mobility. The French chaplain who bravely preached an entire sermon in English on "the good gnu." Widows and widowers who moved, alone, to an unstable Third World country to offer what

335

they could. These were the people we were privileged to rub shoulders with. These were now my heroes.

Our twelve-year-old son provided courageous support as we headed back to Kabul after dropping off his siblings in India. We had to figure between the two of us how to pack so we could haul our possessions through two airports on our way to the United States. I had already taken several boxes of books to Delhi and hired a service in the bazaar there to repack them, stitching them into twenty-seven smaller parcels which could be shipped at a dollar per pound. (They all arrived.) Owen and I arranged our other books, games, bedding and household items around our living room for an indoor yard-sale. I contacted a new family that was coming to Kabul from Hong Kong; they were taking over our house. After reading my list of furniture and appliances, they agreed to buy almost everything. To our relief, they also eagerly promised to keep Nova. (We heard later that she grew fat and happy on Chinese food, and stopped biting people.)

Things that I thought were not worth trying to sell (piles of clothes, partially used coloring books, broken toys, and so on) I laid out on our back veranda as free items. On a Thursday morning (the beginning of our weekend), the *chaokidar* opened the gate and a steady stream of foreign workers and their families poured through the house, snatching up things quickly. By noon we were still left with several books, a video camera, and a stack of board games. I allowed the *chaokidars* to take home anything of interest.

As a final goodbye, I told Owen we would have a combination birthday/going away party. He invited his friends, most of whom were back by now for the beginning of the academic year. I made a cake with homemade ice cream and we planned games to play inside and out.

Just as guests were arriving, we got a call. A pregnant German woman and her husband were eating lunch at a little restaurant nearby when armed men kidnapped the wife. We were all being told to stay where we were.

Some of Owen's friends called and told us they would not be able to come. The others stayed, but most left early. It was so typical of our experience in Afghanistan. My one comfort was that

Owen never wrote an essay about "My Worst Going-Away Party Ever." He seemed to enjoy it, and felt loved by the friends he was leaving behind.

We did it all – sorting, selling, packing, and partying – in nine days. I could never have done it without Owen's help.

As we worked, I reflected on the privilege of having such intimate friends living in close proximity. (The Muellers were down the block; Dan Terry and his wife across the street.) Although our dearest friends in Afghanistan were Americans, when they were in the United States they lived across the country; we could never see them as often as we wanted. They were family, their children nieces and nephews and cousins. The MOLES (Muellers, Oswalds, Lewises, and Extras), as Aidan had dubbed us, had a final dinner together. I thought my heart would break when we said goodbye.

Ibrahim and Nooria wanted us to visit them before we left, but with the kidnapping of the Koreans, security had tightened leading out of the city, and their house was beyond a checkpoint we could not pass. They showed up with all four of their children and I remembered our first meeting, when their oldest daughter and Hannah – both teens now – were just toddlers. I assured them that Rich would try to come back sometime to say goodbye. They urged me to save money to sponsor their family to move to America. I couldn't offer them much hope about that, but I told them we would stay in touch from the other side of the world.

Our *chaokidar's* family also came to say a tearful goodbye. We had been able to help through the hospitalization of their oldest son and the frightening illness of their baby, and in the building of a roof for their new home. I would miss Yusuf's affectionate ways with our children and Nova, and the way he had looked after me while Rich was gone.

The morning we left, an IAM worker came to pick us up in an office vehicle. Ann and our *chaokidar* stood outside the gate, mournfully waving goodbye. We took a circuitous route to the airport – there had been too many bombings lately, and we wanted to avoid main roads. Owen and I schlepped our bags into the airport (only those with tickets were allowed in the building so we couldn't get any help), and were appalled that the authorities wanted to open and examine everything. It was no problem with our suitcases, but I had also packed two boxes of books and toys. Every book was taken out and leafed through (were they looking for drugs? money?) and the few Legos we had opted to cart back were scrutinized with concern. We were questioned about why we had so many books.

"They are school books," I said. "I have been teaching my son."

"My son is a student," the man said. "He doesn't have this many books." It was sad but true; nevertheless, I insisted that these all belonged to us, and we were just taking our own books away. Finally, they allowed me to close up the boxes, drag them to where they could be taped shut, and check them for our flight.

We went through security – as always, a pat-down – and mounted the stairs to the new waiting room. An assortment of foreigners and locals milled around, waiting for one of the afternoon flights. In what had once been a dilapidated, windowless building, passengers could now buy a cup of tea or phone relatives in the comfortable lounge. Unburdened of our luggage, Owen and I sat down.

For years, I had focused my energy on looking, speaking, and acting like an Afghan. Suddenly I decided that it did not matter anymore if I was perceived as a "wild" foreign woman. I pulled off my scarf and folded it up, setting it on an empty seat beside me. I neatened my hair. I could now go back to being something I felt I had not been in a long time: an American woman, with all that meant. The thought was strangely exhilarating.

After Aidan graduated from high school in India the next spring, he and Hannah returned to the States with us. Although Rich and I had spent most of our lives in North America, the same was not true of our children. Each of them had to decide what to do with their past: embrace it? bury it? meld it into something new? For a ceramics assignment, Hannah was told to represent herself as a box. On one side, she put a symbol of her faith; the other three sides, flags – one from Afghanistan, one from India, and one from Arizona. And on the inside she formed a burrito.

338

"That's because I'm white on the outside but brown on the inside," she told me. In that respect, we all have become burritos to varying degrees.

We find Afghan connections where we can; we read the news, greet with alacrity anyone with a name that might have Persian roots, cook *Qabili pilau* for our friends. We cherish the three-dimensionality of what had once been two-dimensional lives.

We miss the heroes we knew. Some we have seen here – the children, we find, are even better than their parents at making trips to spend time together. Some have died of disease. Our friends Tom Little and Dan Terry – along with other expatriates and Afghans – were murdered in 2010 on an eye camp that Rich would have helped with if he had been there. Since then, others have been killed. More of our hearts have been left in Afghanistan than we care to admit.

The Sonoran desert is our home for now. Each day Rich waters plants in a cluster of containers outside our living room window. We are not too picky about what grows; weeds, as I told my father, "are what we call *plants* here." In Kabul, Babur's magnificent park and tomb, established in the 16th century, have been restored; we pray that healing spreads across the country in similar fashion. For our part, we are thankful for how our inner landscape has irrevocably changed by the time we spent dwelling in the warlord's garden.

Sources

"104th Regiment of Foot (Bengal Fusiliers)." *nam.ac.uk*. National Army Museum, 4 September 2013.

"Afghanistan." European Country of Origin Information Network.

"Afghanistan – Air Force." *Afghan Chamber of Commerce*. 1 February 2016.

"Afghanistan: The Massacre in Mazar-I Sharif." *refworld.org*. Human Rights Watch, 1 November 1998.

"Afghanistan – Politics Post-Taliban." *GlobalSecurity.org*, 21 August 2012.

"Afghanistan: Power Struggle." *PBS Newshour*.

"Ahmad Shah Massoud." *Wikipedia*.

"Blood-Stained Hands: Past Atrocities in Kabul and Afghanistan's Legacy of Impunity." *Human Rights Watch*. New York: Human Rights Watch 2005.

Boone, Jon. "A return to magnificence for British diplomats?" *theguardian.com*. Guardian News and Media Ltd., 17 May 2009.

Carter, Jimmy. "State of the Union Address." *millercenter.org*. University of Virginia, 23 January 1980.

"Dr. Najibullah." *Khaama Press*.

Enevoldsen, Jens. *Sound the bells, O moon, arise and shine!* Peshawar: InterLit Foundation, 2000.

Fineman, Mark. "Afghan Leader Najibullah Forced to Resign by Rebels." *The Tech Online Edition.* Massachusetts Institute of Technology, 112: 21, 17 April 1992.

"India-L Archives." *rootsweb.ancestry.com.* Ancestry.com, 27 June 1999.

"In Memoriam." *The Himalayan Journal.* The Himalayan Club, Vol. 62, 2006.

"Killing You is a Very Easy Thing for Us." *hrw.org.* Human Rights Watch, 2003.

"Matching profiles from family trees: Banon." *uk.mundia.com.* Mundia.

McNamara, Robert. "Britain's Disastrous Retreat from Kabul." About.com, 2014.

Rasanayagam, Angelo. *Afghanistan: A Modern History.* New York: St. Martin's Press, 2005.

Reagan, Ronald. "Message on the Observance of Afghanistan Day." *utexas.edu.* University of Texas, 21 March 1983.

"Taliban: Hindus Must Be Labeled." *abcnews.go.com.* New York: ABC News, 22 May 2001.

Wilson, J. Christy Jr. *One Hundred Afghan Persian Proverbs.* Peshawar: InterLit Foundation, 2004.

Made in the USA
San Bernardino, CA
08 March 2020